Give Us This Day

by

David Ivan Vere

Bloomington, IN authorHOUSE® Milton Keynes, UK

AuthorHouse™
1663 Liberty Drive, Suite 200
Bloomington, IN 47403
www.authorhouse.com
Phone: 1-800-839-8640

AuthorHouse™ UK Ltd.
500 Avebury Boulevard
Central Milton Keynes, MK9 2BE
www.authorhouse.co.uk
Phone: 08001974150

First published by AuthorHouse 9/8/2006

ISBN: 1-4259-5381-6 (sc)
ISBN: 1-4259-5380-8 (dj)

Library of Congress Control Number: 2006907204

Printed in the United States of America
Bloomington, Indiana

This book is printed on acid-free paper.

In Memory
To
My Mother, Father,
Elizabeth
&
My Dear Wife Jessie (Poppy)

My special thanks are due to my son, David,
whose contribution to this book made its publication possible.

Table of Contents

Foreword

I still have in my possession an Italian ten-lire note, issued as military currency at the time the Allied forces (the American 5th and British 8th Armies) invaded the Italian mainland in September 1943. In the corners of the ten-lire note from the series of 1943A are printed some ornate scrolls, and with keen eyesight, a pound symbol can be seen in the bottom right-hand corner. The idea was to be able to identify the note against counterfeit money that could flood the market later.

The scene on the front of the note depicts a placid rural setting of a cornfield with the stooks gathered together, drying in the sun. On the back of the note was printed the Four Freedoms: 'Freedom of speech, freedom of religion, freedom from want, freedom from fear'. They were the moral principles set out that every country should abide by at the end of hostilities. It all looked possible with the founding of the United Nations in 1948. But the spirit of goodwill was only temporary. The dream soon ended.

It's very easy to start a war, but you must have the fortitude to bring it to a satisfactory conclusion. The difficult part is when the cost of victory is measured in human sacrifice, the men who never live to see the promised peace. If the planners of the Italian campaign believed that the whole exercise would work to the Allies advantage, that Italy wouldn't be fought over, then their thinking was completely flawed from the start. The terrain of the country was such that it would always favour the defender, and not the aggressor.

The events related here are of my own personal view or record of the war years. The conversations are not necessarily word for word as spoken at the time. However, they are as I remember them after the passing of more than half a century. Also, some of the dates of events may not be strictly accurate, but would fall within the bounds of a day or two.

1. The 'Phoney War'. Dunkirk.

On the eve of the Second World War, being Saturday night, I paid my customary weekend visit to my local cinema, which had the illustrious name of 'The Grand'. It did have a very grand façade, but could not match up to its high sounding name inside. Nevertheless, it was my favourite picture house in the Buckinghamshire town of High Wycombe.

The programme for the evening had for its main attraction a film called *The Road to Glory* starring Warner Baxter and Fredric March. This was a war story about a French regiment of infantry fighting in the trenches of the First World War. The choice of film was not very suitable for showing at this time, for the cinema manager would have booked the film well in advance of its showing and could never have foreseen the tide of events that were about to unfold.

On the morrow at eleven o'clock, the British Prime Minister, Neville Chamberlain, would be declaring a state of war with Germany if we were unable to receive a favourable reply from that country. This was after their invasion of Poland on Friday, 1st of September 1939. If Germany refused, Britain was bound to honour her pact with Poland and, along with France, be at war once again.

So, this was the film I was seeing on that fateful evening with men on the silver screen being slaughtered on the battlefield, and others living without much hope of survival or receiving some terrible injury in the conflict. It was 'kill or be killed'; a daunting prospect for any man trapped in this unremitting struggle for survival.

For me, the most memorable part of the film came when one of the older characters in the regiment, easily recognisable by the lighted pipe he always carried in his mouth, even into battle, was mortally wounded in no man's land. Two of his comrades drag his failing body into a sitting position against a broken down farm cart destroyed by previous gunfire. There with a vacant expression on his face, his pipe still clenched between the teeth, he is just able with his last gasp to mutter, "What a war!" The pipe then falls from his lifeless lips.

I was only fifteen years of age at the time, but the film did make me think about myself. Even then, I was wise enough to understand that if we were going to war, I could one day find myself in a similar plight and that did shock me. It was so easy to suffer the discomfort of others from the safety and comfort of a cinema seat, but what if in reality?

That very morning, I had seen from the wooded hillside overlooking the town, men of the Territorial Army march out of their barracks on the way to the railway station led by the town band. For me it was a most inspiring sight, knowing that their final destination would be somewhere in France. For some of the marching men, cheered on by the Saturday morning shoppers, they would be having their final glance at the town and the places they had grown up in over the years. For them, alas, they would never return to their homeland.

The next morning, Sunday the 3rd, I attended the 11 o'clock service at our Methodist chapel. Having finished the first hymn, the congregation sat down. The vestibule door by the side of the pulpit opened to admit the church steward who proceeded to climb the pulpit steps to whisper in the anxious looking minister's ear. A hushed expectancy fell over everyone. The minister got to his feet to address the congregation with the words, "My dear friends, I have to inform you that war has been declared." With a voice now full of emotion, he said, "Let us all pray."

It was now obvious that the Prime Minister had not received his favourable reply from Adolf Hitler. So, after 21 years of peace, we were back at war again with the same adversary. Nobody in the land, but a fool, would have wished this war on the people after the horrendous casualties and suffering of the last conflict, and the awful memories still in the minds of the older generation. Britain had now started on a journey down an unsure road with no turning back.

From that first night, a strict blackout was imposed throughout the land and would be rigidly enforced. It was backed up by a threat of a fine, imprisonment, or both and would be carried out by having air raid wardens allocated to every street in town and village. My own parents, as memory serves me, found it a problem to comply with owing to the lack of suitable material for making blackout curtains at such short notice. We ended up by folding a newspaper round the lampshade to stop the glare of the lamp directly onto the curtains.

For most of us, life carried on as normal with a few exceptions. Mass assembly was forbidden with the closure of cinemas and stadiums. (Thankfully, this ban was soon lifted after a matter of weeks when the expected air raids on the country failed to materialise.)

The new direction of labour into war work would not affect me, already being employed in light engineering in the town with most of our work for government ministries. The armed services would need to expand with men and women being called up in certain age groups. Some people would volunteer, but not with the same enthusiasm that drove them into the First World War.

The BBC would broadcast government communications to the people. In the event of bombing on the capital, most of its staff and their equipment were moved out of London to the comparative safety of the provinces.

One memory of broadcasting, in the first few days of the war, was the almost continual playing of the theatre organ with Sandy MacPherson. On turning the wireless on, you could bank most times on hearing the organ playing. Without a doubt, it was a good standby for the BBC while they rearranged their programmes to the changed conditions we found ourselves in.

Returning back to work on the Monday morning, I found that most of the conversation going around was rather pessimistic to our chances of victory over Germany. This kind of talk filled me with gloom, but it did not stop me, and the rest of the workforce, from making a greater effort for more production.

During the lunch break that morning, I could see the maintenance staff busy around the factory, filling up sandbags and placing them at the entrance of all the air raid shelters. The windows in all the buildings were painted black and would stay that way for the duration of the war. We each received a badge with our clock numbers on (mine being 88), giving us access into the factory by the security men posted at the main gates. The whole place soon looked under siege with the camouflage painting of the buildings now finished.

On the Western Front, the rival armies were moving into their much vaunted Maginot and Siegfried line fortifications, each side waiting for the other to attack. The country waited with bated breath for the clash that seemed inevitable; but neither Army would commit itself in battle. Germany meanwhile soon overran the Polish forces, about which we could do nothing to help. The Soviet Union, who had made a non-aggression pact with Germany, also invaded Poland, taking possession of almost half of that not overrun by Germany. This did not go down very well with Hitler who had made all of the running and most of the fighting there.

By the end of September 1939, it was all over. Poland now had new masters in their land, and for the Polish nation it was the beginning of a troubled time. The German Army could now turn its full attention back to the Western Front with forces now made available from the fighting in Poland.

After a reasonable amount of time had elapsed, and no German offensive had taken place, we began to wonder what was going on. For this time in our history, the Americans coined a phrase for it – the 'Phoney War'.

I carried on with my work at the factory with the management calling on the need for greater effort in production. It was a very poor environment to work in, with the artificial light, noise and cigarette smoke of around 80 people. It was always good to get away in the evenings if only to return home.

My only pleasure came with a visit to the cinema, in a form of escapism from what was going on around us. Even then, you were reminded of the war going on with the newsreel of the day. They would show, from the Western Front, an officer taking up a crouched position with a revolver in his hand, leading out a patrol into the snowy wastes of no man's land. I was to see this same clip of film many times during the winter months that followed.

The main action of the war was coming from the North Atlantic where the German U-boats were setting about the destruction of our shipping. A film showing a ship just torpedoed, sliding out of view beneath the waves and the crew adrift in open boats, was a grim reminder that we were at war.

Just before Christmas, we had news of a naval engagement in the South Atlantic between British ships and the German pocket battleship, the *Graf Spee* that had been very successful in sinking many of our ships there. The German ship was damaged in the battle and sought refuge in Montevideo harbour to make repairs. The government there set a time limit on their stay in the port. On leaving port, the ship was scuttled in open water. The ship's captain, Hans Langsdorff, later took his own life.

Our first soldier was killed on the Western Front. We could not have more keenly felt it than if we had lost many more in a major battle.

Christmas came as a welcome break for us with the 25th falling on a Monday. At this stage in the war, we did not work on Sundays so were able to enjoy a 3-day holiday.

With the start of the New Year, we were asked to tighten our belts with the introduction of food rationing. This was inevitable with the country being dependent on shipping for our food and raw materials, and the U-boat menace growing with every passing day. Some items of food would vanish from off the shelves and not return for many a long day. My mother, remembering the U-boat blockade of the First World War and the hardships they were made to suffer, not least her then young family, decided to do something about it this time. With prudence, she had put aside selected tins of food for any emergency the war might bring.

It was very hard on parents at this time with the general upheaval of family life going on. They had seen it all before in the last war, and were now being asked to suffer it again with their grownup sons and daughters being called on for military service. It was just one more added burden to worry over. At this stage, I reached my 16th birthday with the consequent task of working longer hours by order of the Works Act.

The sense of well-being, brought about by the 'Phoney War', came to an abrupt end at the beginning of April with the startling news of the

German invasion of Denmark and Norway. This had taken the Allied high command by complete surprise. Our generals, in the main, still geared themselves to the static conditions of warfare in the past, whereas the Germans were now employing a new brand of war similar to that used in Poland. The German plan was simple. Why try and break through the fortifications of the Maginot line when you could outflank them by way of a neutral country? An act of aggression against a neutral state had never been a condition to bother Hitler. He alone was now making the new rules of armed conflict in the most terrorising form, like the indiscriminate bombing of a city.

Without a pause, the German Army now turned their intentions on Holland, Luxemburg and Belgium. These countries were now made to feel the awful power of this new type of warfare. The Germans were scything down all forms of opposition in their paths, as they forged ahead with the tanks of the new Panzer forces.

On hearing the constant bad news over the wireless and seeing the newsreels at the cinema, a state of alarm was growing in the land. A large part of the British Army was now dispatched into Belgium, with the sole aim of stemming the German onslaught there.

When everything now seemed to be falling apart, we had a change of premiership with the resignation of Neville Chamberlain in favour of Winston Churchill.

Back in the factory, men stood around in small groups talking almost in whispers (as if the Germans might hear) about events they could not bring themselves to understand. Why were the British and French armies doing so badly when we had a greater superiority in numbers? This had a bad effect on the people who were rapidly becoming demoralised.

The Germans now sprang the final part of their trap, by breaking through in the Ardennes at the weakest part of the Maginot line. Here, they very soon expanded the breach they had made through the fortifications and now, with large Panzer forces, were driving across France. This bold move had the effect of cutting the French and British armies in two, with the British cut off in Belgium.

The possibility of a great German victory was now beginning to loom on the horizon, casting a dark shadow over our best endeavours here.

Men in the factory were openly talking about smashing the machinery to stop it falling into the hands of the enemy.

With nothing much to stem the flood of their armoured forces, the Germans soon reached the Atlantic coast with a chilling prospect for us all of a possible German occupation of our land.

Decisive action was now taken by the government to disengage most of the forces from their former positions and start them, without delay, to withdraw to the coast. The unfortunate remainder would be used as a rearguard or blocking force. There was a flaw in this plan, in that there was now no major port left (other than the ones now held by the Germans) with the facility of loading on the heavy equipment such as the guns.

We were now to hear on the wireless news bulletins the frequent mention of a place that would now inspire a more spirited effort from the British people – Dunkirk. This was a coastal town in France, near the Belgium frontier, where the bulk of the British forces had converged prior to being picked up by the Royal Navy from the sandy beach there.

This was, without doubt, going to become a formidable task with the enemy so close at hand. We, at home, could only wait and hope for a ray of light from out of the gloom that had fallen upon us all.

From out of the near chaos on the beachhead, some order was at last restored into this vast concentration of men. On the beach, columns of men had been formed, who then waded into the sea till the water came chest high. Here, they waited in the cold sea to be picked up by one of the boats (if they had the strength left to get in), which were filled to capacity. They would then ferry them out to the larger transports, lying offshore. The Germans had completely surrounded our forces there who were now under siege from guns, tanks and the Luftwaffe bomber formations that were also trying to sink our shipping. Many would be sunk with great loss of life before the evacuation was completed.

In the days that followed, the sea remained miraculously calm for the time of year. This enabled the Royal Navy, and others, to lift over 300,000 men from the open water around the beachhead while under continual bombardment. The estimate of recovery put out by the War Department at the start of the operation was a modest 20,000 to 45,000 men at most. They had underestimated the true spirit of the people in this 'backs-to-the-wall' situation.

Some of the survivors of Dunkirk came back in the most wretched condition, having lost their uniforms and equipment, their bodies draped around in blankets or any piece of clothing that could be found. Hundreds of men had lost their rifles in the struggle to escape the carnage on the beachhead. But overall, it was enough to see them return (if not all) safely back on their own soil with a good chance to carry on the fight, when or wherever it would come.

Most of the heavy equipment taken to France by the BEF (British Expeditionary Force) was lost, whereas some of it had managed to slip away before the Germans overran the ports down the coast.

Even after all the fearful consequences that we now found ourselves in, the general mood of the country was lifted by the deliverance of our troops from out of the hands of the enemy. The people now looked on it not as a defeat but a miracle.

German soldiers, standing on the beach at Dunkirk, surveyed the damage they had inflicted on their enemy. With the wreckage of all types of shipping still visible above the waterline, and the beach covered with abandoned service equipment, this then was their victory. One must feel sure that the Germans had bargained for far more than this, and looking now at their handiwork, they could only feel that it was a hollow victory they had won; the 300,000 evading their net and not in captivity. The men were more important than the equipment, which was replaceable. The men were not.

One evening, shortly after, when going home from work by way of the park in the town, I was surprised but pleased to see men of the Royal Artillery with their battery of guns, which looked to me as having a calibre of about 6 inches. The guns and transport were dispersed under the trees with camouflage netting draped over some. They were not taking any chance of a visit from the Luftwaffe, even being over 60 miles inland from the channel coast.

On my arrival home, I mentioned to my parents what I had seen. They, in turn, told me that a number of guns had arrived during the day and were now placed around the bottom of the hillside, at the end of our road. This was the same hillside from where I had watched the Territorials march off for France, now 8 long months ago.

After supper, I paid a visit to the camp they had set up there. The guns were deployed on the grass by the side of a rutted cart track leading onto some old farm buildings. Most of the gun crews were at work on the cleaning and oiling of their pieces, possibly the first time since leaving France?

Watching them at work, I noticed one of the men had a familiar look about him. Moving nearer, I recognised the man who lived no more than two hundred yards away from the spot where he was now standing. After the men had finished their chores and placed camouflage nets over all exposed equipment, to shield them from the eyes of enemy aircraft, they were dismissed. I returned home in the gathering dusk and hoped that the man, who lived so near, would be able to slip away and join his parents for the evening.

Meantime, the French Army, still fighting on with stubborn resistance against the invaders on their soil, were being forced back by the new tactics the Panzer Divisions were now using with such success. Nothing, it seemed, could stand up to this new development in warfare, the like the world had never seen – the combination of ground and airpower working together and smashing through any opposition that tried to stand in its path. The Germans had a name for it – blitzkrieg – meaning 'lightning war'.

Most of the BEF had now been evacuated from France with a trickle of men still coming out to swell the total from Dunkirk. Along with them were many Frenchmen who still wished to fight on if France should fall.

Not wishing to be kept out from the spoils of war, now that the defeat of France looked more certain, Benito Mussolini decided to bring Italy into the conflict with a declaration of war against Britain and France. However, Mussolini was scoffed at by most people who called him nothing more than a 'bag of wind!'

By the middle of June, we were to hear the most devastating piece of news – the fall of Paris – by far Hitler's greatest triumph to date. Within days of this bombshell, we now started to hear talk of an armistice. When it was signed on the 22nd of June 1940, the war was over for that sad nation.

Britain was now standing alone against the might of Hitler's Germany that had just finished overrunning most of the countries of

Europe. Where would he turn next? No one thought that he would be content to sit on the channel coast and do nothing. That was not his way. It was about time we stopped underestimating our enemy, having in mind the gibe about Hitler only being a corporal in the First World War, and a painter by trade. He was now the Supreme Commander of the German Armed Forces. Perhaps it would have been a benefit to our side if we had had a few painters on our own general staff!

The popular song of the day, till now, had been, *'We are going to hang out the washing on the Siegfried line; have you any dirty washing mother dear?'* This, along with other propaganda, now made us feel rather foolish in the light of past events.

The verdict from the workers on the factory floor, over the failure of the BEF and the general conduct of the war in France, was laid fair-and-square on the shoulders of our general staff who it seemed were still stuck in the mud of the 1914-18 war. They had failed to capitalise on the lessons they should have learnt from the fall of Poland, some 8 months before.

2. The calm before the storm.

The government now asked the country's workforce, engaged on war production, to work maximum hours. For us, this entailed working from 8 o'clock in the morning till 8 at night, and would be a full 7-day week. We all groaned at this announcement with its complete abandonment of our own leisure time.

With the tension growing with every passing day, we were now allocated our individual bomb shelters in and around the factory site. Soon, we were having trial runs at getting in and out of the shelters without wasting valuable production time. Departments were split up into different shelters with the object of being able to carry on with production, even after a catastrophe of a bomb shelter receiving a direct hit with heavy casualties. This was a good company policy, showing that someone at the top could see a crisis ahead.

The month of July had come and gone without the enemy putting in any appearance over here. Not that we wanted him to. But come he would when he was ready. There were skirmishes over the Channel with the Luftwaffe probing at our defences and being chased off by the Royal Air Force.

One thing for me, which came to an end with the working of maximum hours, was my association with the Methodist chapel after ten years of good fellowship there. Some of my friends, being somewhat older than I, had already been called up into the Armed Forces, and the chapel, alas, would never return to its golden past. I shall always remember the kindness and goodwill shown at any gathering, religious or social, that took place there.

In 1938, when the talk of a possible war and rearmament was in the offing, we were asked by one of the stewards at the chapel if we would sign a petition in favour of the Reverend Frank Buchman's 'Campaign for Moral Rearmament'. I think all the young men, with ages ranging from fifteen to twenty, signed in the frail hope of peace. It had very high ideals, but it came to an abrupt end at the start of the war.

The traditional holiday month of August came in, and within days saw the start of the long-awaited German onslaught against our island. Targets first attacked by the Luftwaffe were airfields and radar installations along the coast. The Royal Air Force was repulsing these with losses on both sides. The airfields damaged were a cause of great concern with the result of the planes having to fly onto undamaged fields. This, in turn, upset the balance of our own defences.

Back at the factory, we made many visits to the bomb shelters when the sirens sounded. In later days, we would have our own aircraft spotters, up in a tower, only sending us to the shelters when they deemed it was necessary for our own safety. And in doing so would completely ignore the sirens sounding in the town.

During this troubled time when none of us could know what each new day would bring, we eagerly turned to the wireless for information and guidance from the war leaders. Churchill made a rousing speech in regard to resisting any German attempt at invasion on our shores. He said that all he could offer us was 'Blood, Toil, Tears and Sweat', and we would fight them on the beaches and in the hills if necessary. This was very powerful stuff and went down very well in the country.

In the meantime, the aerial battles had increased in number and intensity with hundreds of planes taking part, weaving and dodging in the skies above us, leaving telltale vapour trails behind them as they each struggled for supremacy. The daily losses of both sides were very heavy.

One big advantage we had over the enemy was that if one of our planes was shot down and the pilot survived, he would fight another day. However, the enemy in the same situation would find himself out of the war, and in a prisoner of war compound.

The Germans came very close to a great victory with their strategy of bombing the airfields out of existence and denying us their use. If they had carried on with this policy, they could have won the battle. But by the end of the month, they mysteriously changed their tactics to the bombing of the capital. Within days, they started out on a nightly bombing campaign in an all out effort to terrorise the population into submission.

The air battles by day, over our shores, had been won by the Royal Air Force driving the enemy from out of the skies with the unacceptable losses of their men and machines.

Each night now after dark, my family and I could walk out of the house into the garden and see the evidence of the bombing on London. By looking due east, up the valley, even at a distance of 30 miles, we could see fires raging away and casting a red glow, lighting up the night sky. Enemy aircraft were raining down death and destruction on the city, killing the brave firemen who were striving to control the flames. Some of the fires burning in the docks were out of control. Searchlights probed through the red gloom of fire and smoke. With their fingers of bright light trying to locate the enemy above, and make them, in turn, targets for the antiaircraft guns. We were witnessing a most awesome sight, and felt thankful for the fact that we could go back inside the house and not have the dreadful fear that the people of London were being made to suffer.

At this vital stage in the war, when it looked a probability that all could be lost, we found a new champion in the form of J.B. Priestley. He came to the microphone, in Broadcasting House, for a series of postscripts following the 9 o'clock Sunday night Home Service news. The talks started after the fall of Dunkirk, and lasted over a period of several months.

Priestley was able to raise the spirit of the nation, and place it on a higher plane with his brand of good Yorkshire style commonsense in our cause for freedom and justice against Nazi tyranny. With a few well-chosen words, he seemed to have the gift of talking his way out of the desperate position we found ourselves in – if we kept our nerve, all would turn out well in the end. The postscripts were an inspiration and acted on the people like a good tonic. Priestley voiced the same problems that Churchill had spoken of, but the very way he said it, it sounded more acceptable to the people. Churchill had only offered a stick, whereas Priestley had found a carrot to tie on the end of it.

By the end of September, we were still having enemy planes over the country in daylight. Some of their bomber formations numbered many hundreds of aircraft. This development was forcing us into the factory air raid shelters on most days of the week, resulting in a total loss of production of hundreds of hours work.

With a workforce of over eight hundred personnel employed in the company, the stoppages were causing some concern to management. When the bells throughout the factory started to ring, everyone could be relied on to reach the shelters in double-quick time with it being an issue of a matter of life and death. But on the 'All Clear', it turned out to be different in many ways.

The true situation can be summed up in this memo to all staff in charge of shelters at the time:

Special note for Staff in charge of Shelters.
1st October 1940

Please note the following points and they must be strictly adhered to under all circumstances

1) There must be no smoking in the Shelters. This is absolutely essential, as the air must be kept as fresh as possible. Should the sirens go in the Town, no notice should be taken of them until the bell rings.

2) Persons in Shelters are to remain as quiet as possible, since Spotters are listening as well as trying to see any Aircraft in the vicinity.

3) Staff are to see that persons return to work quickly. There was a lot of lingering about yesterday. The all-important part of the Spotter System is to save as much time as possible. This was defeated yesterday. Also, see that all persons move to the Shelters quickly.

4) There must not be a crowd round the entrances at any time, whether there is danger or not. Keep

everyone, except one person nominated by you, inside the Shelter during the alarm period.

The Factory Owner

It was signed with a fine flourish by the factory owner and dated 1/10/40. This then was the situation we lived under, at the time, always waiting for the unexpected to happen.

Britain could only respond to the German attacks, wherever they would come. We were not strong enough yet to mount any attack in strength against Hitler's new empire.

Work was carried on, day in day out, in boring and repetitive jobs. However, we did know that our products were essential to the war effort. Loudspeakers had been installed in all departments at the onset of war. Now they were used to broadcast music from the BBC programmes. Also, the factory owner introduced his own record requests over the system, with an afternoon and evening session played at the request of the workers for the price of two pence per record. The proceeds would go in aid to one of the many war funds.

Recordings by Stanley Holloway and Bernard Miles were very popular with their light-hearted monologues, with jazz, light and classic music. The two programmes each day were always looked forward to with great interest. The boss would make some subtle comment with every record played, causing some consternation to some of the subscribers to the good cause. I always thought that he made a very commendable job on his turntable, making life a little more bearable.

In mid-November, during the hours of darkness, the centre of the city of Coventry was totally destroyed by the Luftwaffe, and its magnificent cathedral reduced to a pile of rubble. Not least was the shocking loss of life there running into hundreds. This was another grim reminder for us. It showed once again what measures Hitler was prepared to take, to bring us to our knees and complete his run of conquests in Western Europe.

I always felt sure that the German intelligence service must have known of our existence in the town – being an old established company in the electrical instrument-making field with a reputation second to none in the land. A large part of our instrument production found its way into the cockpits of all fighter and bomber planes flown by the

Royal Air Force. Some of them had our firm's title still on the dials, advertising where we were located in the land.

We also did work for the admiralty, demanding a very high standard from the workforce. There were other big contractors in the town engaged in a variety of war production. Some in the shadow factories built before the war with government aid, and turned over to war production at the onset of hostilities with Germany.

One of the contractors, making tanks, even had a railway branch line laid to dispatch its work from the factory. With all of this war potential now growing in the town, we could be looked on as a military target.

Christmas came round once again, giving us a welcome break. However, before the old year was out, the Luftwaffe set the city of London on fire in a night raid with most devastating results. Once again, I could see from the garden path the extent of the fires being far worse than anything seen before. It could have been Hitler's final fling of 1940, at his failure in not having conquered Britain, in this, the year of his greatest triumph, and he gave vent to his feelings in ordering this terror raid on the capital.

What kind of a year would 1941 bring to our embattled island? Until now, we had managed to ward off the enemy air attacks made in daylight, but the nightly bombing campaign continued with all of its problems for the citizens of London. The invasion of our shores had been ruled out for the time being after the dispersal of the German invasion barges from the French ports. But Hitler was still casting his eye around for more conquests to add to his growing empire.

Britain, in her empire, still held all of her bases in the Mediterranean and the Far East. Australia, along with New Zealand, India, Canada and South Africa had all come to our aid with the generous help of their sons in the shape of new divisions to fight alongside our own troops.

In Egypt, the British Army under General Wavell was making a move against the Italians where from Libya, Mussolini had been flexing his military muscle. The Italian leader was trying to prove to Hitler that whatever he could do, he, Mussolini, could do also. Mussolini had already invaded Greece without informing his German partner. This, in turn, forced the British government into sending forces into Greece to help them repel the invader. The fighting was still going on there, but the Italians were being held on all fronts.

It was a job to keep up with events now that our troops were fighting on two fronts many hundreds of miles apart. Looking at the maps in the daily papers, the British had a strong military base in Egypt, but the troops sent into Greece looked, even to my own untrained eye, out on a limb.

Back on the home front, we carried on the best we knew how with the rations received each week. Mother tried out some of the wartime recipes that Lord Woolton, the Minister of Food, had recommended to us. If they were short of some ingredients, you could say they were adequate, but most of all filling.

War is not just about fighting at the battlefront. It raises many other issues that have to be taken care of. Food being one of the main problems we faced. With the heavy losses taking place to our shipping, mostly in the Atlantic, it was essential that our food supply be maintained at a high level.

Hitler was now trying to starve us out, so we came back with a 'Dig for Victory' campaign. Now that we were growing most of our food, more people were needed to produce it. This problem was solved with the formation of the Women's Land Army, and with this new influx into agriculture, some men were released from their farming duties and called up into the forces. It would prove to be a tough job for the ladies moving into what had been, till now, a man's domain. The war had turned them into the new 'Sons of the Soil!'

Most of our entertainment now, other than going to the cinema, came from our friend in the corner – the wireless set. It was a welcome relief after a hard day's work at the factory, especially in the long winter evenings. Never arriving home before 8.20pm, and after getting cleaned up, all one could do was drop into a chair and switch the wireless on. There was always a plentiful supply of good comedy shows on most nights of the week, making for very good listening and taking our minds away from the war for an hour or two. The enjoyment the characters in the shows gave turned them into household names and did much to bolster morale at a time when it was sorely needed. The BBC was never more appreciated than at this time in its short history. What would we have done without it?

At the factory, we had a visit from a naval officer, and at a later date an officer of the Royal Air Force. The purpose of the visits was to try and boost extra production from the workforce with a pep talk from each of the officers. Both of the talks took place in the factory canteen in our tea break.

When the factory owner introduced the naval commander to us, he asked for, and received, a big hand for the man from the senior service. This officer, who must have been over fifty years of age, had most likely served in the First World War. His main theme in the talk was about the Battle of the Atlantic and the struggles they were having in getting the convoys through, coming from all parts of the globe into the British ports. He kept us in complete silence while he outlined what the admiralty had done to counter the U-boat menace, and he finished off by thanking us for our own efforts and the importance of the work we were doing.

Having at last finished, the commander received applause for his naval view of the war, telescoped down into a twenty-minute speech. When the applause had stopped, the factory owner was soon on his feet, reminding us all to get back to our places of work, the tea break having overrun by five minutes.

When the flight lieutenant of the Royal Air Force came down to deliver his pep talk at the factory, I suspected at the way he subsequently behaved that he could have made a visit to the company boardroom, where they kept liquid refreshment for visitors of such standing, before coming to the canteen.

The factory owner, who told us that the officer had been on bombing missions over Germany, introduced him. This won the lieutenant a big hand when he got up to speak, but not before a murmur had passed round the canteen from some of the ladies in the audience. This bordered almost on adoration at the figure standing before them. In comparison with the naval officer, whose uniform was smart but had seen better days with a lived-in appearance to it, this man was immaculately turned out as if he had stepped out of a shop in London's Saville Row.

He started his talk by telling us about the planning of a bombing raid into Germany, then on to the mission itself. The talk was quite interesting until he started to describe flying over the Alps and seeing the full moon rise over the mountain peaks. "What a wonderful sight," he said with a touch of emotion in his voice. Some of the ladies gave another sigh. "Oh yes," he said, "it's a most wonderful sight and most … romantic!" He carried on, by repeating it in different ways about his lovely moon, with the ladies just about near to a mild form of hysteria, conjured up by this handsome Royal Air Force officer standing before them with a very flushed face. The pep talk was fast turning into a giggle for the men in the audience.

In the end, he was able to conclude the story of bombing missions over Germany. The boss, who had sat throughout the talk with a look of embarrassment on his face, now jumped to his feet and started to applaud his guest of honour. We all joined in to various degrees of enthusiasm for his effort, and would long remember the flight lieutenant and his beautiful, romantic moon!

Back to the fighting in the Western Desert, the British forces had done well in forcing the Italians out of their strong positions and had them on the run. But our victory was short-lived. By the end of March, the German Army started to arrive in Tripoli in the shape of two divisions. The main aim of the new troops was to stiffen the resolve of the flagging Italian divisions who had come close to a rout in their last encounter with the British forces. The new commander of the German-Italian force would be a German with the name of Erwin Rommel.

We were to encounter the same problem with our forces fighting in Greece, where once again the intervention by the Germans took a hand in helping their Italian allies to push us out of Greece.

From the start, we had not been there in sufficient numbers to influence the battle. So, after a brief campaign there, all of our forces were evacuated by the beginning of May. This was indeed very bad news, showing us once again that we did not have the men or equipment yet to be able to match the German war machine.

I scanned the *News Chronicle*, our daily newspaper, for information about the fronts, but could find nothing more than I already knew from the news broadcasts. News was always tight when we were on the defensive and it could just be one of those times.

The fighting in the Western Desert had taken a turn for the worse with the intervention of the German forces, and would make life more difficult for our 8th Army. It was the most dreadful of places to wage a battle, with all the discomforts the desert could inflict on anyone having to fight there. I sincerely hoped that I would never be called on to serve there in such a barren and inhospitable place.

Now that I had attained my 17th birthday, there was now only a year to run before I became eligible for military service. One thing I had decided on was to join the Army if called up.

On the 10th of May, we had a surprise – the landing in Scotland of Rudolf Hess – Hitler's deputy and a man of great standing in the Nazi Party. Why did he come here, and why had he fled his own country in a stolen aircraft? After his interrogation, Hess was imprisoned here. The whole affair became shrouded in mystery with a wall of secrecy drawn tight around this amazing episode in the war.

It could be coincidence, but that very night London suffered one of its most severe raids. By this time, Hitler would have surmised that his late deputy would have been taken to the capital for interrogation. In his wrath, Hitler ordered the Luftwaffe into action, knowing that Hess would hear, if not feel, the power of his late master. With the bombing alone, Hitler could guarantee Hess not receiving a good reception here, especially after the killing of many more innocent civilians.

The flight of Hess from Germany made a good subject to talk about at the factory. With all of the ideas put forward, some could have been near the truth. But in the end, we would all forget about Hess and his reason for coming as the war moved on to a further surprising event. This one single event would dramatically alter the course of the war.

3. Reprieve. Japanese treachery. Call-up.

On the 22nd of June 1941, Germany, with untold savagery, turned on Russia, whose troops on the borders fell back in disarray before the German onslaught. The shop floor, after sharing views on the new situation, could find no answer to it all. Why had Hitler turned on Russia (when they had both signed a non-aggression pact) when he still had us (the old enemy) to deal with? It must have been him showing his contempt for us, knowing full well that we were in no position to take advantage of him switching his forces from the Western to the Eastern Front.

Germany was now fighting on two fronts with a third looming in the Mediterranean, with the involvement of German forces there attempting to inject some starch into the flagging Italian Army.

Within weeks, the German forces had pushed the Russians out of Poland and were now making wide inroads into Russia itself. No one could doubt the power of the German Army, but at least it had lifted the threat of invasion from our own shores.

It was usual on Thursday mornings, at around 10.30, to be paid a visit by the chairman and founder of the company. He would arrive at the factory in his chauffeur-driven car. He would then come into the shop, we being first on his round, and walk slowly passed his employees who would be working away at bench or machine under the noisy overhead belting that ran the length of the shop. He rarely engaged in conversation on the shop floor unless interested in some process that he would like explained. I think he was too much of a gentleman to complain on the spot with something he did not approve of, but later take up the matter with his son, the managing director.

Then, without having a long illness, we received the unexpected and sad news of the chairman's death. He was a thoughtful man and treated his employees fairly, being way ahead of his time with better social conditions, like paid holidays, a pension fund and a sports ground.

A works committee was set up to commemorate his passing with a bronze plaque. A donation was asked for, of sixpence from each employee in the company, and was collected without dissention from the near nine hundred staff employed there. How they ever found the bronze to make this, with a war going on and the metal at a premium, I shall never know. After it was finished, the plaque was placed in the hall, and what a magnificent job the foundry had made. Thinking of the calibre of the man, the use of the bronze was more than justifiable to his memory.

Back to the war, with Hitler expending most of his fury in Russia, he was still able to devote some considerable part of it here with raids by the Luftwaffe by night, mostly on the capital. This, on the whole, created a deep sense of insecurity into the minds of the longsuffering people. For them it was no easy task whenever the sirens sounded, to trudge to the shelters with their few treasured possessions. And this could happen several times in any given week. Their failure to do so was to risk death or injury.

On one of my Thursdays off from work, along with three other members of the family, we decided to go and have a look at the damage there. This, we could see before our train reached its destination at Marylebone with plenty of damage alongside the tracks. We made several journeys around the city, viewing from the top of a bus, which made a fine vantage point for us.

I remember a news broadcaster on the radio stating that you had to take a bus ride to find the damage. They were right. When you did, you could only be shocked by the sight and magnitude of the damage before your eyes. In some places, acres of rubble was all that remained of large buildings and homes. Some of it was still smouldering from past raids, and was being hosed down by members of the fire brigade. I noticed they were wearing a simple emblem in red over their breast pocket and on it one word – LONDON. Without doubt, they were in the most hazardous job one could ever be called on to do, constantly exposed to danger while fighting the fires with the raiders overhead feeding the fires with more incendiary and bombs.

After returning from a visit to see the damage at Dalstone Lane, Hackney, where the Germans had paid many visits in the past months, we decided to go and see a place that had taken no damage so far. Our destination was St. Paul's cathedral, and our timing was most fortunate in that one of its famous lunchtime concerts was in progress there. Arrayed around the steps into the cathedral, a Dutch military band was performing before a very enthusiastic audience of several hundred. They were enjoying the fine music and the unusual setting for the event, of the magnificent towering dome. It was a most moving experience after having seen the destruction in some parts of the city, and here was the cathedral still standing in all its magnificence.

Countless thousands of lives had already been lost in the struggle for our survival. The fact that we still had to win the war was a cold and sobering thought.

Going back home on the train, I was glad that I had seen the damage at firsthand. It made us feel all the more conscious of other people's suffering. Three things of our visit, I would long remember: The inspirational playing of the Dutch band at the cathedral – a memory that would last forever. Many miles of hosepipe lying criss-crossed in the roads, some of it leaking with jets of water springing from their damaged casings. And lastly was a large billboard we saw in the city with the words, 'If you can kneel before your God, you can stand before your Enemy!' I could fully agree with the sentiments of the first part, but could not come to terms with the second.

The German advance into Russia continued apace with some major cities falling to the aggressor. Even Moscow was now under threat, and if it should fall it would be a calamity not only for the Russians but the war in general. Our own forces fighting in the desert had started out on a new offensive, this time from Libya against their new enemy, Rommel and his newly reconstituted Afrika Korps. The Italians were now showing more vim since his arrival with the German force. This was bad news for us, alongside the latest events from the Eastern Front.

At home, a remark by my father helped us keep our sense of humour at a time when there was little margin between laughing and crying. One night, after having retired to bed, we were awakened from our slumbers by the wailing of sirens in the town, bringing all of us downstairs in various stages of sleep. We could hear the drone of the aircraft flying overhead, no doubt on their way to bomb targets in the Midlands. After an hour or so had elapsed without the 'All Clear' sounding, my father, who worked very hard and was approaching retirement age, decided he was going back to bed – danger or no danger. We were all rather concerned for his safety, more so when we could hear the bombers returning.

My mother, who was now in a state of some agitation, went to the foot of the stairs and called up in a shaky voice, "Dad, the German planes are overhead, you should come down!" A curt reply came back from my father, still in bed and unmoveable, "I don't care if they are Spanish!" This attitude of my father's made us smile and, much later, would make us laugh at the sheer cheek of the remark. The 'Spanish' planes would become, in time, a family byword.

With the beginning of December 1941, it was time for thinking about gifts for the family; now very hard to find in this, the third year of the war. This would be my last Christmas at home if I were called up for military service after my 18th birthday in March. Our thoughts of a peaceful Christmas were somewhat shattered by the news of the Japanese attack on the United States fleet, at Pearl Harbour on the 7th, causing crippling damage to the Pacific fleet.

Within days, America and Britain declared war on Japan. Then, in turn, Germany and Italy declared war on the United States of America. Sides had been taken, turning the war in Europe into a global conflict. Britain now had America and Russia on her side in the fight against Hitler, giving us a more than even chance of survival than we ever held before. However, the picture coming from the Far East was not so good.

The Japanese wasted no time; with great speed, they invaded the Philippines, Burma and Borneo. Then the terrible news broke of the naval losses of HMS *The Prince of Wales* and HMS *Repulse*, sunk with great loss of life off the Malaya coast in trying to stop the Japanese invasion forces. The very thought that two capital ships of such calibre could be sunk in so short a time filled us with dismay, bordering on disbelief at such a tragedy so soon in the new war.

Bad news became a daily event from the Far East and the Pacific; with a new kind of warfare, none of us could understand. Remembering my schoolboy jargon, I could say that the 'Yellow Peril' were most definitely on the march against us. One good piece of news did reach us before the Christmas Holiday, this time from the Desert where the siege of Tobruk was raised and Benghazi retaken.

With the war now in the Far East, the Germans at the gates of Moscow and the fighting in the Western Desert taking place, it was hard to think of Christmas in terms of peace and goodwill to all men. Nevertheless, we still managed to enjoy our Christmas with a two-day break from our everlasting, repetitive jobs at the factory. Even so, it was far more acceptable than the hazards of most service life and the loss of all home comforts, or leaving home.

The New Year 1942 had come and gone but not, unfortunately, our troubles with bad news from most fronts coming in daily. The German and Italian forces had started a new offensive against the 8th Army in the Western Desert. However, the German advance into Russia had been stopped by the severity of the cold weather. Whereas in the Far East, the Japanese were roaming at will in their conquest of lands in the Pacific. It would take the Allied forces a long time before they overcame the supremacy the Japanese had gained by their act of treachery at Pearl Harbour.

The sheer scale of the logistical problems for the United States Navy was graphically shown on a newsreel at the cinemas. With the help of a large-scale map covering the United States Western Seaboard and the Pacific Ocean, a naval officer, with the aid of a graduated rod marked off into 24 hours of steaming time for the naval ships, was showing how difficult it was to reinforce the danger points now under threat of invasion from the 'Land of the Rising Sun'.

Back home, in the comparative safety of 'Fortress Great Britain', thousands of miles from the main battlefronts, we had rather a bad shock. The German battleships *Soharnhorst*, *Prince Eugen* and *Gneisenau* moved out from their base at Brest. The battleships had been trapped in the port, and now Hitler wanted them moved for raiding in the North Atlantic. They came sweeping up the English Channel at full speed, keeping well into the French coastline and out of range of our coastal batteries.

The audacity of the action took the services completely by surprise. All our forces could muster in trying to stop the ships were the old, outdated Fairey Swordfish torpedo-carrying planes. The crews in the Swordfish did their level best in trying to stop the ships from escaping, but most of them were downed into a cold sea before they could even make their torpedo runs by the accurate and withering defensive fire put up by the German vessels. The enemy also had the advantage of a fighter escort from the Luftwaffe, flying out from their French airfields only minutes away in flying time from the actual engagement.

It was a very sad day, not only for the loss of the men, but no reward gained for the courage and effort made. Angry questions were asked in Parliament about the action in the Channel. Why had we not been able to mount a stronger and more aggressive force against the ships that got away?

The failure of the British Navy to stop the ships was well talked over on the shop floor. But we had little time for it to sink in before we were shaken to the roots of our very existence by a further blow.

Within days of our naval setback, we had a second humiliation. This time it was the staggering news from the Far East of the fall of Singapore, the once impregnable fortress of the British Empire, now conquered by an inferior force of the Japanese. The garrison in Singapore was under the command of General Percival with 130,000 men at his disposal. Why then did he surrender and see his men marched off into captivity? Newspapers were full of pictures of the surrender; pictures you did not wish to look upon and feel happy about.

The irony of the situation lay in the fact that all the large guns, for the defence of Singapore, could only traverse seawards from where a traditional attack, the British said, would come. The Japanese did not oblige the British and came through the jungle to take them in the rear. The Australian troops and a few other units put up a spirited fight, but in the main, they just gave in for lack of good leadership at the top. It was a major disaster for British Arms, the worst of its kind in our history.

In our first engagement on land with the new enemy here, we had managed to lose without a fight. Nearly half the total number of men that the Navy had picked up from the beach at Dunkirk, at such great loss in men and ships, just to see it all thrown away by surrendering to a force of about 30,000 men of the Imperial Japanese Army. To say the public were in a state of bewilderment, at the loss of Singapore, was incorrect. In fact, they were downright furious at the scale of our misfortune there.

What was going to happen to the poor swines led away into captivity? The Chinese had never been treated very fairly by their Japanese conquerors over the past ten years of fighting on the Chinese mainland. We had seen evidence of this over the years, from the newsreels at the cinemas, with the most brutal scenes imaginable on the silver screen in front of us, of men and women in captivity being killed off by their barbaric captors without any sign of mercy shown. One thing we were aware of, from the start of the Japanese conflict, and that was they would never abide by the Geneva Convention.

It was now March and I had attained my 18th birthday, and in so doing had made myself allegeable for military service. For me it became a most unstable time, waiting for something that was going to change my way of life, in the form of a letter from HMS.

Time went by and no word came. But the battles still raged with the fall of Rangoon to the Japanese, and more set backs for us in the desert war. The only light on the horizon was the great success of the Russian Army, forcing the Germans back on the defensive with very heavy losses on both sides.

Our own battles in the factory went on with the management asking evermore for more production. No one, to my knowledge, was ever paid an extra farthing for the large increase in production achieved there during my time in the war.

With all the windows in the factory painted black from the first days of the war and bolted shut in summer and winter, we never did see a lot of natural daylight. Now, even the most athletic and robust of men and women had a face with a whitish pallor, no doubt the consequence of working too long under artificial lights.

On coming out of the factory into the bright sunlight, you had to shield your eyes from the glare while you adjusted to the changed condition. I had been suffering for sometime with very severe headaches. The only remedy that would ease the pain was a quiet darkroom.

With the months slipping away into summer, we found our fortune on the fighting fronts at its lowest ebb since the war started. British forces were in big trouble in North Africa where Rommel was forcing our Army into making many bad decisions. In the Far East, the Japanese were still on the rampage and it was difficult to see how they could be stopped. On the Russian Front, where they had done so well, the Russians were now in retreat on all fronts before a big German counteroffensive. I could never see how the war could ever change in our favour. At times like this, victory looked far from certain.

I now received a letter, not the one I had expected, but a notification from the municipal council office telling me to report at the police station for enrolment into the civil defence (ARP warden). After work on the day stated, I presented myself at the station. The desk sergeant, having read the document, looked me up and down, shrugged his shoulders and said, "Don't bother with this, son. They appear to have made an error." And that was it; my role as a warden, strolling round blacked-out streets of the town, was not to be.

I felt sure that my name was on a list somewhere, just waiting to come up like all of the others who were waiting to join the queue of silent, unknown men. They would have the same kind of fears as me at leaving the comforts of home life, however humble they may be, for the rigorous existence of the armed forces.

Walking home from work one evening and going through the park to bypass the town (where over two years before, I had seen the camouflaged guns of the artillery standing under the trees after the retreat from Dunkirk), I was made aware of a strange noise up ahead that for the life of me I could not identify. Rounding the bend from the park and coming to the main road, I could immediately see the reason for this unusual sound. On reaching the road at the entrance to the park, I was confronted with a sight that lifted my spirit of mind no end.

There, marching along in front of me, were many hundreds of American Army Air Force servicemen. The strange and unfamiliar sound was coming from their marching feet; the men all issued with soft-soled boots but looked very serviceable and smart.

From my vantage point on the corner, I had a wonderful view of the column of marching men. They stretched away over the high street in the town and up the hill to the railway station yard, and still they came on. The head of the column had, by now, disappeared round the bend in the road, leading out of town with another hill to climb before they arrived at their base – a very well kept secret from us all. It was a most heart-warming sight, watching the men who had come from all parts of the United States, crossing the hostile Atlantic to give us a helping hand in the war with Germany.

I was made to wait on the corner for about ten minutes before the tail of the column had passed by, and enabling me, at last, to cross the road. The sight I had witnessed was reminiscent of a scene you might see at the cinema – the marching men symbolising the march to freedom.

Two years ago, it could well have been German troops marching down from the station in their jackboots. The noise would have been something quite different to what I did hear on that unforgettable evening. The American 'soft shoe shuffle' approach or the 'strident crunch' of the German jackboot, and I for one was glad and most grateful that the Americans had arrived here first. Any thought or threat of invasion of our land had finally been lifted with the arrival of new reinforcements from the New World.

The Army Air Force was quick to get its bombing campaign underway, flying out of airfields in southeast England. Squadrons of planes, we saw flying over, came from around Oxfordshire. They passed over at altitudes of many thousands of feet, in combat formations ready to ward off the German fighter planes they were bound to encounter when they crossed the French coast.

The Flying Fortress was now the frontline bomber with the American Air Force, so-called for its massive firepower onboard. All missions flown over enemy territory were done in broad daylight, a necessary aid for navigation and precision bombing.

I very rarely saw them fly out on a mission but did see many return, flying at a much lower altitude than when they were starting on the mission. Sadly, you would see many empty spaces in the formations, a clear indication to us, on the ground, of losses they had been forced to incur in carrying out the mission.

On one occasion, walking over the hill on my day off, I was fortunate to see some of them return from such a mission. I could hear them long before they made their appearance, flying up the valley. I was completely surprised by the aircraft when they suddenly came into view. Flying at no more than a few hundred feet from where I was standing, I could see the damage the planes had suffered. Some propellers on the engines were not revolving, showing the engine was dead or shut down. One plane had a large piece missing from its tail section, showing how close it had come to going down, out of control. With a deafening roar, the planes passed on into the distance.

What I could not see were the casualties they must have had onboard, possibly some dead, and others wounded, lying on the fuselage floor waiting for medical attention. Until now, I had seen no evidence of the real war except for the bomb damage I had witnessed in London. Seeing the planes with their damage at such close quarters was a grim reminder of the war still to be won.

Our fortunes had taken some very nasty knocks over the past months with the enemy regaining the upper hand on all the major battlefronts. The Americans had some success in the Far East, at the Battle of Midway Island. A great naval victory for them after so many setbacks at the hands of the Japanese who still managed to control the North West Pacific, and wreaked havoc wherever they raised the flag of the 'Rising Sun'. All of the forces fighting the Japanese were having a tough time in trying to contain them. The 'Yellow' horde seemed to be everywhere in that area of the world.

Back home, the BBC announced an item in the main news broadcast that a new general had been chosen to command the British 8th Army. His name was Bernard Montgomery. It was hoped that he would have more success than his predecessors in the post, now that we had been pushed back over the Egyptian frontier. Losing Egypt altogether would be a catastrophe of the highest order.

I received a letter from the Ministry of Labour and National Service, to submit myself for a medical examination before a medical board for grading. It went on: 'Failure to do so will result in a fine, imprisonment, or both,' if I failed to appear on the afternoon of the 21st of September 1942.

The medical board had taken over a church hall in the town, fitted out into cubicles with hanging curtains to carry out their task in some privacy. Here, a team of doctors, all specialists in their own field, examined us for any defects we may have from our eyes and ears to the soles of our feet. The doctors were very thorough in their work and any malingerer would have had very short shrift from the panel. They all asked me questions about any past illnesses, or if I had ever been an epileptic: "Have you any distinctive marks on your body for identification purposes?" "Yes! A large scar under my right knee."

Lastly, you were set an intelligence test. I was given a book with a series of pictures on every page. The task set before me was to state which picture, on that particular page, did not match or correspond with the rest of the set. The first pages of the book were simple to work out, but with the turn of every page thereafter it became more difficult for the brain to cope. However, in the end the examiner was well satisfied with my effort and, after waiting sometime, I was given a grade card with the grade written in red ink – I (One).

The medical ended with an interview with a lieutenant colonel. He told me, "Your company has placed a deferment order on your call-up." So I asked him, "Would I eventually be called up for military service?" His reply to that was, "You could very well be in the near future." He then asked me, "Are you prepared to be called for service, regardless of the deferment order placed on you?" "Yes, sir!" I replied. "One more thing," he asked, "what service do you have preference for, if you are called?" "The Army, sir!" The interview was over.

I had, in no way, volunteered to join the service, but at the same time I was unable to standby on the sidelines, knowing that others in my own age group had been called up while I stayed with the company.

I had been in this church hall many years before, on an exchange visit with our own Sunday school, less than 200 yards away. Now I was here for an entirely different reason altogether. Having been given the remainder of the day off, I returned home for tea, a privilege I imagined would very soon come to an end.

I completed the rest of my day off by paying a visit to the cinema where the film *The First of the Few* with Leslie Howard was being shown. It was a very good film, but not fully appreciated by me. In the less interesting parts, my mind was taken up with what the colonel had told me. I must admit that it put a damper on fully enjoying the film.

On returning to work the next day, I was asked innumerable questions about the medical and interview by my friends. They would still have to take their own in good time. I thought it best not to tell them too much about the details of the interview. It could very well get back to the management who would be most annoyed at my apparent ingratitude to the company.

On the 23rd of October, we received some good news over the radio. The 8th Army under its new commander, Montgomery, had gone on to the offensive with a massive artillery barrage on German and Italian positions at a place called El Alamein, not many miles from our naval base at Alexandria.

Within days, the 8th Army were able to pierce the German fortifications in many places and, by the beginning of November, had the Germans and Italians in full retreat. This, we felt, seemed a more substantial victory than other battles that had taken place in the desert. It was strange to think of Rommel on the run, when up till now he had only a string of victories to his credit.

On Thursday the 12th of November, which happened to be my day off, I received an official looking letter by the 8 o'clock post that told me it was on His Majesties Service. On opening it, I found that I had received my call-up papers, telling me, or should I say instructing me to report to Meanee Barracks, Colchester, on Thursday the 19th of November 1942.

It went on: 'If you fail to comply with this order, the police will be informed of your absence. You should arrive at the barracks early rather than late in the day, using the travel warrant enclosed for the railway journey. Bring along your razor and toothbrush. Also, a travelling case for returning your civilian clothes back to your home address'. The colonel had been proved right. It was sooner, not later.

What I had to do was inform the company of this new development in my personal situation. After showing the shop foreman my letter, he in turn passed it on to the office. They were holding documents I now required to pass on into the Army administration. While I was waiting for the foreman, I passed down the lines of benches and machines saying goodbye to my numerous friends in the shop. The foreman returned with the documents and my pay, in full, and after a friendly chat and wishing me well, I walked out of the factory into the street, leaving all the noise and bustle behind me that war production entailed.

Walking back home, I now felt some misgivings about the suddenness of events that had overtaken me. From a job of complete security and a good home, to 'God knows what'.

I had the whole week to get myself prepared, and firstly I was hoping that I might be able to buy myself a watch to take with me. After conferring with my mother about the likelihood of obtaining a watch, after three years of war, she just said, "Leave it to me." Later, after a visit into town, she returned in triumph with a watch at the cost of £2. It would be a week's wages used up in getting the watch.

Thinking ahead, it would be most unlikely that I would receive any leave this side of Christmas or New Year. So again, with my mothers help, we decided to go Christmas shopping for the rest of the family, and niece and nephew and their parents who would all be at home on Christmas Day with mother and father.

The week soon sped by and on the last day I went to my regular barber for a haircut. I explained to him that I needed it to be cut very short, and he did just that for me, having no wish to be pulled up for long hair on my first parade.

My father called me early the next morning, for me to get a quick start. Having said farewell to my parents with the promise of writing home just as soon as was possible, I started out on my journey into a cold, blacked-out morning with my few belongings in a near-empty suitcase.

In the past week, I had found out that a few of my old school friends had also been called up, and were also going to Colchester, but only one of them going to the same barracks as myself.

A brisk walk through the darkened streets soon got me to the railway station where I soon teamed up with the others. The train appeared out of the gloom, and we all piled on with the rest of the passengers about to depart on their own daily tasks. I felt very envious of the other passengers in the compartments. They were not carrying, like us, the telltale sign of the suitcase. They would be returning home after their day at the office or factory. We would not.

The train pulled away from the station, taking us away from our past ways into a new existence. We spent the journey to London Marylebone talking between ourselves at how we would fare on arrival at our destination, the garrison town of Colchester. This old place, dating back to Roman times, has always been a military camp for the training of soldiers.

On arrival at Marylebone, we took the tube for Liverpool Street station where the place thronged with Army personnel, coming and going with a great deal of intervention by a large contingent of military police – redcaps – checking the passes of one and all with a uniform on.

After a short wait, we boarded the train for the final part of our journey. It was a slow train, stopping at stations along the way, but at last the train pulled into a station that could only be our destination, confirmed by the porters calling out, "Colchester … Colchester!" I moved out of my seat with some reluctance.

In the station yard, a number of 3-ton lorries were waiting for us with the driver of each vehicle calling out the name of the barracks they would be leaving for. My friends moved away to their own lorries, leaving the two of us bound for Meanee. I climbed up into the vehicle with a host of others (all new faces), ranging in age from nineteen to the middle thirties. They would have come from all walks of life, into the melting pot of the Army.

4. "Keep your name off the village war memorial!"

The lorry, now full, started off on its journey, passing through the town on its way to the barracks. I noticed on the way there that one picture house was showing the film *Tortilla Flat* starring Spencer Tracy. Without thinking, I decided that I would pay the cinema a visit at the weekend.

Moving up a slight incline at the edge of the town, we were there, passing through large wrought iron gates into the barracks. A wide road ran down the length of the post with the accommodation blocks, two storeys high, running along the right-hand side with small ancillary buildings on the other; the first one inside the gate being the orderly room and guardhouse.

After removing ourselves from the vehicle, we were ordered by an NCO (non commissioned officer) to form up outside a reception building. In single file, we passed by officials documenting details of each man in the new intake. Questions we were asked: next of kin, religious denomination, trade on enlistment and a host of other details when, at the end, I was given a slip of paper with some numbers on – 14356964. This was to be my new identification, and I had been posted into D Company. Unfortunately, my friend was posted into another company.

After waiting some time with an ever-increasing group of men, who would be serving together in the same platoon, we were taken to our quarters on the ground floor of one of the barrack blocks. Here we deposited our belongings onto bunk beds. I selected a bottom berth on the side of the room away from the mainstream of men coming and going. If all the bunks were filled, there would be forty in the room. A Lance Corporal Wickham now arrived on the scene. He would be in charge of us, and billeted in the same room.

His first task was to march the platoon to the mess hall for the midday meal. I, by this time, had been without food and drink for about six hours, and was looking forward to my first meal in the Army. In this I was rather disappointed when one of the cooks at the serving counter placed a ladle full of stew onto my plate, which comprised in the main of carrots swimming in greasy looking water with half a slice of bread per man to go with it. I had never been able to eat carrots in my meals back home, so a decision had to be made there and then. It was a simple choice – eat the things or starve!

Sitting down at one of the mess tables with my newfound companions, I could hear that they were making a few unpleasant remarks about what they had in front of them. I cleared my own plate and wiped it dry with the bread.

After the meal was over, we formed up outside and marched back to our quarters where we found the platoon sergeant waiting for us. He introduced himself saying, "I am your platoon sergeant, and you will always address me as Sergeant Atterbury. You must always stand to attention when you speak with an NCO or an officer, and you will call him sir!" He continued. "Never speak to an officer unless spoken to. If you wish to speak with an officer, you must first notify an NCO of the matter. Don't forget to always salute the officers."

Sergeant Atterbury went on. "My job in the next six weeks is to take you through basic infantry training; in small arms, drill and fieldcraft." The sergeant now looked very seriously at his new intake and continued. "Always pay attention to what I tell you, if you want to keep your name off the village war memorial!" He then went on to say, "You have no rights in the Army. Your only entitlement is to be given three meals a day."

The sergeant continued. "Everything you receive is a privilege, like pay and leave." He also made reference to a book that he carried with him, titled 'Kings Rules and Regulations' that left us in no doubt that we were in the Army now. "Don't forget," the sergeant went on, "to listen to the bugle calls in the camp, and recognise the different calls played. Reveille, mess calls, fire picket and lights out are the main calls that should interest you. Lastly, if any man feels unfit for duty, he must first notify an NCO to place his name on sick report for sick parade. Before we go outside for a guided tour of the camp, I can tell you that you will be issued with your Army kit tomorrow and get your civilian clothes posted home."

Before he marched his platoon off, the sergeant put us through our paces with some drill. "I can't have you going around like a rabble, even when you are still in civilian clothes." When our drill had improved to his own satisfaction, he marched us off with our first stop at the main gate and the guardhouse. "Make sure that none of you end up in there. Keep out of trouble and obey without question all orders given you."

We moving on, working our way around the camp, and were shown most places that would affect us in our stay here. These including among them, the barber's shop, armoury, ·22" rifle range, the straw-shed and a building containing a gas chamber, in which eventually we would all have to pass through as part of the training.

The tour of the camp over and back outside the billet, the sergeant, with his platoon standing to attention, walked along the backs of the three ranks of men, tapping some of them on the shoulder in passing with a comment made in a quiet voice, "Haircut."

I stood there in complete confidence that he would walk by without touching me on the shoulder. But he did. "Haircut." My first reaction was to reply to him that I had visited a barber only the day before, but stopped by a visionary glimpse of the dreaded guardhouse for answering the sergeant back. He moved to the front of his civilian platoon, reminding some of us to make a visit to the camp barber that evening. "Corporal Wickham will now take you over to the straw-shed to get your palliasses filled. Take over, Corporal!" and the sergeant was gone.

An empty palliasse was on each bunk. This was a canvas pocket with ties down its side, into which we were about to stuff with straw. Taking orders now from Corporal Wickham was of a more light-hearted nature after our spell with the 'Grim Reaper'. The corporal told us not to stuff too much straw in; otherwise, it would form lumps and be most uncomfortable for sleeping on. The straw was a very poor substitute indeed for the beds we had left behind. After our task in the shed was complete, we carried back our mattresses in our own time, marching together with them being impossible.

After hearing the mess call, the corporal had us form up outside and marched us off to our tea. This comprised of bread with margarine and jam, about a 3oz slice of fruitcake and tea served out in a pint enamel mug. Our meal over, we walked back to the place that would be our new home for the next six weeks, taking us up to the New Year.

For those of us that needed the attention of the barber, we made our way across the darkened parade ground and made our entry. It was rather a dingy place, no frills in this establishment. When my turn came round, I sat in the chair and he wrapped a cloth around my neck and shoulders with a complete absence of nicety that I had received in the hands of other barbers. It must have been obvious to him that in our civilian clothing, we were a new intake who had fallen foul of our overzealous sergeant. In my case, he would soon 'correct' the error I had made.

Taking up his razor, a cutthroat, he set to work on the back of my neck, where in no time I began to feel most uncomfortable with a burning sensation creeping round my neck from his excessive misuse of the razor. What the so-called barber had done for me would have no doubt ruined his reputation outside, in a high street shop, with a black eye for good measure but, in here, he was king. Once again, the shadow of the guardhouse had cast its influence over speaking out.

Outside again in the dark, I gingerly placed my hand on my neck, trying to gain some comfort from it, only to find it had more of an aggravating effect than before. I decided there and then, that in future I would have it cut outside the camp, and better not to draw attention to it with my new friends.

When we had all returned to the billet, the corporal called for our attention and to sit around on the bottom bunks. Firstly, he called our names from the roster with our answering call of "Corporal!" Finding his list was all present and correct, the corporal got on with his role of informing us of more rules and regulations we must comply with. "For instance," he said, "you must read the company orders every day for any duties you may be detailed to carry out. You will find the noticeboard with the words on 'Read and Digest Thoroughly'! Make sure you do."

The corporal continued. "The washroom door is by the side of the noticeboard, and some of you may have noticed already that we only have cold water on tap, but you must shave every morning before first parade at 6.30, reveille being at 6 o'clock. In the first half-hour, you must wash, shave and make up your bed in a uniform manner. You can see how I make mine up in the morning. By the way," the corporal went on, "I should have mentioned this before to you. Don't try and leave the camp for any reason, you are all confined to barracks for the next few days. During that time, you will be given a series of inoculations and vaccination by the MO (medical officer). Anyway, it will be a good chance over the weekend to work on your kit, polish the brass work on the webbing, give your boots a coat of dubbing and so on."

The corporal filled us in with a mass of information, and good tips of sound advice to follow in the future. He was not a bad chap, only doing his job of turning us into soldiers. Meanee Barracks, we were told, was run by the Royal Sussex and Royal Berkshire Regiments, he being in the Royal Sussex and his sergeant in the Royal Berkshires who he mentioned had been on the Mission to Moscow, led by Sir Stafford Cripps. The sergeant must have been good at his job to be chosen for the mission. However, he was no longer a young man and could be in his forties, twice the age of the corporal who could be a year older than me.

The session with the corporal over, he took us along to the cookhouse to see what was on offer there. I came away having had a good portion of bread and cheese and a mug of hot sweet tea.

We just talked with each other for the remainder of the evening, and by the time of lights out at 10 o'clock, we had made our beds up with the three Army blankets provided, and a round bolster we would use like a pillow. Before the bugle sounded at 10 o'clock, the corporal warned us that it would soon be lights out. The rest of us, not already in our bunks, crawled or jumped in depending on what level you were on. I was glad from the start that I could crawl into bed, while some on the top bunks made very hard work of it.

The trouble on my neck flared up again when it came into contact with the coarse blanket on the bolster. All I could do for relief from the burning pain was to lie on my side and bury my face into the bolster where after a time it did feel better. I would always remember my first day in this camp, not only for the injustice at the hands of the camp barber, but a host of other things that one was now involved in.

The bugle began to sound lights out, and the corporal obliged by plunging his platoon into darkness. The straw in our palliasses rustled away with the men getting settled in their beds. I lay and thought to myself about the other men lying in the dark. Would they have the same problem of not being able to sleep away from their homes?

It was the first time in my life that I had been parted from my parents and home, leading me on to think of the old quotations about home we had grown up with: *'Home-Sweet-Home'*, *'Go east or west, Home's best'* and the last one saying it all, *'There's no place like Home'*. I guarantee that most of the men, lying there, would have been thinking along the same lines and endorse my sentiments. After all, we were still wearing civilian clothing and not turned into soldiers yet.

Sleep was very hard to come by, being unable to shut the mind off at will. Now that we had started a different kind of existence, of a more physical nature, we would need all the sleep we could get.

I could hear a most unfamiliar noise going on and opened my eyes. It was still dark, but not for long. The light blazed on in the room with the bugler sounding reveille – a most chilling sound to hear after coming out of a deep sleep. And to cap it all, the final realisation of where you were. We were soon out of our beds and on our feet, not altogether due to the sound of the bugle but the sound of the corporal's rousing voice.

I managed to get a place in the washroom and started shaving in the cold water, it was the best we had on offer, but it did make hard work of it. Washing round my neck, I found it less painful but still sore to the touch. Back in the billet, I made up my bed in the prescribed manner and waited for the parade to begin.

It started at 6.30, and was held in the room. Over the wintertime with a complete blackout outside, it was the only way to get the training done. The corporal called the parade to order, and told us to form a semi-circle round the table he was standing by. He then moved to his bunk and pulled out, from underneath, a Bren gun procured from the armoury for our first encounter with a weapon that could kill.

"Pay attention now and listen, it's in your own interest." The corporal then gave us a talk on the use of the Bren gun in its role in an infantry section, and later the more technical details. He finished by dismantling the weapon into its main parts, and then selected some of the men to assemble it again. The corporal was good at his job of instructing; otherwise, he would never have managed to be on the training staff. He had also done his training there and retained after finishing his own General Service Corps training.

The lesson with the Bren over, the corporal marched us off to our breakfast that comprised of porridge with salt, one sausage with beans, a slice of bread and a cup of tea to help it down.

Later in the morning, and still in our civilian clothing, we were marched to the camp's administration building. Here, Army clerks now worked on our documentation for Army records, and our new 'Army Book 64: The Soldier's Service' and pay-books, part one and two, replacing our civilian identity card which had now been confiscated.

One of the many pay clerks there asked me, "Do you wish to make a contribution home each week to your next of kin, deducted from the pay in increments of 7/- shillings?" It had come to our knowledge that if a single-man made no contribution home, then their next of kin would receive no pension if the man lost his life in the service. I thought it a rather ruthless attitude for the authorities to take, such an unfeeling position. The married men had no say in the matter. In their case, deductions were automatically made. In my own case, I wished to make a 7/- shilling a week allowance to my parents and, if sent abroad at a later date, I would double it.

A great deal of information was required for part one of the pay-book, this being in retrospect a complete record of the man at the start of his Army service.

Our next port of call was a visit to the MO. On entering into his domain, the platoon was ordered to stand in a single line. With our coats off and shirtsleeves rolled well up, each of us would slowly advance towards him, and turn for inoculation in the left arm, then turn about, then into the right. I felt some trepidation, waiting there for my turn.

The scene here, in front of me, was reminiscent of a James Cagney film I had seen in the past where he, having been called up for military service in the First World War, awaits his turn in a file of men for inoculation with some of them not too keen to have it done. Cagney boastfully tells them, "There's nothing to it. I can take it!" When it's Cagney's turn, the medical officer takes his arm to inject, only to find that the man's passed out and on his way to the ground. I hoped that none of us would 'Cagney Out'. And no one did.

The corporal reminded us that we would all be back here in the morning for vaccination, and warned us again about leaving the camp. We were all placed on light duties over the weekend; giving us all a chance to recover from the two inoculations and the vaccination still to come.

After our midday meal, in what was called the cookhouse by all and sundry, the platoon was notified to parade at the quartermaster's stores at 14.00 hours for the drawing out of our kit. Having marched to the stores, we filed inside and reformed into three ranks. The quartermaster was there, along with his orderly store men waiting behind a counter for the command, from him, to start kitting us out from the numerous racks piled high with Army stores.

The quartermaster addressed us so. "Don't forget to take care of the articles you are being issued with. They cost a great deal of money and have to be paid for by the taxpayers in the country." The entire platoon would have loved the opportunity of telling the officer that, indeed, we had been paying our tax till the needs of the Army decided otherwise. But none of us did tell him.

The first man in line went to the counter and was given a kit bag, and proceeded down the counter accompanied by an orderly, who must have been a tailor, calling out the garment size for each man. At the end of the counter, the kit bag was full to overflowing with the items received. They were:

Anklets webbing	Belt webbing
Blouse Battledress	Boots ankle
Braces trousers	Braces webbing L&R
Cap	Drawer's cellular
Field Dressing	Gas-Cape
Gloves knitted	Greatcoat
Ground Sheet	Helmet steel

'House-wife'	Jack-knife
Jacket Khaki Drill	Jersey Pullover
Knife, Fork & Spoon	Mess Tins set
Mug enamel	Overalls
Pack large	Pack small
Pouch Ammunition 2	Respirator
Shirts	Shoe Brush
Shoes canvas	Shorts Khaki Drill
Socks woollen	Towels
Trousers Battledress	Trousers Khaki Drill
Vests woollen	Washing Holdall
Water Bottle	

Having returned to the billet with our overloaded kit bags, the corporal wasted no time in telling us to get changed into the new garments, with denim jackets and trousers to be worn.

Each man started to shed his smart, individual clothing, of colourful shirts and ties discarded and replaced with garments of a drab uniformity. Personally, having changed into the new clothing, it felt very strange and would take a lot of getting used to. I sadly missed my silk shirt, now replaced by the serge that increased the irritation in my neck. The boots I found were the most comfortable of footwear, being very supple and supporting the ankle at the same time, and should always have 13 studs in each sole as it was a chargeable offence to have one missing without proper reason. On the whole, I think we all felt a touch of embarrassment in our new uniforms at this stage in our training. We, no doubt, looked on ourselves as one of the awkward squads.

Having now finished with our civilian clothing, it was time to get it packed away into our suitcases for sending home. I had already prepared a short note home with my new address to go along with the case. Also, the return of the watch my mother had gone to so much trouble over, feeling certain it would never stand up to the rigorous infantry training I was about to set out on.

The corporal had managed to get a goodly supply of tie-on labels, string and brown paper sheets from the stores to bind round our cases.

When our cases were ready, the GPO were notified, and late that afternoon they were collected and taken down to the railway station on their first leg back home.

Saturday morning, after our first parade inside the billet, we were marched to our breakfast, the first time dressed as soldiers. However, not before the corporal had given us a wigging for what he called our slovenly attitude when on parade, making us come to attention many times before he marched us off.

On our return to the billet, we found Sergeant Atterbury looking round our kit layouts on our bunks and seemed well satisfied with our effort. The sergeant then had us outside on foot-drill, marching us up and down between the barrack blocks, though not on the barrack square which no doubt would come soon enough.

Vaccination parade followed the drilling, when after this was over we returned once more to our drill with the sergeant and corporal warming to their task. At long last, the parade came to an end, but not before the sergeant had called out a short list of names, mine included, on a detail to report to the officers' mess on Sunday morning at 10.00 hours. All parades finished on Saturday at 12.00 hours where the men not on camp duty could go into the town, but not before being inspected at the main gate by the camp police for any infringement in dress or lack of soldierly bearing.

For us who were confined to barracks, we got to work on the toecaps of our boots. These required to be highly polished. Also, all of the brass work on our set of webbing had to be polished until you could see your face in it.

The break in our routine also enabled us to chat with other members of the platoon, and form some kind of short-term friendships with each other. On the whole it seemed a good balance of men to be with, all coming from a similar type of background, that is bar one man. Most of the men were a lot older than me, some of them being well into their thirties, and a good many also married.

With our individual chores finished, it was teatime and we just wandered to the cookhouse in our own time (it was nice not having to be marched there) where we had a better tea than usual waiting for us in the half-empty camp. At 18.00 hours, we could light the coal fire in the billet, but never before, not even in the most atrocious weather were you allowed to. The rest of the evening was spent talking round the fire, mostly about films they had seen in the past at their local cinema. Others wrote letters home or found company in books.

On Sunday morning, I reported with the rest of the detail at the officers' mess for our duties there. At the door of the mess, the orderly sergeant, wearing his red sash of office, waited for us. "Wipe your boots and take your caps off!" he shouted, leading us through the doors into a large hallway where he detailed us off to our separate tasks. Mine, and one other member of the detail, was to scrub and wipe dry the hallway floor. Before he started us on our chores, he said, "If you are spoken to by any officer, you will stand smartly to attention and reply. Now let's get started."

We reported to the kitchen for our buckets of hot water and soap, along with scrubbing brushes and cloths. Getting onto our knees, we started on removing the dried mud from the tiled floor, with occasional visits from the orderly sergeant checking on our progress. Towards the end, my knees started to develop a dull ache, no doubt from kneeling on the cold tiles all the morning with only the thickness of my denim trousers keeping out the cold. It was hard work for what they called 'light duties'. After the orderly sergeant dismissed the detail, the rest of the day was our own.

After our Sunday dinner and back in our billet, the corporal intimated that the platoon officer could very well be paying us a visit, now that the real training of the platoon was about to commence. The corporal, with his very words, left us in no doubt that Sergeant Atterbury would expect a good performance from his squad when we moved onto the barrack square.

While he had the floor, the corporal also told us that during the coming week, we must blanco all of our webbing at a place provided for it, especially making sure of belts and anklets that would be worn on the church parade by all men who were in the Church of England. They could expect to find themselves on the parade every Sunday where the officers would inspect them before being marched away to the garrison church for a service there.

The men of other religious denominations were excused the church parade and allowed to walk into the town to their own place of worship, but not before having been inspected by the police at the main gate.

The corporal had said all he had wanted and a lot more beside, anyway it was teatime.

After our Sunday tea was over, it was soon time to light the fire again where we spent the evening in much the same way as the evening before. We just had nothing better to do with no books or wireless in the billet. Most of the men were in their bunks long before lights out.

When reveille sounded next morning, I found that placing my feet onto the ground and standing was a most painful task. I found that both knees were slightly swollen, obviously caused by them being in contact far too long with the cold, hard tiles on the floor of the officers' mess. By all things reasonable, I should report to Corporal Wickham and ask to be placed on sick parade, but I had no intention of becoming the first medical casualty in the platoon.

After just four days in the Army, I had been all but scalped by the fool of a barber, and now I had a touch of bursitis, or the more common name used of housemaid's knee. I was going to find it hard for myself on the barrack square.

After the first parade and breakfast over, the corporal had us outside for a warm-up session with our drill. Sergeant Atterbury, whose very presence on the parade made us all stand taller, soon joined us. He now marched us onto the main parade ground where other platoons were being drilled with a great deal of shouted orders coming from the sergeants.

Sergeant Atterbury decided, with the aid of Corporal Wickham, to demonstrate the correct way to drill, and gave him the order to "Stand at—ease; Atten—tion; By the Left, Quick—march, Left—Right, Left—Right; Move to the left in Diagonal march; Left incline; Right incline; About—turn." After the corporal's solo effort had been halted, the sergeant said, "That's how it should be done and that's how I want it done by this platoon."

The drill started and went very well at first, that is until one of the men got confused between his left and right, moving the wrong way and making the platoon just fold up on itself with the men aimlessly walking about trying to reform the broken ranks. The sergeant looked about due to have an epileptic fit there in front of us. "As you were!" he called out, making us cringe like an unguarded flock of sheep confronted by a wolf. "Fall back into three ranks," he cried, "and look sharp about it!"

When the platoon had sorted itself out and standing to attention, the sergeant gave us a good dressing down for our incompetence on the parade ground. He told us the remedy was more drill, so back to pounding the parade ground. Even giving our sergeant our undivided attention to being drilled, we could still see and hear with some satisfaction that other platoons drilling on the square were having the same problems; possibly more so by some of the language that was being addressed to the numerous squads there.

An officer made his way onto the parade ground, and then walked over to where Sergeant Atterbury was doing his best to forge us into a unit more suitable for use in the brigade of guards. The sergeant, now having seen the officer approaching, called the platoon to a halt and, after an exchange of salutes and a few quick words together, the sergeant turned back to his platoon and gave the order, "For inspection; Open order—march; Eyes—right; Straighten the line; Front rank, arm's length from next man; Eyes—front; Stand still."

The sergeant turned back to the officer, saluted him, and while so doing reported, "Platoon ready for your inspection, sir!" The young officer, with the rank of second lieutenant, stepped forward and walked down the three ranks of men, sometimes stopping to speak to some of them. With the inspection over, the officer and his sergeant walked back to the front of the platoon, about-turned and faced the platoon. The sergeant now giving us the order, "Close order—march; Keep still." Then with a return of salutes again, the officer walked off the parade ground.

The officer seemed a very good man, not a lot older than me. We would have a chance to find out what he was really like in the days ahead.

Sergeant Atterbury soon had us back at work after this short interlude with the officer's inspection over. He had us pounding away till we were rescued by the sound of the bugle with midday mess call.

The parade over and back inside the billet, I examined my knees for any detrimental change in the housemaid's knee situation. Both of them were still swollen, but added to that our legs were tired and leaden after our efforts on the parade ground, and if having put up with that they got no worse, I felt sure that in the end nature would take its own course.

Our identity discs were issued out to us. The pair of discs were made from an indestructible material, and had our name, number and religion stamped into them. They were joined together with waxed string, one loop for going round the neck and a shorter loop for holding the second disc to the first. Once placed round the neck, they should never be removed for any reason, and must be displayed outside your battledress on all kit inspections. Not to have them on was a criminal charge. At the end of the day, if you should 'Fall' in what they call 'Your Duty', the second disc will be removed from your person with the tag going on to Army records. This was a most grim and sobering thought that it could ever happen.

From this time, things moved on apace with our first visit to the gymnasium, which was only a short march away and was to be a twice-weekly event. I found no problem with the physical training, but always felt uneasy in the presence of the staff instructors who seemed to display a rather sadistic disregard for the men in their charge. They would pick on the new recruits to the extent that it did no credit for morale or Army discipline.

They picked on one man for supposedly having a dirty neck. "Don't you use a mirror when you wash your neck?" the poor man was asked. "We don't have a hand mirror in our washroom, Sergeant." "That's no excuse!" he howled back at the unfortunate man. "Get one!" We would all like to have the washing facilities the instructors enjoyed in their gym, with hot and cold water available to them while we had cold water and cramped conditions in our washroom. Afterwards, we could see no sign of a tidemark on the man's neck.

After our physical training sessions, we were always pleased to find Corporal Wickham waiting outside to march us back, even if it turned out to be a square bashing parade.

The platoon made a visit to the armoury to draw our rifles and bayonets. The rifle was the Short Lee-Enfield. It would make our drill all the more difficult now with a rifle on our shoulder.

We had, at this time, two lectures on consecutive evenings, held in the mess hall for the benefit of the new intake of several hundred men. On the first evening, the floor was taken by the medical officer of the depot. He pulled no punches in addressing us, in general terms, on health and hygiene while in the service and our duty in making sure that we were always fit for the job we would be called on to do in the future. We had all been before a panel of doctors at our local medical boards, and were classified Grade One. He finished with, "Make sure you stay that way!"

The personnel selection officer gave the second lecture. He gave his talk on the way they selected each individual to fit into the right kind of employment while in the service. He went on to say, "If you were a baker before you came here, we may find you better suited to become a driver, and so on." The officer carried on with, "I know too well that you would all like to become drivers, but that's not possible. We have a much greater need for infantrymen (groan) than any other part of the services, but you will be given a series of intelligence tests shortly and that will help us in deciding, eventually, where you will be posted."

Back with the training, we had our first lesson in fieldcraft, by marching out to the training site, way out of town and into the countryside. We came to a place with irregular shaped fields, hedgerows, trees and plenty of mud and water around.

The platoon officer had joined us for this exercise, but he gave Sergeant Atterbury full control of events. This he did with a demonstration by Corporal Wickham on how to crawl over the ground with the minimum of exposure to the enemy. Head well down, elbows fully extended for gaining purchase on the ground, inching yourself forward on alternative elbows with the aid of the boots for that extra push, and the rifle carried over the arms and clamped down with your jaw. That was the way it should be done.

The sergeant called out, "Get into extended line across the field and when I give the order, drop onto the ground then wait for the order to advance over the field. No one must avoid the ground in front of him, crawl through it. Let's get started then. Down! Don't worry over the mud. That will come off. Ad—vance! Keep down there."

We started off over the wet and muddy ground, trying to keep a low profile as we moved forward. It proved to be a slow and laborious task, needing a great deal of physical effort and good stamina to move any great distance.

The sergeant at last called a halt, telling us to stand and look back at the distance we had covered. We found it to be about forty yards from the start with some of the men way back down the course, and one in particular had not done very well, possibly due to his girth. Getting back onto our feet had exposed to us all the condition we were now in, from our contact with the wet ground, finding ourselves plasted on our fronts with wet mud. This would take a lot of cleaning off later, and done in our own free time with cold water.

The training session was not over yet, but while having a short break, standing round the officer, Sergeant Atterbury had our attention about when he was on the Russian Front as observer to the battle conditions there. He went on to tell us how the Germans used their mortars with such devastating effect. "If you have a mortar round land in your immediate front, then one in your rear, you know full well they are ranging rounds with the next ones falling around you. So take my advice, move out fast if you can and take up other positions. It will help to keep your name off the village war memorial if you do."

After our training session had ended, we marched back to the barracks in the failing light of the winter afternoon, the front of our uniforms now stiff with the dried mud and our webbing looking no better. It would take all the evening to get this lot cleaned up and our webbing re-blancoed for parades next day.

Friday came around and with it our first privilege of payday. The full company paraded for this in the afternoon before tea. Our sergeant had already been over the procedure for pay parade with us. Firstly, the company would be standing at ease, and then the colour sergeant would call out the name of a man, in alphabetical order. You spring to attention and call out, "Sir!" then advance to a table where the officers are sitting, halt in front of the table, salute and move over to the end of the table to sign your name on the indentation form, while the officer in charge would be signing your pay-book for the amount you will receive. The second officer places your money on the table. You collect up your money and pay-book, take a smart step backwards, salute, about-turn and march off.

Some of the men did their pay drill all wrong, and in turn were pounced on by their sergeants at the rear of the company lines. I, unfortunately, was one of them, having trouble in picking the money up from the table (in my case the sum of fourteen shillings in small change).

I was unable to hold all my money and pay-book in my left hand, leaving the right hand free for the salute. So, with some degree of dexterity, I did my best to conceal the last coins betwixt my thumb and forefinger, and stepping back one pace, saluted the officers and marched off. But not very far before Sergeant Atterbury caught up with me and in a very quiet kind of voice, almost friendly for him, said, "I saw what you did. Make sure, next time, to scoop all of it into the left hand. Now get on."

Taking into account the sergeant's usual bluster, I thought he had been rather lenient with me. But then I had given of my very best, not only on the parade ground but all other activity the platoon had been engaged in and carried out with enthusiasm, knowing no other way.

Later in the billet, I would contemplate on all the trouble I had been subjected to in the past week for the princely sum of fourteen shillings. Twenty-one shillings if my allowance home was taken into consideration. That sum being about a quarter of my gross earnings in my civilian employment. In my new employment, the wages would never come that easy.

I had received my first letter from home with the good news that my suitcase had arrived with contents intact. I would have to reply over the weekend.

With our last parade over on Saturday morning, and our visit to the cookhouse for our midday meal finished, a few of my new friends decided to go into the town for a look around, see a film, and try and find something to eat afterwards. But first, we had to make sure we would be able to pass the scrutinising eyes of the regimental guard at the gate who, we were told, would pick on you for any detail of incorrect dress or deportment.

So, wearing our serge uniforms, highly polished boots, with webbing belt and anklets blancoed and their brasses polished, we advanced to the main gate, and standing to attention were inspected and passed out through the gate.

Colchester, being a garrison town, was full of troops and people scouring about, doing their weekend shopping for goods and food that was less abundant as the war progressed. All the troops I saw were on their best behaviour, no doubt helped by the presence of many redcaps on duty.

After seeing around the town, we descended on one of the picture houses. This one was showing an RAF film about a mission over Germany. Not exactly a very good choice of film for a touch of escapism all of us wished to find from our labours of the past week, but there was not a lot on offer at the other places in the town.

We trooped into the foyer and were confronted with a board, on which read 'Soldiers in Uniform – Price three-pence' with a broad arrow pointing to some stairs. All of us had to be prudent with our money, so the price looked very compelling. After having paid our money over the cash desk, we started up the stairs with our three-penny tickets, making a horrible noise on the wooden steps in our hobnail boots. We climbed even higher up the stairs till we came to a curtain in our path.

Pulling it aside, we found ourselves on a narrow balcony with seats, but where was the silver screen we had come to see? Looking over the side of the balcony, we were astounded to find the screen way below us. From the viewing angle we found ourselves in, the screen appeared to be elongated with the characters in the film appearing very distorted and comic looking. Nevertheless, we made the best of it with a future thought to make it our first and last visit here.

Coming out from the cinema, we found one of the numerous tearooms in the town, and enjoyed some cake and a large pot of tea whilst having a good conversation about things so far since being called into the service, being less restricted than our talk in the billet. They were all of the opinion that the platoon officer was all right. Also, the two NCOs came out very well in the judgment of this 'tearoom court'.

It was a unanimous decision for our return to the barracks for the Saturday evening meal, which last week had been first class. Returning back into the barracks was easy, it's the coming out that poses the problem. None of us were disappointed at our early return into captivity, our reward being a goodly portion of Welsh rabbit to round off the day.

It was Sunday morning with a later reveille, but this week was different for us in that all the Church of England people had to attend the weekly church parade and was compulsory for all ranks. The rest of us, in other denominations, would also have to be well turned out, but could find our own way into town and find our own places of worship.

There were about half-a-dozen in the platoon who were Methodist, so I was in good company. One of them was Arthur Lewis who had come from a Welsh Valley and lived in its harsh reality till being called up. Arthur made a very nice comment about the difference between the Church of England and Methodism, saying, "To me, Methodists are more down-to-earth people in their religion with an over-the-garden-wall approach to it. Whereas the Church of England have a more stuffy attitude and lack the friendship shown by the Methodists." Having come out with that, Arthur, being a much older man and more worldly-wise than the rest of us, became a kind of leader for us in the Methodist camp.

The Church of England parade started long before our leaving time to walk into town. We could hear the shouts of command coming from the parade ground that sounded less religious by the minute. We were most thankful for being Methodists, and not on the parade ground along with the others. Anyway, it was time for us to leave and reaching the main gate were asked, "Where are you going?" by the regimental policeman on duty. "Church!" was our reply and, with a cursory glance at us, he waved us on.

Very soon, we found a Methodist chapel and removing our caps went inside, finding a goodly part of the congregation were soldiers. The minister seemed a very good man and, when the service was over, he thanked us for being there and hoped he would see us again.

5. End of General Service Corps training. Moving on.

Monday came, bringing all of us back into our routine of mastering the techniques of the infantryman. We had moved on to the sighting of a rifle mounted on a tripod; this taking place on the perimeter of the parade ground with targets on the far side. Each of us took it in turn to sight the rifle onto the centre of the target.

After each man's turn, the NCO in charge would push the rifle off target so not to give the next man an advantage with his own sighting. Some of the men were unable to lay the rifle on correctly, giving an impression they had no wish to become a sniper in this Army.

The platoon was fast becoming more proficient at drill, more apparent after every session spent on the parade ground. One or two of the men were still failing to come up to the sergeant's standard, but they never would if drilled on the square till kingdom come. Drill must have taken a third of our working day. The rest of the time was filled with our lessons on the Bren gun and now the Mills 36 hand grenades, respirator training for gas attack, long marches in battle-order for toughening us up, and the obstacle course thrown in for good measure. And we must not overlook our twice-weekly visits to physical training.

The platoon was now due for a demonstration by the weapons training officer, a captain with a fierce looking countenance and a reputation to go with it. We marched to one of the many battle-training areas outside the town. This one having high earthwork embankments on their sides with a brickwork enclosure, making sure of stopping everything fired into it from a range of about one hundred feet. A tier of sandbags had been placed in front of the brickwork as a safety factor from any ricochet.

I also noticed a dummy on display there suspended from a wooden frame. Its head and body full of straw, and always represented the enemy in bayonet practice or drill. I could see no reason, at the time, for it being there.

The captain started his demonstration by blasting off a few rifle rounds at random into the sandbags. Then refilling the magazine of the rifle with ten rounds, he fired them off in rapid succession with a very quick manipulation of the bolt. Then moving on to the Bren gun, he blasted away at the sandbags, never firing at a definite target. He then tried a Thompson submachine gun, turning its muzzle towards the sandbags and pulling the trigger of the weapon. It started spitting fury from its barrel, tearing the jute sandbags apart with the impact from the heavy calibre bullets.

The last item in the captain's arsenal was a Boys antitank rifle, a formidable piece of equipment for the infantryman to have to lug around, with its weight not far short of forty pounds. For this demonstration, the captain stuffed his ears with cotton wool, giving us a clear indication of what to expect when the rifle was fired. But none of us would dare place our hands over our ears to try and minimise the coming blast from the Boys. Lying down behind the rifle, he took aim and fired—Crack—making some jump and our eardrums complain. On firing, the recoil of the Boys rifle was powerful enough to push the officer back along the ground.

Having now shown us the way to handle and fire the various types of weapons, he now turned his attention onto the dummy. "Have any of you had bayonet practice yet?" he asked. We all chorused, "No, sir!" "Right then, I shall give a demonstration on how it should be done." Taking up his rifle, he fixed a bayonet into position. "Pay attention!" he shouted. "When you bayonet your man don't tickle him with it, stick the damn thing in like this." And he launched himself at the straw-filled dummy, sticking his bayonet and half the rifle in with the ferocity of his attack. Pulling the bayonet free from the dummy, he turned round to us and, speaking with all the harshness he could muster, said,

"After bayoneting and you can't remove the blade, what you must do is this." Advancing once again to the dummy, he stabbed the bayonet into the straw chest and cried out, "If you can't remove it, shove a round up the spout and pull the trigger,"—Bang—, "and blow the bugger off!" the captain ended.

The effect on the platoon was one of revulsion that he had been able to brutalise the brutal act of bayoneting a man to death. What we had seen take place became a talking point, back at the billet, for many a long day.

It was the turn of the platoon to pay a visit to the indoor rifle range. Inside were four firing positions on a thirty-yard shoot at 6" square targets, using standard ·303" rifles converted to fire ·22" ammunition. The platoon officer made a few points to observe while firing was taking place, along with the help of Sergeant Atterbury and Corporal Wickham, making sure the very strict safety rules were enforced.

The four firing positions consisted of one sandbag on the floor for each man to lie in a prone position with his rifle resting on the bag. The first four men took up their positions with the officer reminding them, "Make sure you fire at your own target, and I shall be observing your rounds with a telescope to record your success or otherwise." He turned to the sergeant. "Are we ready, Sergeant Atterbury?" "Yes, sir," the sergeant replied, "but first could I make a suggestion, sir?" "Yes, carry on, Sergeant."

Sergeant Atterbury addressed the men so. "When you take aim on the target try not to move your body, otherwise the rifle will also move off the target, and remember before you squeeze the trigger hold your breath, the body will then be motionless." The sergeant having finished, the officer said, "That's a very good piece of advice, Sergeant, and I hope they will benefit by putting it into practice. Right then, load your first round into the chamber and fire when ready."

Crack—Crack—, the rounds sped towards the targets, but no one could see where the bullets had penetrated from that distance without the aid of a telescope. With the officer giving a running commentary on the results, it would seem the sergeant's words, for the most part, had gone unheeded.

Most of them had spent their five rounds when I took my place along with the other three. The officer gave the order, "Load the first round then fire when ready." Taking careful aim and remembering the words of the sergeant, I squeezed the trigger and waited for the comment on my first shot, which was, "Bull's-eye to the right of centre, good shot." Numbers two, three, four and five were fired without comment from the officer, but after clearing our rifles, he asked for 'Number 2 Target' to be handed to him.

After looking at the target, he then showed it to Sergeant Atterbury. The officer addressed himself to me. "Have you ever fired a rifle before?" he asked, to which I replied, "No, sir." "Then how about this?" handing the target over to me. I examined it with some embarrassment before the rest of the platoon, who had now gathered around me for their own look at the card that had five perforations on the right side of the bull's-eye in a group that a halfpenny would cover. Three of the holes were breaking into one another. "I think you should keep the card," the officer said, "and send it home to your parents. That was indeed some very excellent shooting." "Thank you, sir," I said.

We started a series of intelligence tests that lasted over several days, making a nice change from the routine we had settled into after the last few weeks of our training programme. The tests were conducted by a group of scholarly looking men in uniform. They could very well have been personnel from ABCA (Army Bureau of Current Affairs).

Our first test was a question and answer paper; place your tick in the box you think to be correct. A good example was of two pictures showing trains having crashed on a bend in the track. One train derailed on the inside of the bend, the other on the outside. Which of the two pictures is correct? Some of the questions were not so simple and became more difficult the farther you advanced. All the aptitude tests we passed or otherwise would decide on our future employment while in the Army. Whereas the personnel selection officer had already informed us that the real need was for more infantry, and that being the case, we had very few options open to us.

With our intelligence tests out of the way, we had two other items to work into the training programme with a visit to the grenade range and a walk through the gas chamber – with and without a respirator on.

Firstly, our visit to the grenade range was preceded by a lesson on arming the grenades prior to their use. They were prepared in the billet under the ever-watchful eyes of Sergeant Atterbury and Corporal

Wickham, who had us unscrewing the base plugs before priming them with the combined percussion cap with its seven-second fuse. The grenade must be held in the throwing hand with the hand clenched tight, holding down on the firing mechanism in the shape of a steel handle which in turn is held down with its safety pin.

It goes without saying that we had already received our customary warning from Sergeant Atterbury, with the reminder to keep our names off the village war memorial with the careful handling of the grenades, which were very dangerous if treated without due care and attention.

With the boxes of grenades now primed, the platoon marched out from the barracks, but was now accompanied by our officer who led his men alongside the sergeant with the corporal in the rear. Our officer had formed a good working relationship with his sergeant and trusted in his judgment from many years of service life.

After leaving the town, there was a complete absence of traffic on the road, not that there were many vehicles about in the town other than an occasional delivery van. Petrol rationing had taken its toll. The countryside was very quiet, running down for the winter. With us now halfway into December with the leaves now off the trees and hedgerows, it was all damp and silent here, but was now broken by the sound of forty-three pairs of boots pounding the empty highway.

We turned off the road and onto one of the numerous tracks till we came to a field surrounded by hedgerows. In front of us, standing at the entrance, was a large white painted sign warning the public it was WD property and a dangerous place to venture on.

In the field, I saw what appeared to be a miniature fort made with sandbags. On closer inspection, I found it to be a cleverly constructed piece of engineering, made not for looks but with a guaranteed safety factor built into its walls of sand and wooden frames. At the front was the throwing bay with high walls of sandbags on the sides and back, and a wall about five feet high in the front where, hopefully, our grenades would go. A passageway led back into the main part of the building with a ninety-degree turn, thus neutralising the effect of fragments and blast should an accident occur in the throwing bay. This main part of the building housed the platoon while they waited their turn to throw. The building was finished off with an observation platform above the main quarters, with access via a wooden ladder. Here, the officer would observe where each bomb landed and remark on the competence of the thrower and his two grenades.

Sergeant Atterbury was in charge in the throwing bay; it being his responsibility to clear any mishandled grenades that failed to leave the bay at the first attempt. The throwing got underway with Corporal Wickham sending the men through with their two grenades. The sergeant took care of the second round while the first was being thrown.

The solitude of the countryside was broken by the blast of eighty bombs exploding at short intervals, sending their lethal pieces of steel in all directions. The fort was being hit time out of number, especially those dropping short from where they should have been with the offenders getting a right reprimand from the officer and backed up by Sergeant Atterbury.

My turn came and I walked into the bay, the sergeant taking one grenade from me. "You know what to do," he said, "throw when ready." I gripped the grenade in my right hand, making sure the firing lever would still be held in place after pulling the pin. Then pulling the pin free, I straightened my throwing arm at the same time making the other arm act like a counterbalance. Giving it all I could muster, the grenade left my hand at the top of its travel, setting in train the mechanism to destruct the bomb in the space of seven seconds.

The sergeant and I looked over the top of the sandbags to locate where it had fallen, then his hand pulled me down behind the barrier. Bang—, the grenade exploded, sounding much more deadly out in the open bay than inside the holding section. After my second attempt, the officer was pleased to call down, "Two good throws, well done."

The platoon, having now thrown their grenades, made the place tidy by collecting up the oddments. The platoon then marched back to the barracks in the gathering dusk with the hope of a decent tea in prospect for us all.

A day or so later, the platoon was down for a visit to the camp gas chamber. The Army still looked on gas warfare as a growing possibility now with the tide of war turning in our favour, which in turn may make the enemy resort to using their vast stocks of gas they held in reserve in trying to regain the initiative on the battlefront.

The Army always took the threat of gas being used very seriously, not least in the platoon having spent many hours on the subject with the anti-gas equipment issued out to us. We had a gas-cape for overall protection, respirator and an anti-gas wallet that held anti-gas swabs and cream for use on infected skin. It was all taken very seriously, and that was why we were being ordered to walk through the gas chamber here to feel the effect of what it can do to a human being in a matter of seconds.

The platoon was marched to the gas chamber with our respirators in position on the chest, and also wearing our steel helmets. We arrived at this bleak looking building that had a door at each end with a long enough distance between the doors to force a man to draw breath in going from one end to the other.

The officer was rather tense while addressing us on the drill for this exercise, which had some element of danger in the process. "Firstly, you must all walk through the room with your respirators on, then do the same with them off. Corporal Wickham will be standing near the centre of the room next to the gas-candle, which will give off the conditions you would find yourselves in under a gas attack." The officer carried on. "I shall be on the entrance door making sure that you go in, with Sergeant Atterbury on the exit door making doubly sure you all come out. You can light the candle now, Sergeant."

First, the sergeant placed his respirator on and returned his helmet back onto his head. He then walked into the room, switched on a single light bulb hanging there (which I thought was rather odd, not being all that dark in the room), then put a match to the candle and came out closing both doors behind him. Removing his respirator, the sergeant said, "By the way, I shall be able to tell by the condition you are in whether you came through holding your breath. Don't try it on, otherwise you will be made to make a return trip!"

Within minutes, I could see the reason for the sergeant switching the light bulb on. For now the room had turned into a murky gloom, the light from the bulb almost obscured by a moving fog of gas.

Corporal Wickham, with his own respirator now on, took up his position in the room. The platoon was now ordered to place on their equipment and, in single file, started to walk through the murky room, this being the easy part of the exercise. I stepped into the room breathing quite well in the respirator. Even then, my vision started to mist up, even after using a demisting cloth on them. Walking passed the corporal, I was soon outside with the sergeant telling us, "Remove your respirators." After taking mine off, I could smell the effect of the gas still in my clothing, enough to irritate the eyes.

Having now all passed through, the platoon made ready for the crucial part of the lesson which I felt sure would not be very pleasant. The officer had a final word for us. "I can see that you have returned your respirators back into their containers, so we can get started back through. And when you come out the other end, you can make your own way back to the billet."

The first man started on his way through and with his first steps, we outside could hear him gasping and coughing for breath as the first whiff of gas reached down into his lungs. One man followed after another through the doorway, all confronting the same problem the second they set foot inside the room. My own first step caught me unawares with the potent nature of the gas, causing the throat and lungs to burn and the eyes to smart and run like the nose in sympathy with the rest. I moved passed the corporal, feeling the effects in the room more so with every step taken. Sergeant Atterbury, still wearing his own respirator, helped those who needed it most through the doorway and into the fresh air.

Having come myself into the clean air and breathed in its life giving qualities, I felt better but not very good. Some members of the platoon were in a very poor state, coughing and spluttering from their ordeal. Unfortunately, a few were sick and looked pale-faced from their nauseous condition.

Much later, after the platoon had sufficiently pulled itself together with the exception of one or two who still looked rather poorly, the sergeant decided on taking his men for a run, hoping it would clear away the remnants of the gas we had in our systems. It was an effort at the start, but the run turned out more successful than anyone could have anticipated, and all of us felt the benefit from clearing our lungs of the obnoxious stuff we had been forced to inhale. Breathing in the cold air of that December afternoon did us a power of good, borne out next morning with an empty sick report.

Many incidents took place during our first six weeks, some worthy of mention, others not. For instance, we had an air raid alert one evening. The drill was to evacuate the entire barracks and move out to one of the training areas where we filed into a zigzag trench system, about four or five feet deep, that had been dug for our protection. The trench looked very exposed to any form of sustained aerial bombardment. Fortunately, in this case, it was not put to the test. After hearing a few explosions in the distance (whether made by the enemy or us, I couldn't tell), the 'All Clear' sounded out soon after enabling the shivering occupants of the trench to return to the warmth of the billets.

I also did a fire picket duty with seven other members of the platoon. Our main task was to patrol the sleeping camp during the hours of darkness, making sure all was well. There was one big snag that went along with the fire picket duty, and that was being held responsible for next day's requirement of peeled potatoes at the cookhouse for round about a thousand men. During the evening, the duty officer called in to see how much progress we had made into the mountain of potatoes. While here, the officer gave us a lecture on the need to peel them with as little waste as possible. "Don't forget, if you peel them thinly it will save on shipping which in turn will help the war effort. Carry on."

I made mention, way back in the narrative, about one man in the platoon who had most decidedly come from a different background and society to our own. He was a big man for eighteen years of age and must have weighed in the region of around fifteen stone or more. Not a great help in infantry training.

The man, Private Charity, was at times on the butt end of remarks made by both the sergeant and the corporal, at his inability to perform with the same enthusiasm as the rest of the platoon showed. We had been issued with a holdall for keeping our shaving kit and other requirements in, while our own toilet bags we had taken into the Army were returned home. Thirty-nine members of the platoon would comply with this order; one would not by still taking his own toilet bag into the washroom. The bag being the size of a miniature kit bag to hold all of the items he had in his possession, all of them expensive looking articles.

One other ploy he used for getting around the rules was over nightwear, wherein you retire for the night in the Army you would sleep in your underwear, but not he. He would get into his top bunk bed in his underwear and then the transformation into a pair of pyjamas would take place after lights out, and under cover of his blanket. This worked in reverse with the first notes of reveille sounding – off with the pyjamas into his underwear.

The best story must be about the regular food parcels he received from home. These must have contained around half-a-dozen boneless pork chops, each made into a sandwich from crispy bread, giving it the appearance by its size to a 'Dagwood Bumstead' sandwich (of *Blondie* films fame). The chop in every sandwich would represent a whole week's meat ration for one person. But he would scoff them in the billet, not giving a thought to what others may think of his scrumptious gifts from home.

We had now come into the last week of the general service training with Christmas coming in-between, so Friday the 25th would be a holiday. Christmas came without the good cheer of former years to make it worth celebrating. This, our first Christmas away from home, could never come up to the expectations of a family together at this most wonderful season of the year.

Come Christmas morning, we all turned out to the main thoroughfare of the camp to see and hear the band playing a medley of popular tunes. Afterwards, the fife and drum section of the band marched and counter-marched up and down between the hundreds of men watching the display. I don't think there could be many soldiers standing there who would not have shed a tear during this so very emotive time.

For our Christmas dinner, our own officer waited on us at the table. He did his level best to please us in this gesture of goodwill towards his platoon. Each man received one pint bottle of beer. Not being a drinker myself, I passed it over to one of the lads who accepted it with gratitude. Our Christmas dinner was reasonably good, well above the usual fare we received each day. This may have been due to the large number of officers on duty at the table as to why it was above average, and the fact it was Christmas.

One good concession we had for the day was a fire that made the billet a far more comfortable place. After our Christmas tea we all settled round the fire and just talked. Arthur Lewis told us some amusing stories about his own life back in the Valleys. It did help to pass the Christmas night away without thinking too much of what was taking place at home.

One little titbit made us smile when someone mentioned, not in his presence, that Charity had received among his presents from home a package from his aunt. Inside, he found an Army side-hat; unfortunately, for him, he would be unable to wear this superior looking creation without finding himself shut up in the guardroom. So the aunt had sent her dear nephew an Officer's side-hat! Did she think he was due for promotion?

So ended Christmas Day 1942. How many more would have to be spent in this manner?

At reveille, on Boxing Day morning, I found it most difficult to rise out of my bunk. And it came to me the realisation that I was once again about to succumb to the same trouble I had suffered with over the past year or two, when I had been working in the blacked-out factory under artificial lights.

Today of all days, we were down for a visit to the assault course and on that account alone I had no wish to dodge-the-column. Anyway, if I did report sick they would accuse me of too much high living from the day before. There was only one course left open for me and that was to try and tough it out.

I managed to get through the first parade held in the billet and even went on to breakfast, but found myself unable to touch it. Then we all prepared in battle-order for our visit to the assault course. Much to my own consternation, it got around that the company commander would accompany us on this exercise, going along for the jaunt to rid himself of the excesses of the day before. It would become more difficult for me to conceal my own condition now. I must have looked downright lethargic to those around me as I positioned myself in the middle of the platoon and just hoped I would make it there and back.

By the time we had reached our destination, I was all but dead on my feet. Thankfully, we were fallen out for a rest and smoke before starting over the various obstacles of the assault course.

The platoon officer must have seen that all was not well with one of his men and came straight over to enquire what was wrong. I came to attention at his approach and he asked me, "Did you have too much to drink yesterday?" Standing fractionally taller, having been somewhat stung by the remark, I replied, "On the contrary, sir, I had no intoxicating drink yesterday. This, what I have now, only came on this morning, sir. I should have gone sick but decided to carry on, having had the same thing happen to me in the past." The officer was satisfied with my explanation to him, but said, "You can't go over the assault course in your condition and we don't want any accidents today. So just keep standing by me and as far as I'm concerned you will already have been over the course." I did just as he told me, standing there with him as if detailed to do so.

The first men got away over the numerous obstacles, it being a very punishing course, and most of them were soon in some kind of trouble with most of it happening at the rope-over-the-water obstacle. Here you pulled yourself along the rope with your hands while you dragged your legs, also over the rope supporting the weight of the body. There was one difficulty in doing it this way; you were moving along headfirst, hand over hand looking up at the sky, when you should have a view of what was below.

A good number of men fell off into the water, or slipped back down the muddy bank back into the water. Standing there behind the officer, I felt most grateful that I was on the sidelines and not taking part in the Boxing Day revels. By the time the platoon had completed the course they looked a sorry lot. A few of them still had dry uniforms while the rest were wet and muddy.

The company commander called out, "Have you all been over?" and after a brief silence he said, "Right, let's get formed up and get on our way back." I must say that my memory of the return from the assault course training ground is indeed rather hazy but for the one recollection that I still carried my own rifle. No one around me would relieve me from the burden of carrying it.

Back at the billet with parades finished for the day, I removed my kit from off the bed and quickly took its place. The men still left in the billet realised by now that I had some kind of problem and kept the noise down so I could rest. Later, one of the men returned from his tea with a full mug and asked me if I would like it. I took it with gratitude.

The platoon officer called into the billet enquiring about my condition. "How do you feel now?" he asked. "A lot better now I've rested, sir. I should be back on my feet in the morning after a night's sleep. Also, may I thank you, sir, for helping me today." "That's alright, get some rest now," he replied and left the billet.

Next morning, being Sunday, it was a late reveille that served in my favour giving me extra time for rest. When I moved off the bed, I felt somewhat shaky for a while but was well enough later to walk down into the town with Arthur Lewis and the others to our weekly visit to the Methodist chapel. This could very well be the last time with our new postings due any day now. It was rather sad after going through so much together in the last six weeks and the new friendships we had made, that we should be going our separate ways, never knowing what befell the men who were called up together for war service on the 19th of November 1942.

The next morning after our first parade and breakfast, Sergeant Atterbury had us on the parade ground for drill. This could well be the last time he would drill us, and so it turned out to be. He was just going to run over what we practiced here on the square over the last six weeks. Calling us to attention, the sergeant then went on to run through the different drills, sharpening our movements up till even he was satisfied with the proficiency of the platoon. On the whole, we had been very fortunate with the sergeant and corporal. Would they be as good in our next posting?

We were told that the platoon would be informed of our postings with a visit to the personnel selection officer, where we would all be having a personal interview with a Lieutenant Tappet. He would tell each of us how well, or otherwise, we had fared in the intelligence tests.

I waited in his outer office with some of the other men, waiting to learn our fate in the decisions already taken by the selection board. It was now my turn to go in and closing the door behind me, I saluted the officer sitting at his desk, giving my name and number to him. "Sit Down," he said in a most friendly manner. "Let's see, here we are," he said looking at the report in front of him. "You will be joining the Royal Berkshire Regiment as of the 31st of December, staying on here in the barracks but in new quarters. After having done quite well in the tests," he continued "you will be joining Headquarters Company for a course on the 3" mortar. You know the kind of thing, er, like a length of drainpipe! The course also includes carrier driving instructions and wireless procedure in the sending and receiving of messages." He went on. "If you fail on any part of the course, you will be excluded from the mortars. Any questions?" he asked. "No, sir!" "Right then, good luck." The interview over, I stood up, saluted and left the office.

Later, when everyone had seen the selection officer, I found there were two others in the platoon who would be joining me in the mortars; one of them was Charity. The platoon was winding down with all of us getting our kit together for the move. Some were leaving the barracks now they had been posted away to their battalions, wherever they would be. Whereas we were more fortunate, that our move to the new quarters was only some 150 yards away.

The platoon officer came in to wish us well in our new postings and good wishes for the future. On the whole, he had been a very good officer to all of us. He must have had very mixed emotions at our departure from his control. I felt the same way. I believe we had been his very first command. What type of officer would we get this time?

After having said a reluctant farewell to my friends of the last six weeks, I left the old billet for the last time, but not without a twinge of regret at its passing.

6. The mortar platoon.

I found my way with my kit to the new quarters. It was a vast improvement on the old billet, being a single storey building of wooden construction. There were several units of this type of building there and housed the entire complement of Headquarters Company, of which the mortars, signals and carrier platoons were part.

The men in the mortar hut were in various stages of their training with some about to finish and others coming along at two-weekly intervals. Once again, I was most fortunate in obtaining a bottom bunk bed, but my elation was short-lived in finding myself beneath Charity on the top bunk. This type of building also had the luxury of hot and cold running water. That was not the end as it was also able to boast of a wireless set, giving the hut a kind of five-star classification. No doubt, it would spoil us when we had to move on at a future date.

The next morning one of our first duties of the new intake into Headquarters Company was to have a lecture from our new company commander, a Captain Hewlett. I had seen this officer at various times around the camp and having seen him once you would always remember him. Short in stature, but not in girth, having to have a large V-shaped gusset let into the rear of his trousers being the only way he could ever wear a uniform.

All of us in the new intake paraded at the headquarters for our lecture. The sergeant, having called the parade to attention at the arrival of the captain, now told us to "Sit down and keep quiet."

The captain had a good look around at his new intake and started off in this kind of manner. "I am Captain Hewlett, your company commander, and you have been drafted into this company for specialist training after having done well in the tests set for you." He went on. "All of you here were found to be of above average intelligence, but don't runaway with any grand ideas about yourselves. You will all be expected to put your utmost into your training while you are here, while failure on your part at any stage of training will result in you being returned back to your battalions." He continued. "At the end of the course you will all sit a written exam, so pay attention to your instructors and carry out their orders."

He wound up his talk with a real bone-shocker for us all. "None of you will be receiving any kind of leave till the end of the course. Not even a twenty-four hour pass will be issued out till the training is completed." He ended with, "The war effort must take priority over all other considerations."

After the captain had finished and the parade dismissed, we were able to discuss between ourselves what he had said along with "No leave!" We still had then sixteen more weeks of training in front of us before any leave was possible. That, we all thought, was rather unjust having to serve over five months without returning home. After all 'Kings Rules and Regulations' do state that leave is a privilege and not a right.

We soon settled down to the two extra weeks of infantry training before moving on to the mortars. The training was much of the same already covered in our first six weeks, but the fieldcraft was of a more arduous nature, coming back most nights covered in wet mud that must be removed by first parade the next day.

One event that's worth a mention was the early arrival of the platoon sergeant one morning into the hut, not long after reveille, and caught sight of Charity in his smart pyjamas. The sergeant stared in disbelief at the man in front of him and bawled out in a most scornful manner, "Don't you know that even … I have not the right to wear pyjamas! Get them off and lose them, other ranks don't wear such things!" With this, the sergeant turned and stomped out of the hut in a cold fury.

The reason that Charity had been caught in the first place was that some of the lads in the hut had given him a light-hearted ragging about his ritual under the bedclothes every morning, in the removal of his sleeping garments. He had then inadvertently left his bunk, still in his pyjamas, to face up to his would-be antagonists round his own domain when the sergeant intervened in the proceedings. Charity should have been put on a charge for disobeying standing orders, but not him.

At last, with our infantry training over, we started on the mortar course. For the next fourteen weeks, we would be expected to master a simple but still complex piece of weaponry.

The introductory talk for the benefit of the new intake was made by the platoon sergeant. "My name is Sergeant Piggot and you have been selected to come here on a programme of 3" mortar and carrier driving instruction, which takes place on Friday mornings on the roads with the afternoons spent on driving on the rough country training ground." He continued. "You will be split up into pairs of three, which makes up a gun crew, with an instructor who will be giving out orders that you will carry out, especially with some effort in the mortar drill." He went on. "Lieutenant Ford is the platoon commander, but at this time remains absent on sick leave. You may see him at times running out or into the camp trying to regain his health from an accident." He then detailed us off to our instructors. I was with a Lance Corporal Warwick who seemed on the face of it a pleasant enough man.

On the first day of our training, the corporal marched us to the mortar stores for the collection of one 3" mortar. We all found out soon enough, lifting the parts for the first time, the sheer physical strength required in handling the parts. They were in the region of well over forty pounds each in weight with a harness provided for the transportation between places. The harness went over the right shoulder and would cause some pain in the shoulder blade after a 'long-carry'. This was the term used for an extended march with your piece of mortar, at times a journey of many miles making you feel like a beast of burden.

Corporal Warwick marched us out of the barracks to one of the training sites for our first lesson. He had chosen one of the places far away from any other activity taking place, and away from prying military eyes. "Right," he said, "what I shall be doing will be to demonstrate the correct way to assemble the three parts which by now you know are very robust, but take great care of the gun sight which is more fragile, so treat it with some respect. We shall be having a lesson on its use at a later time." He continued. "I shall be needing an extra pair of hands later so if someone would like to volunteer, so much the better."

The corporal walked out about twenty feet in front of us and pushed, what could only be, an aiming post into the ground with the heel of his boot on a hinged bar at the base and one in the centre for folding it together. The aiming post was decorated in black and white bands with its diamond shaped aiming point at the top.

"We have an extra aiming post for each crew, used for more accuracy and to hold a night aiming lamp, but I won't go into that just now," the corporal said. "This is the sequence you have to follow so pay attention. You will be exercising this drill many hundreds of times over the next fourteen weeks, and later timed with a stopwatch for speed and progress."

Then picking the baseplate up (with some effort), the corporal placed it back down onto the ground in the general direction of the post. He moved it around on its cast spikes under the base, until he was sure that the barrel recess and sides of the plate were of equal portions to the post. Next he lifted and placed the barrel into the socket of the plate, giving it a quarter-turn, locking it into position and making it secure from leaving the socket when fired.

The corporal kept up a running commentary for our benefit. He explained at this point that the base plug held the firing pin at its centre and automatically fired the bomb on contact.

With help from one of the men, he removed the leather barrel cover that kept it clean and dry and unhooked the retention spring on its side from its keeper position. The bipod, now with its legs fully extended and locked in position, was placed by its solid brass yoke over the muzzle and slipped down the barrel to its retaining collar. The retention spring, now placed by its toggle into the split brass claws on the side of the yoke, held the mortar parts firmly together but still flexible.

The corporal now returned the cover to the barrel. "I hope you have been following what's been done so far?" he remarked. "Now we can go a step further by placing the gun sight onto the tapered spigot, here on the yoke, and lock in position." And here, the corporal removed the sight from its protective case and with due care put the final piece into place.

"That was just a rundown in slow-motion," the corporal explained, "in the procedure for mounting the gun. Taking it down goes in reverse order with a few exceptions from time to time. Some of you may have noticed a clamp handle over the top of the legs on the bipod," the corporal said, "and in the event of having to mount the mortar on uneven ground, this takes the barrel out of the perpendicular. So you must correct this error, by Number Three first placing his hand on the barrel above the yoke, supporting it while he turns the handle on the clamp, releasing it from the serrated quadrant plate, and moves the barrel to a vertical position before relocking the clamp."

The corporal went on. "One more important thing in the drill must be that every time you dismantle the mortar, the first thing you must do will be; Number One will unlock the gun sight, turning the longitudinal deflection table back to zero degrees and the range scale to zero yards, before returning it to the box. Next, he will return the yoke to the centre position of its travel by the traversing handle that turns the buttress thread, moving the yoke while Number Two will have removed the retaining spring from the yoke." After a pause, he continued. "Number Two now waits for Number Three to wind down the vertical lift or range handle to the bottom of its travel. Now, with the help of Number Two, they slip the yoke from the top of the barrel while Number Two now returns the spring to the barrel and removes it from the baseplate by giving it the quarter-turn."

The corporal, having finished his rundown of the dismantling sequence, asked, "Have any of you any questions you would like to ask?" The men remained silent. "Right then, you first three take the parts and mount the mortar," he ordered them. The first crew did make an effort, but they struggled with the parts, getting in each others' way and seeming to have lost the thread of the assembly order and doing no better in taking it down. Whereas the subsequent crews did much better, learning from the mistakes of others.

At the end of the day, the corporal marched us back from the cold training ground for our tea, and later the warmth of the billet where we talked over our first day with some of the men who were more advanced with their training. Some of them had less than two weeks before they finished with the prospect of home leave at the end of it. One thing they all agreed with was that the mortar course was most demanding and certainly no picnic with the burden of the carrying and working of it imposed on the individual. I was glad that being robust myself I could tackle the task that lay in front of me.

Some of the platoon, even after their eight weeks of physical training, had found it almost more than they were able to cope with. Even a large man like Charity, who should have been strong, found it very hard to come to terms with. One wonders at the time if Lieutenant Tappet, the personnel selection officer, had given any thought to the physical requirements necessary for this type of training? I suppose the answer to this question must be no when I remember his explanation to me that the 3" mortar looked like 'a length of drainpipe!'

In the new intake, I was most fortunate in meeting and starting a friendship with one of the men. His name was Robert Manley, a few months older than myself and had left school at the age of fourteen (like myself). Bob had worked till being conscripted into the service, also on the same day as myself, but drafted into a different company to my own. He had survived the Blitz along with father, mother and younger sister, in an area that had seen a lot of the bombing in and around Dalston Lane, Hackney. I had seen the damage for myself in Dalston on a day visit to the capital in 1941.

Bob was the most amiable of men, always cheerful but never pushy, the kind of man who was good company. Being short in stature gave him the appearance of looking portly. Even some of the men would later call him 'Barrel'. For all that, Bob was strong and also very bright, making him a good candidate for the mortars.

For most of that first week, the corporal persevered in his efforts to speed us up in the first stage of just mounting the mortar before moving on. We not only had our daily visits to the bleak training ground, we also had lessons in the warm mortar stores on the gun sight, but not often enough for our liking.

Out on the training ground, Corporal Warwick mentioned to us that he thought it was time we changed over to the full mortar mounting drill. The result would be of starting the drill lying on the ground in a prone position behind your piece of mortar. On the command of "Action", you were expected to jump onto your feet, taking your piece of mortar with you on the run to the mounting position where you carry on with the original drill. Dismantling the gun was in the same sequence as before, but now you run back to your starting position with your piece of mortar, throwing it and yourself behind it into a still prone position.

"By the way," Corporal Warwick said, "some of you may be feeling that carrying out this drill is just a waste of time and is done only for the sake of enforcing discipline, for instance like drilling on the barrack square day in day out without much reason. But here," the corporal continued, "it's the first discipline, just one of the many you have to master on your way through this course. And some day, you may find the reason or purpose for this training. It's inevitable, seeing that you are now being trained in the use of the mortar, that most of you will ultimately find yourselves posted to a mortar platoon with some battalion on active service. You may find there," the corporal emphasised, "the speed at which you get in and out of action might just one day help you in your own survival." That was the end of Corporal Warwick's sobering comments.

After more drill, he marched us away from the training ground, where we spent most of our days, and back for our tea. We had a peaceful evening in the billet, enabling me to write a letter home.

Giving us a change from our mortar drill, the dozen men of the new intake crowded into the mortar stores for a lesson on the gun sight. Corporal Warwick had drawn extra sights from the store man, who being a regular soldier gave the impression that all the stores were his very own property and not that of the War Department. The corporal passed the sights round to each group. We had, of course, used it already on the drill but we had never tried to zero it. Now we could examine it at firsthand.

It was of brass construction throughout and one of its main features consisted of a curved sliding scale ranged off in increments of twenty-five yards. There were two separate scales with a zero position or pointer reading off the range on the scale. They were a charge-one and charge-two range scales that worked on the principle of removing half of the propellant charge from the bomb; charge-one being the minimum range, charge-two the maximum (at that time being one mile). The moving scale was locked into position by means of a large wing nut situated on the right side of the sight.

At the top of the sight was a small optical device. This held a triangle with a translucent background mounted in a metal tube. This was only used when night aiming was required with the aiming lamp fixed onto the foremast of the two aiming posts. The open gun sight was fixed by the side of the tube and consisted of two sturdy metal triangles about two inches apart and were used for general sighting of the gun.

The corporal throughout had been giving a running commentary, trying to explain the intricate parts and their technical terms and functions. He moved on, this time to the turret head. This carried the two aiming sights, making it a fixture with one exception. You could move the optical night aiming sight by means of an adjustable screw, enabling it to be lined up with the aiming lamp in position on the far post.

The turret head could be made to rotate by means of two knurled knobs, one either side of the turret, linked together by a worm drive (concealed). These, in turn, drove a gearwheel fastened to the centre of the turret. On the base of the turret were engraved calibrations in degrees and half-degrees ·30 minutes. Facing the turret, the operator would find that the 'degrees left' are on the right side, while 'degrees right' on the left side.

At this stage one in the group asked, "Why are the degree scales reading in reverse, Corporal?" "It's like this," the corporal explained, "if you had the mortar mounted and zeroed on the aiming post, and get a command like this – left 5° ·30 minutes. Number One will first move the turret from its zero position, engraved in the base, by twisting the knurled knob to the required position where the reading on the turret of left 5° ·30 minutes should correspond with the zero on the base, and all of you with a gun sight should now set yours on the same." Having moved their sights round, the corporal continued on his way. "Now we can see that having moved it left accordingly to the engraving on the turret, the sight most distinctly will have moved right of the aiming post. That's why the degree scales read in reverse. So, Number One must correct this by working the traversing handle and moving the sight back onto the aiming post, and in so doing the barrel will follow, moving now with a 5° ·30 minutes left to its former position."

The corporal continued with his mass of information, knowing full well that some of his group had lost touch with him. "Now we have manually moved the mortar by making it go to the left, then its two levelling bubbles are no longer in their central positions. I hope you are all following this with due attention?" the corporal asked of us. "Then now having moved the gun, its levelling bubbles (spirit levels) would have run outside of their central position tolerance lines, you can see etched into the glass. What Number One and Two must now do between themselves is to restore the levelling bubbles back into the tolerance lines. This is done by turning both handles of the vertical or range and the traversing or longitudinal handles. Both of the levelling bubbles will be on the move, so Number One and Two must converse with each other, confirming that their own bubble lies central. The talk between them need only be 'central-central central-central' till both bubbles are centralised. After all this, Number One must make sure that his aiming triangle will be looking at the aiming post. Have you any questions?" To ask a question would only have complicated things in our heads, already buzzing from the amount of information we had been expected to digest.

Corporal Warwick suggested it would be in our own interest to record the lessons in a notebook for future help in our exam when the course finished. Most of us had soon taken his advice and in the town, looking round the shops, found there was not a lot to choose from. Myself ending up with a hardcover, narrow looking account book, complete with its £.s.d. columns at the side of the page. This gave my mortar notes a kind of profit and loss to them!

We still had to attend the physical training sessions where the staff always made the men feel uncomfortable. We looked on it with as much favour as a visit to Gestapo headquarters. None of my fellow soldiers in the platoon liked them with their overbearing sense of physical superiority, and liked them even less when they picked on Charity because of his flabbiness and inability to move with any great speed.

Friday morning, the 15th of January, was to be for the new intake our first driving instruction. Greatcoats would be worn along with steel helmets. All of us were rather apprehensive at the thought of driving a vehicle for the first time, and it could be your last if you failed to pick up the fundamental aspects of driving. That would entail getting kicked out of the mortar platoon training. You must be able to drive a mortar carrier to be an integral part of the crew, being able to function in every roll.

We marched off to the motor pool suffering a great deal from a lack of confidence. On arrival, we were portioned out to four men to each vehicle that turned out to be 15cwt trucks that had undoubtedly seen better days, wrecked at the hands of hundreds of would-be drivers of which I would soon be joining. It came out while we were at the pool that we should be transferring to the tracked vehicles for next Friday's lesson. The trucks would be best for us to start with.

We had a middle-aged sergeant for our instructor and his first question was, "Can any of you drive?" Charity, who was in our party, made it known that he had driven his father's car from time to time, so the sergeant suggested he could be the first candidate behind the wheel. The sergeant, who I could see was a careful man, asked us all to "Pile into the back of the truck, I shall be driving it out of town. We don't want any accidents here do we?" Having left the town behind us and now well into the countryside, the sergeant stopped the truck and changed to the other side of the cab inviting Charity to take his place.

"You know what to do then?" the sergeant asked. "First you release the handbrake, but keep your hand there till you start to pull away. Now then where your feet are from the left, we have the clutch, brake and acceleration pedals, and finally the gear change lever of four forward and one reverse." After a short pause to let the information sink in, the sergeant said, "Right, place it in first gear and pull away when it's clear."

This, Charity did, pulling away with a great deal of protest coming from the region of the gearbox, of grating and grinding of unmeshed teeth. However, he did at last manage to get it through the gears and into top, but by then he was in trouble. He seemed to have no true sense of direction, moving from one side of the road to the other, forcing the once placid sergeant into action by placing his hand on the steering wheel, bringing the truck onto the correct side of the road and running in a straight line. The sergeant then told Charity to "Change down into bottom gear and stop."

Charity at last came to a halt and the sergeant said, "You told me that you could drive, so why then did you almost run into the ditch back there, and by the way you were driving too fast!" Charity answered in his most condescending manner. "You see, Sergeant, my father's car has a very long bonnet which helps me to line it up with the road ahead, but this is just a flat-fronted truck with no bonnet to guide me." "That's just plain rubbish and you know it!" the sergeant thundered at Charity. "Get into the back of the truck and let one of the others try."

The next man fared no better, but he could drive in a straight line. It came to my turn and moving into the cab next to the sergeant, I did all of the things the others before me had done, only perhaps worse. I managed to get it running on the road and in a more or less straight line, but after coasting along for some way, he made to remind me to "Change the gears down when you come onto bends in the road. Don't just carry on, use the gears." "Yes, Sergeant," I replied. However, at the next bend I failed to make a smooth change down, rattling the gears and forcing a comment out of him that was lost to me in the noise but felt it was not very complimentary.

After the last man in the truck had tried his luck and found he had none, the sergeant returned us back to barracks for our midday meal. "Before you go," he said, "make sure you all perform better when we go out this afternoon. You must show more aptitude towards driving, so just sit in the cab and get on with it. Off you go then."

During our break for the midday meal, our only topic was of our poor showing by all the groups who had made their first attempt at driving. That is with the exception of Charity who claimed he could drive. What did they expect of us first time out? In fact some of the men would have been more likely to have driven a horse-drawn conveyance, like a milk float, coal cart, bakers or greengrocery, all delivered to our homes by the horse. The ownership of cars being very low with most of them now garaged for lack of petrol. You could say it was a new thing for most of us and we were ill-prepared for it.

That afternoon, the sergeant drove us out of the town for what we thought would be another lesson in gear-grinding. Before he called for the first victim, he decided to have a chat with us about what he called 'the doubling of the clutch'. "Every time you change gear, you should do so by first depressing the clutch pedal as far as it goes. While at the same time place the gear lever into neutral, take your foot off the pedal, and having selected your next gear, you depress the pedal for the second time and slip the gear from neutral into its selected place. Have you got that?" the sergeant asked of us.

There was only one answer we could give him – all of us did better with far less crashing of the gears that helped with our confidence after having lost it that morning. After we had returned to the barracks for tea, the sergeant let it be known that we could go out in the carriers on the following Friday. So, we had managed to get over our first hurdle with a good few more to come before finishing our training days.

Saturday morning finished the first week of mortar training, giving us a break from our physical exertions of which there had been many. It was still not an idle time for us, having to clean and blanco our belts and anklets, polish our boots and clean our brasses for church or chapel next day. We also had to find time for writing up our notes before they slipped from memory, with another lot due starting on Monday. None of us had time to leave the camp and go into town, but even then we were rewarded with a first class tea and evening meal that was always special at my time in the camp. Then time for a letter back home and a chat with the rest of the men was all we could do before the notes of lights out forced the camp into silence (that is with the exception of a few men still whispering to each other in the dark).

Over the weekend, two other men joined Bob and me in our group who seemingly would fit in very well in our long winter evenings of small talk. Their names were Peter Dorset and George Govey.

After our rest over the weekend, on Monday morning our training started again in earnest with an upgrading in our mortar drill. The drill starts with the mortar pieces lying on the ground, just a few feet apart, and about ten paces from where the three crewmembers are standing at ease, aligned with their respective mortar part. They will then receive the command of "Attention" where the crew spring smartly into that position waiting for the next command of "Action" requiring them now to run forward, and with all the energy they can muster, throw themselves onto the ground and slide into a prone position behind their piece of gun. Here, lying dead still, they wait for the next command of "Action". On command, you must leap onto your feet, literally snatching your load from the ground, and run forward with it to its mounting position where it must be assembled and laid onto the aiming post in the minimum of time. When all set, Number One of the crew calls out, "Ready to fire!"

Again to dismantle the mortar with the command of "Action", the crew must take it down in double-quick time and run back with their parts to their former positions they were in and stand to attention behind them. You could be expected to run through this drill, without letup, three times with the crewmembers changing their roles round to fill every position in the crew.

By the end of the day, after having grovelled around in the wet grass and mud, our denims had taken on, just once more, the appearance of a well-used back doormat. They would, of course, have to be clean and dry for the first parade of the day. These were still held in the hut before our breakfast on some aspect of the mortar.

The first full parade of the day was held outside Company HQ office, on a small parade ground tucked away from the main camp. One reason for this muster was to count the men on parade and call the role. Headquarters Company was formed up into three sides of a square by platoon with Company Sergeant Major Webb calling the role and Captain Hewlett just strolling around looking at his men. The CSM, having counted his flock, then called the parade to "Attention" and marched towards the company commander with a good deal of foot stomping. Halting in front of the captain, he gave the customary salute with some vigour and informed him that "The Company is all present and correct, sir!"

The captain returned the salute with his customary wave of the hand before addressing the men on parade. "Some of the men in the 3" mortars will be finishing their course this week, and will end with the firing of live ammunition on the mortar range. The new intake will accompany them, guarding the perimeter of the range during the firing. However, they will be able to see the mortar fired at close hand before starting on their guard duties. Right, Sergeant Major, dismiss the parade." "Sir", called out the CSM. "Officer on parade, dismiss!" We all turned to our right and saluted the captain, who then sauntered away displaying the gusset let into his trousers of the victory sign.

On the day of the mortar shoot, we were briefed about the part we would play in keeping civilians away from the danger zone. There was access to several footpaths in the area, although were marked by large red warning flags flying at the safety margin of the perimeter. We were also told to wear our steel helmets and not to wander away from our guard positions once they were set for us.

Our transport was a 3-ton lorry that would take us to the firing range, with the men who were going to do the firing. They were already waiting in their loaded carriers with the mortar parts strapped into position at the rear, and carrying the full complement of 88 x 10lb HE (high explosive) mortar bombs in cases of 3, in racks around the carrier.

After waiting there sometime, Captain Hewlett emerged from the HQ office, ambled over to our transport and proceeded to mount into the cab. We were then very soon on our way with the carriers bringing up the rear, the tracks making a fearful din on the road. It was a journey of several miles before we arrived at the range, which I could see was mostly scrubland with saplings interspersed over the rest.

Our group standing in the background looked on while a mortar was set up by the platoon sergeant, Sergeant Piggot, who was doing so with meticulous care, or so it seemed to us after the way we had all been throwing it together in our drill of the past few days. At last the platoon sergeant was satisfied with his effort, and it became obvious to us bystanders that the aiming post and mortar were lined up on some large wooden barrels in the distance at a range of about six or seven hundred yards. I could see that a good deal of the area, in and around where they were standing, was almost devoid of vegetation. The bombs fired from this position over a period of time had scythed the landscape flat.

Meanwhile, the captain had been walking back and forth waiting to get things started, eventually turning his attention onto our group. The captain called out, "Govey!" "Yes, sir?" answered George, springing to attention in the most enthusiastic manner. "What is the target?" the captain asked of him. "The barrels, sir!" said George. "The barrels!!!" exclaimed the officer, "I'll kick you in the balls, Govey!" shouted the captain, shocking the men with his profane outburst. "Charity!" he called out. "Tell them the target." Charity came to attention before addressing the captain, and when he did, it was spoken with a note of triumph in his voice. "The ENEMY, sir!"

I found out later that the whole group, had they been asked, would have given the same reply that George Govey had made to Captain Hewlett. Even I, had I been asked, would have said to the captain, "The barrels, sir!" without hesitation of any kind.

After this episode, I don't think Charity would have many friends around him, if any. In trying to make George look foolish, he had indeed blotted his copybook. As for Captain Hewlett, with his bombastic manner and personal castigation of George Govey, he was not to know at the time that a year on, George would be returned to England after having been wounded on three separate occasions while fighting on the Italian peninsula. And some of the others with us that day listening to his outburst would also fight there, only they would never return to their homeland.

With the captain's temper spent, they soon started firing, turning our minds away from the previous event. The first bomb away surprised me, making a thump rather than a loud bang. With a keen eye, you could pick up the bomb in flight, speeding away to the apex of its high trajectory before falling back to earth, slowly at first then speeding up till you all but lose sight of it before the explosion takes place.

After we had seen all they wished to show us, we were taken round to our guard positions where two of us were dropped off at every point on the footpath, located by a large red flag, with a warning from the NCO not to move away from that spot.

In time, we heard the thump of a mortar being fired and knew that the bomb was on its way. Even then, we were taken by surprise with the detonation of its charge of high explosive and complete disintegration of the missile, dispersing its lethal fragments of shrapnel over a wide area, making the most vicious whining sounds in the process. At the end of the shoot, we could hear all the mortars firing together by the rapidity of the distant thumps. These were soon lost to us by the explosions of the bombs falling to earth. It seemed closer than before, enough to make us lay down on the pathway with our faces buried in the tufts of coarse grass at the edge of the track. While in that position, a piece of shrapnel zipped into the grass, landing no more than one foot from my friend's face.

The mortaring had stopped by now, and reaching out, he picked up the bright fragment of steel with its jagged edges. It was still warm from the explosion that had forced it here. I had a look at the piece of shrapnel, being almost two inches long, and after a good examination of this deadly piece of material and its wider implications for us in the future, I passed it back to Arthur who told me, "I shall get this mounted and wear it on my watch-chain!" What a bizarre idea I thought, carrying round a piece of metal that had come very near to killing him. This was not the Arthur Lewis I mentioned in the general service days; he had moved on to an infantry regiment of the Royal Sussex. Soon after, we were picked up from our guard duties and returned to barracks.

At the end of the day in the privacy of our billet, our home from home you could say, we talked over the behaviour of the company commander. We all came down on the side of George who had obviously taken it rather badly. One of the men pointed out that the captain would be unable to physically carry out the task he had threatened George with that morning.

Friday turned out a nice day for our first carrier driving instruction. With its open top and sides exposed to the elements, the carrier was not exactly the kind of ride to match sitting in the back of a covered truck. However, it did the job it was designed for. Like the week before, we were marched to the motor pool that was tucked away in a corner of the camp, where we were handed over to our instructors who doled us out four men to each of the three carriers.

Our instructor was a very large sergeant and he let us know from the beginning who was in charge. Having driven us out of town, he pulled up at the foot of a hill running out into the countryside with no sign of any traffic on the roads. "Have any of you ever driven before last week's lesson?" the sergeant wanted to know. "No, Sergeant," we all chorused back. "Right then, let's have the first one then," the sergeant replied.

I had already decided beforehand that I would take the risk of making a fool of myself and get it over with. I climbed over, into the driving seat, threading myself passed the steering wheel. Sitting down in the seat, I found the wheel only inches from my chest. The sergeant gave us a general rundown on the procedures you should follow in this type of vehicle. One thing I did notice was the gear-changing lever confined in a slotted brass plate. The slots were in the shape of the letter H, numbered at each corner giving the gear position from 1-4 with a cutout for REV. I later found out it was a gate-change box, and I must say it made a vast difference to my own driving and helped the other men in the same way, being far better than last week's bonnet-less jalopy of Charity fame.

Starting off on the slope of the hill with the engine running and the brake released (foot and hand); I found that by imposing a slight lock on the steering wheel, the carrier was stopped from running downhill. Now with more advice from the sergeant, he told me to "Pull away and give the engine more power ... that's it. Now change into second ... and third. It should be able to get up here in third, but not top. Don't forget this must weigh over seven tons, we don't want to strain the gearbox do we?"

I did most of the things right and was pleased with my performance in the driving seat. However, it was very soon spoilt by the sergeant beating tattoo on the top of my steel helmet with the flat of his hand for not removing myself quickly enough from the seat, and the comment of "You dozy man" for good measure didn't help.

Most of the men did well that morning, and returning for our midday meal we all looked forward to the afternoon and our cross-country driving. It looked better still when we returned to the motor pool and our instructor of the morning had been exchanged for a lance corporal. He was not a young man, but he soon proved he was a first class instructor and soon put us right when we did wrong in a more dignified manner than some we had lately.

The training ground used by the carriers was made up of light woodlands and innumerable footpaths, some of which were deeply rutted by carrier tracks and the carriers themselves were in danger of being bellied on their hull. The plain fact was they rolled over from time to time and the occupants inside crushed. Only the man on instruction and the NCO in charge were allowed in the carrier. This was an Army order of one man in the carrier going over dangerous ground. One feature in the training ground where this could very well happen was a hole about a hundred feet across by twenty feet in depth, flat at the bottom with very steep sides all round. We would have to become more proficient before attempting a run at that.

There was no doubt that the corporal was a good man at his job, and by the end of the afternoon all of us had been made to benefit by his attitude towards us. We hoped that he would be made available for us on the following Friday. Driving over the uneven paths was like a ride on a rocking horse and in any other time you could very well say that you were enjoying the experience, but not when you know what the total result of this training would eventually lead you to.

With the exception of Friday's driving, lessons on the mortar and its component parts were carried out every day. Most evenings were now spent in writing up our notes for the day in our odd looking notebooks. There were evenings in the week when Bob and I would go into the town, but only if they were showing a good film.

One did come to our notice, that being *The Great Mr Handel*, the moving story of George Fredrick Handel's work on his ultimate masterpiece, *'The Messiah'*. Possibly, the greatest piece of music ever to find its way onto paper; the very name itself giving him the inspiration to complete the work in a matter of three weeks. It was a most wonderful film, taking our thoughts away from our daily dosage of aggressive intent that had no part in our true natures.

On the way back to the camp through the quiet blacked-out streets, I asked my friend of his opinion on what he had seen and did he like the music? To this he replied, "It was a good film and very well acted …" Bob hesitated before going on. "Do you know, I sometimes doubt the existence of a God who lets us be punished in this way with all this killing and bombing going on. There can't be any justification in making the people suffer in this way. What do you think about it?" I responded, "I liked the film and music, making one feel better for having seen it. As for the other things, I don't know the answer Bob, I only wish that I could tell you but it's way over my head." Bob was satisfied with what I had said and finished that part of our conversation with his favourite quotation, "You die if you worry; You die if you don't!" Bob soon returned to his jovial self that always made him such good company, even in the blacked-out streets.

It was Friday again, a day off from the demands of the 3" mortar. Before, when we had been out driving, we had never strayed very far from the outskirts of the town. So it was good news to hear that now we had become more proficient, we would be taken out on a longish run.

The route was a new concrete road made not long before the start of the war. This particular road made its way to Clacton-On-Sea, a journey of fifteen miles or so. For me, personally, it would be a day I would long remember.

We started our journey on the empty road with no traffic coming or going. We had the open road to ourselves, taking a turn each to sit behind the wheel. This week the senior sergeant of the motor pool supervised us. He stopped us now and again during the trip and had us backing the carrier into any leafy lane. This was no easy task. The driver had to stand at the controls and turn his head and body round till he could see over the top of the engine cover before trying to reverse. Not very easily done in a narrow lane, we all found out, a manoeuvre that does take some practice.

The sergeant turned out to be a very friendly man, telling us that when we arrived at Clacton he knew a place where we could get a cup of tea and a cheese sandwich somewhere along the seafront.

Long before reaching the town, I could hear a number of explosions taking place up ahead, even above the noise of the engine and the carrier tracks making a din on the road. At last, passing through the town and emerging from the buildings therein, we came out onto the seafront. My eyes gazed in wonder at my first sight of the sea and its curvature on the horizon. I was taken completely by surprise with it all, a most wonderful sight and very memorable. As for all the welcoming committee making the noise, they were made up of a row of Bofors guns spaced out along the seafront, blazing away at a windsock being towed offshore by a light aircraft with a goodly length of tow between it and the sock.

The noise was deafening, so having reached our destination, the sergeant climbed out and made hast into the café doorway; we needed no invitation to do the same. The sergeant was right about the quality of the food. The bread and cheese was wonderful along with a large mug of hot sweet tea. It was just what we needed after our cold journey. Where did the extra rations come from, for they were very generous with the portions we had?

Returning from Clacton and once again taking our turn at the wheel, we arrived back at the camp for our midday meal. Afterwards, we spent the rest of our driving session in the mud of the wood and thickets, churning up the ground when we moved off the footpaths. The moving mechanical parts, such as the sprockets, bogie and tracks soon got encased in mud – a good way to practice real service conditions.

It's rather strange but we were never asked nor did any cleaning of the carriers, even after getting them in the most appalling condition. But they were always clean when taken back onto the road.

7. End of training. Posted overseas. The reality of war.

The weeks were flying by now, making it more difficult to take all the information in our stride, like being told that a sergeant was coming over from the signal platoon to teach us wireless procedure, in the sending and receiving of messages on the two types now in use – the WT17 and 22 sets. The '17 set had a place where it could be in the carrier but had a short range of operation, whereas the larger '22 set had a wider field of operation and in most cases was carried around on your back, a considerable weight to carry.

The sergeant showed us how to net two sets together on the same frequency, enabling messages to be passed between one and the other. "All conversations over the airwaves must always be carried out using correct wireless procedure. Always keep a message simple and short, and by the way," the sergeant added, "don't forget, everything you say gets monitored by the military authority, so watch what you say. Just one more thing," the sergeant asked, "do any of you know the phonetic alphabet – Able, Baker, Charlie and so on? I can see by the head shaking that you don't. Never mind, you can learn it, the quicker the better." He, the sergeant, would be taking us for other lessons to be fitted into our already overcrowded training programme.

Charity received a mysterious package in the post from some member of the family. He would have informed them of the terrible task he was made to carry out once or twice a week of keeping his webbing blancoed. Therefore, his dutiful family had sent him a superior brand of Blanco that could be painted onto the webbing with a brush. Everyone blancoed their webbing belts and anklets for the Sunday church parades for the Church of England and Methodists.

No one seemed to notice till it was too late that Charity's shade of green was far brighter than the rest of ours. Someone suggested that he looked like Robin Hood! There was no backing out from the parade, he had to go and face the consequence of his own folly. We were told later that he received a right roasting on the parade from NCO and officers alike, but the fact still remained that for this misdemeanour he was never charged with a break in Army discipline.

For a change, we had lessons on 3" mortar ammunition with Corporal Warwick. "On active service they are carried around in a strong container of three bombs – 30lb in weight – but are kept in a steel container of six when in store and must always be kept dry." He continued. "Taking one of the rounds out of the container of three, you have the bomb around 12" long with its aluminium safety cap on the nose. By the way, I should have told you at the start to get this information down in your books. This being the kind of question that comes up in the exam," the corporal warned. "Right then, the safety cap only gets unscrewed at the time of firing and protects a thin metal cap over the detonator that reacts instantaneously on impact with the HE, that is high explosive in the bomb, and ends with a highly dangerous spread of steel fragments."

"It's impossible to let you see the whole picture without going back over things again," the corporal commented. "The bomb only becomes armed or made ready to explode from the moment it is fired. The velocity of the round from the barrel causes the mechanism inside the detonator, of a steel ball and spring, to drop into place and made un-returnable to its former position. Now the bomb will have become armed."

The corporal continued. "You will have seen that we have a raised band on the top, or the full diameter of the bomb, and is called the tolerance or driving band which fits reasonably well into the barrel, but never tight. Here, at the tail of the round, we have a waterproof cover attached to the round at the top of the fins with a tape also attached to the cover by a pop-rivet. The tape goes round the fins and tied with a bow so it can be removed without any fuss of knots at the vital time of firing. Also, at the bottom of the cover, we have a cupped steel base formed inside to stop any accidental firing of the cartridge in the centre of the fins if the round was mishandled in anyway."

"I shall have to go back to the barrel in explaining the next part," the corporal said. "You may remember, if you don't you should. The firing pin at the bottom of the barrel comes into use when you drop the bomb down, into the muzzle, and the weight of the round hitting the pin automatically discharges the cartridge into the propellant charges of nitrocellulose yellow. These are in capsules set out around the tailfins and held in position by close wound springs, which in turn are kept in position by running through holes in the fins."

"You may have noticed," the corporal remarked, "that the fins attached to the bomb are in pairs and are stamped out and formed to fit the hollow tube at the base of the bomb. The fins are spot-welded onto the tube and must withstand the blast to project the missile on its way. Should one of the fins break away, the bomb becomes unstable and liable to fall just about anywhere other than the target area. If you can get all of this down in your notebooks tonight, you will have done a good job. You could, of course, ask your friends if you can copy their notes, but it's far better that you write your own. You learn more that way." The corporal then ended with, "There will be more for tomorrow, but now let's get our tea."

The next day was more of the same. Corporal Warwick carrying on where he had left off the day before, giving us loads of information to get down on paper. "We have talked about the 3" mortar round at some length, so we can fill in some of the details now about where, in fact, you could expect your round to land if fired at a target. On charge-one, when we fire the mortar over a shorter range by removing three of the capsules of nitrocellulose yellow from around the tailfins, the bomb will travel a shorter distance and will always be more accurate. But when you change over to charge-two, we have the six capsules in place giving the mortar a range of one mile. However, in so doing we are less accurate in placing our rounds on the target."

The corporal went on. "We have a name for this theoretical place the bombs should land in, called the beaten-zone, and worked out by a number of factors. They could be the armourer incorrectly zeroing the mortar sight or gun, or even wear in the barrel. The lack of attention by the crew in laying the gun on, like the centralising of the bubbles in the spirit levels. The slight variations in the propellant charge, and lastly the weather with a wind being the most dominate factor. All of them together account for the size of the beaten-zone. With the mortar's rapid rate of fire, it can place around and on the target a good concentration of fire, even with the rounds that fall away from the target it would cause concern and confusion on the ground."

Again, the corporal closed with, "Have you any questions before we finish off ... no? Right then, tomorrow we best catch up on our fieldwork. Can any of you dig?" the corporal asked. "Well, I can tell by your silence that you can't so I had better teach you then."

Next day, the detachments were taken out into the countryside. We travelled in carriers, carrying the mortars, dummy ammunition cases and a good number of picks and shovels. The corporal had us gather around him. "Now today we are going to construct some mortar pits, which must hold the three crew members, mortar and ammunition, plus giving you room to work in. Every time you confront the enemy on the battlefield you would be expected to dig the mortar in, secretly at night in a more exposed position to digging one in daylight where you wouldn't have concealment from the enemy."

"When you move into a new position, the mortar can be mounted and ready to fire before you dig the hole. And seeing that only two or three can be digging the hole at the same time, the rest of the detachment should be digging their own personal slit trenches, but taking a turn with the mortar pit. It's for your own safety to get below ground level with only the leather muzzle cover and the gun sight in view. Now, mount one of the mortars," Corporal Warwick ordered, "but always make sure it's on firm ground when you do."

When the mortar was ready, taking up a pick, Corporal Warwick made a line with the pointed end about six inches in front of the bipod's feet. "Now we need the gun crew. Step forward and take up your correct positions at the gun. First, we have Number One in position, giving him space to crouch down so I can make a line at right angles, giving him just enough room, and that would also apply to Number Two and Three, giving him extra room to place his ammunition cases. So, if a line is drawn at right angles passed the bomb cases, we now have to link the two sides with a parallel line with the front leaving the crew room to move around in. Now if you remove the mortar you can start digging in the outline we have made on the ground. The rest of you can start digging your own pits and I suppose we can call it a day at three feet deep or thereabouts. Get on with it then."

The corporal watched the marking out of the two other pits and seemed well satisfied, but he soon had some comment for the men digging the slit trenches with a rather grim warning. "I know this is not for real, but some of you should be reminded to always dig your own trench far enough away from the mortar pit in case of some unforeseen event like taking a direct hit. While you are safe in your much smaller slit trenches from the fragmentation of the bombs, I'm not too sure about the blast effect at close quarters. Anyway, it's better by far to be on the side of caution."

We spent most of the day in making the pits, then trying them out for size with the crew, mortar and ammunition, finding in every case we needed more room to function in. We had been told beforehand that the holes would have to be filled back in. And on its completion, all of us were very weary from our efforts. After our tea, no one was willing or could bother with their notebooks, some of them just turning into their bunks while others just sat around talking over the day's events.

There was one part of our training that I was never able to perform properly or come to terms with. That was working with a respirator in position on mortar drill, from a prone position (lying on the ground behind your piece of mortar), jumping up at the command of "Action" and running forward with it to its set position.

Before using your respirator, you would make sure it was clean and the eyepieces wiped with an anti-misting cream, stopping them from fogging up when being used. However, in my case with the respirator in position and carrying out the drill, by the time I had lifted it from the ground and ran forward with it to its mounting position, my eyepieces were both fogged up by the time we had the three parts linked together. Then if I were Number One or Two on the gun, responsible for the zeroing of one of the two bubbles and laying it onto the aiming post, I would be completely lost not being able to see a single thing.

With all of the respirator drills, with the actual mounting of the mortar, I was never able to carry out successfully. When it came to this particular test at the end of our training, Lieutenant Ford never asked or looked into the reason of my failure and would consequently have given me 0 out of 10 for my efforts, leaving me rather dejected.

Looking back now, with years of hindsight, it must have been one of two things. Firstly, I could have been issued with a faulty respirator, or my approach to all mortar drill had been the cause of my own undoing. I always carried out the mortar drill with vigour and possibly, in the process, I was burning off more calories than I need have done, hence the forming of more water vapour than the demisting cream could cope with inside the respirator.

We continued our training on communications with the signal sergeant. Gradually we became more proficient with the walkie-talkie sets (portable radio transmitting and receiving sets). We were also introduced to the self-powering field telephone, whereby a detachment commander could communicate along a length of cable back to the mortar position and his Number One. The microphone was strapped around the neck and throat, the power being induced by speaking into the throat-microphone and the electrical impulses would then be picked up in the earpieces at the other end. It also gave the freedom of both hands in the adjustment of the mortar without having to hold a telephone in one of the hands.

Other means were used in the communications field between the mortar crew and detachment commander, but the throat type microphone was in common use at the time.

New men were coming into the platoon every second week. At the completion of our mortar training programme with the firing of live ammunition, we were now due for leave, or what they called privilege leave after having had none in almost six months since being called up.

But first, we were told of our exam results on our knowledge of the 3" mortar with favourable remarks from Mortar HQ, though some of the men did not make the grade. Then there was the driving test where I passed with a Grade 'A'. Upon return from our leave, we would be posted to our respective battalions, the Royal Sussex or Royal Berkshire regiments. One piece of news that filled the men with disgust was that Charity, of all people, had been posted to Ireland to join the Intelligence

Corps! All the men in the platoon were dumbfounded. Charity's social status had clearly played its part.

It was good to be going home again, seeing my parents and one or two other members of the family. Time on leave went very swiftly by, and I soon found myself on the train back to Colchester along with my friends.

Back at Colchester, we had to spend two weeks without doing too much but wait before being posted to the 9th Royal Berkshire Regiment, a holding battalion in Norfolk for a programme of intensive mortar training.

We left Colchester by train for Norwich, where here we changed onto a branch line for North Walsham, then Mundesley-On-Sea. Here we were taken by Army transport to our destination and received a shock to find we were going to be billeted in a wonderful park in the grounds of a stately home, used only for the purpose of Company HQ. We were billeted in bell tents surrounded by trees and magnificent rhododendron shrubs.

The nature of the training was very severe with long carries of the mortar by the crews. The distance of the carry was in the region of two or three miles that had to be done in a certain time with part of the course being done on the run, the only way to complete the distance in the time allowed. Your piece of mortar would weigh in the region of forty pounds plus. We also had to deal with the heat of high summer, which indeed was very hot in 1943.

While we were at the camp, a very bad tragedy took place. A young Scottish soldier received a letter from his lady friend, telling him their engagement was off. It did not seem to occur to her that he was about to go abroad and could do nothing about the new situation. He was so badly affected by the news that when on his own with his thoughts he placed his rifle in his mouth and pulled the trigger. A bloody hole in the bell tent was testimony to what he had done.

After the mortar training was completed, we moved to an old holiday camp at Mundesley-On-Sea, just a few miles away. This was a place from where you were posted abroad and soon we were given leave for just that.

On our return from leave, they started issuing us with kit that had all the hallmarks of the Far East. Then there was an about-turn on this. The powers that be decided that half of us were too young to go on a draft abroad. So us underage soldiers were formed into a platoon and told by the camp commanding officer, "You will all have another six more weeks of infantry training before being eligible for overseas service, but will be having another seven days embarkation leave at the completion of the course. Your platoon officer will be Lieutenant George of the Wiltshire Regiment who I know will serve you well."

The lieutenant was a first rate officer. We worked hard, but he was always fair with us, joining in with everything he asked of us. I think, without a doubt, he was the best officer I ever served under. In training, we did a six-mile run and walk in full battle-order, then a ten-mile run and walk, and both had to be completed in one and two hours respectively. He also climbed up and down the sand cliffs with us on Mundesley beach, which were over a hundred feet high and very dangerous in places.

My very good friend, Bob Manley, had some trouble in coping with this. One evening, Bob and I went onto the sand cliffs on our own. I was able to impart some confidence into him and soon he was able to climb unaided. Bob was most grateful for my time spent with him.

Bob and I also used to go into Norwich on Saturday afternoons, when we could get a leave pass to see a film. The most outstanding one was *Random Harvest* with Ronald Colman and Greer Garson; both of us being very impressed with it and a most moving film.

With our six weeks training coming to its close, one or two of the men in the platoon broached the subject to the officer about the seven days leave that had been promised at the beginning of the course. The officer said, "I will look into it with the company commander at once." We waited in expectation for the officer to report back, and when he did, we were somewhat shocked that there would be no leave for us. The platoon, to say the least, was very dejected at the news.

After telling us the worst, Lieutenant George looked over his platoon with a very thoughtful look on his face. He said, "Have I your permission to approach the company commander and tell him, without the thought of mutiny in the ranks, that the men will go abroad with very bad feeling after the promise made to them in good faith was broken?" Later, the issue was passed over by the company commander to Brigade who sanctioned the leave without question. So, we had our seven days leave, all due to the kindness of the lieutenant who was an exception to the rule.

On our return from leave, we had a kit inspection and were fitted out with clothes for overseas service. The next was an inspection of our kit by the brigadier, the last before we left for foreign parts. The draft was confined to the camp till we left and that was not long in coming. We moved out of the camp in transports. The date of the move was at the beginning of August 1943, and could have been Bank Holiday Monday.

We were taken to the station and boarded the train for our final destination, wherever that was for we had no idea. The train passed from daylight into darkness and back again. Then it was mentioned by someone that we had passed Carlisle. So, we had arrived at the Scottish border and could now be on our way to the only port we could think of – Glasgow. The train rumbled on passed buildings in outlying towns till we came to Glasgow with its workshops and warehouses in abundance, then at last we came to the end of the line.

We moved off the train with all our gear, formed up in threes and marched off along the quay that contained a ship in dry dock with a list from end to end of around about 10° degrees from the vertical. It was a strange sight. We did not bypass the stricken ship, but were halted at its gangplank and ordered to file aboard. This was going to be our billet for the next day or two.

The ship we were on now had been torpedoed in an Atlantic convoy, had limped home to go into dry dock, and now awaited repairs to her damaged hull. We slept on the mess decks, neither better nor worse for being in the open.

At last, our ship arrived in dock and it was not long before we had transferred our belongings onboard. The name of the ship was the *Bergenfiord*, and it was not long before other groups came onboard to make up the numbers. It would be a tight squeeze for us all.

The officer in charge of the troops onboard came over the loudspeakers for a pep talk with us, going something like this: "I'm well aware that we are short on space, but we must all make the best of it for the sake of the war effort. We shall be joining the convoy soon, so we shall soon be underway and I expect every man to play his part. Thank you."

In fact, we were soon away, pulling out into the Clyde, moving passed the shipyards on our way to the Firth-of-Clyde and the open sea. There were ships being made and ships being repaired along the length of the Clyde, and when our ship came into view, the entire workforce had turned out along the rails of their ships and were cheering us like mad. I was very moved at this show of goodwill towards us and at the same time, I thought to myself, it might be the last time my friends and I would see the 'Old Country' again. It was a sad moment.

We passed by Greenock and the rolling hills out into the Firth-of-Clyde, and then out to the open sea where the convoy awaited. The sea became very choppy when I saw what could only be the pilot's boat. The boat came out to head the convoy through the channel and was being tossed about like a cork in the rough sea. It was hard not to laugh at the spectacle, but within twenty-four hours, we found out the power of the sea and the last laugh was on us all.

The convoy steamed well out into the Atlantic before making its sweep for the Mediterranean. After around six days of steaming, this was reached with no trouble that we were aware of. The Mediterranean was different in that the enemy planes dropped in from time to time for target practice on the ships, but mercifully, they didn't put in an appearance. After a few more days had passed it looked to us that we should soon be making landfall, and so it was.

I came awake at the reveille call, and the realisation dawned on me that the vessel had stopped during the night. We dressed and had our breakfast. While doing so, we were told over the ship's loudspeaker system by the transport officer that we had arrived at our destination in North Africa, at the port of Philippeville in Algeria. After his address about our behaviour and conduct, while in this land, he finished by thanking us for our cooperation onboard ship, living in such cramped conditions that he justified for the sake of the war effort.

Later, when we had got our kit together and cleaned our quarters, we climbed the stairs out of the well of the ship onto our drill deck. The ship was lying about a mile offshore, giving us a wonderful view of the coastline in the fresh morning sunshine touching the whitewashed villas of the town. A sight you would long remember.

Later in the morning, the ship moved under its own power into its berth on the quayside. I, along with some of my friends, had been detailed off to take care of the officers' baggage. They would be moving into the same camp as us. The officers were not known to me by name or sight and had obviously come from other holding battalions, now alas back in England. I had only seen them at our boat drill stations and coming from their own quarters, a more superior part of the ship and strictly off limits for other ranks.

Our party had to wait on deck while watching the hundreds of men stagger down the gangway with their kit, and very soon loaded onto open-sided trucks and driven away to their various destinations.

After all the troops had left the ship, the baggage party went into action removing the piles of officers' luggage, which we found very different from our own; camp beds, folding washbasins and the like we were not allowed to have in our own kit. Working in the hot sun, we removed theirs and our own things onto an open-sided vehicle. The baggage party ended up by sitting on top of this pile of luggage. I had my last glimpse of the *Bergenfiord* as we moved away from the docks and through the town into the poorer Arab quarters.

We could see from our vantage point on top of the luggage a small boy of around four or five years of age, waiting by the side of the road. Pulling level with him, he placed his hands on the bottom of his robe and hoisted it as far as it would go, revealing a naked torso from bare feet to armpits. He was not finished yet as he called out in a high-pitched voice, "Up your pipe, Tommy!" We looked at one another in complete astonishment. Although never expecting a welcoming committee, it showed there was a bad feeling towards the occupation of their land by a foreign power.

Travelling eastwards, we soon cleared the town and out into the desert where the road was in sight of the sea with the land, the other side, made up of sand dunes stretching away south into the far distance. It was hot and dusty on top of the luggage and I would be glad when we came to our destination.

We could see the road ahead now had a slight incline with a bend at the top leading into higher dunes. And from this an officer appeared as if out from nowhere, holding his hands on high for us to stop. He was in a very agitated state when he called out to us to "Get off the truck and come with me!" We followed him with some haste to the top of the incline where we met an awful sight of a vehicle that had come off the road, had rolled down the bank, crushing its cab in the process and was now turned upside-down with its wheels pointing skywards.

That was my first impression of the accident, still unaware as to what had really happened till coming close. Then I was met with the most ghastly sight of men's limbs protruding out from under the steel sides of the vehicle, trapped by the crushing weight, their limbs pushed into the encrusted sand. That was not all, there were men crying out in terror inside the overturned hull. We had no idea of the number inside, but one thing was obvious, they were severely injured along with the dead and dying, waiting to be rescued from their torment.

The officer, in a not very hopeful voice, suggested we try and lift it onto its side, but after trying, we had to give in. If we had digging tools available we would by now have freed the survivors.

When we had lost all but hope, we could hear a tracked vehicle approaching and came into view at the same place where the unfortunate accident had occurred. It was a medium-sized tank that slithered down the bank and came to rest. With the trapped men still crying out from inside, upon hearing the tank, they must have thought they were about to be rescued. I, along with the others, could not see how the presence of the tank would help. It had no lifting equipment or digging tools so it seemed.

While this was going on, we found out that the occupants of the vehicle were soldiers of the Free-French forces. This, in turn, explained our failure to grasp what they had been calling out to us. I now watched in despair while the tank crew fitted a cable to the side of the hull, and when they were ready the engine roared away, pulling the cable taut and making the hull shudder with the men inside now going frantic at their new oppressor. The hull began to move, dragging the men inside along with it, inflicting more pain and suffering for those still alive.

More attempts were made and all ended in failure. Then, without any reason, the officer told us to get back onto our transport and leave. The men returned to our pile of luggage and sat in silence at what they had witnessed.

The transport moved off from this frightful place, down the coast road. I was thinking my own thoughts without conversing with the others about this tragic event, and the inhuman cruelty the men had been made to suffer. We had possibly seen too much for the officer's liking back there. The whole event would be a cover-up and regarded as 'never happened'. The French military authority would most likely report the men dead, killed in action for the good of their country. I honestly believe that some of them could have been saved from the tons of steel trapping them, before the intervention of the tank and crew with their display of gross incompetence against the lives of their fellow beings.

The transport rolled along down the coast road with no sign of habitation of any kind till after many a mile we came to our transit camp, a sight that did nothing to raise my flagging spirit.

The camp was made up in rows of two-man tents. The occupants' kit neatly displayed in front of each of the open flaps. Only the military mind could have devised such a way of keeping discipline in this place, miles away from anywhere.

At last, the transport came to a halt at a timber built administration office. We unloaded the officers' equipment and our own before we were marched off to our battalion draft lines and the welcome faces of our friends. Our own NCOs were in charge of us but not in control of the camp, which came under the camp staff.

The next morning, the CO of the camp inspected our kits. He was an elderly looking captain who later had the draft assemble in front of the administration office for what could only be called a pep talk from him about camp discipline. Standing on the veranda, the officer had a long hard look at the one hundred and twenty or so men in our draft.

He pulled himself up and said, "My name is Montgomery, and I shall expect the same high standard of results as the other man received!" And after he had paused for effect, he went on. "No one must leave the camp or try to visit the town. But drill and training must be carried on with while you remain here, and the breaking of camp standing orders will be severely dealt with." He carried on till even he ran out of steam, but not the men who had been forced to listen in stony silence. Of course, we had no choice in the matter but to listen.

The captain eventually dismissed us, and it was clear that most of the men were furious at his treatment of us. There weren't even facilities for a cup of tea and a bun. They, who ran the camp, could have done something for our off duty spells. Was this the correct way of treating men who would very shortly be laying their lives on the line when they came into contact with the enemy? My impression of the pompous captain was in linking his own name with the illustrious general, who I feel sure would have been very peeved indeed at having his good name taken in vain by this upstart of a captain.

A day or so later, the men of the draft were marched off into the desert to a training area some distance from the camp. There, we were told, we would see a demonstration by a Guards unit on the taking of 'Long Stop Hill', one of the battles of the desert campaign and would be carried out using live ammunition.

To accompany us for this exercise, we had the camp CO who was going to give a running commentary on how the attack developed into a rout of the enemy forces there. We also had a few of the officers from the draft coming to watch the display.

Coming to the place where the demonstration was to be held, we were dispersed into groups of two or three on a sandbank which ran about two hundred feet in length, and in turn faced into a valley of some considerable length of half a mile or more till it ran into some sand dunes and out of our vision. The floor of the valley was quite flat in places and as wide as the bank we now occupied. The banks running down the valley were of various heights with defiles in places running into the desert. The only things growing in this barren landscape were a few stunted bushes and scrub, also a few along the bank where we were standing.

I also noticed that the CO and other officers present were standing on the flanks of the rest of us. Normally they would be controlling events from a central position of the men; otherwise, we would be unable to hear the captain's explanation of what was going on. Some prearranged signal must have been given, as we could hear the captain calling out about keeping our eyes on the head of the valley for any movement.

At last, we did see some movement up ahead, but at that distance they were still too far away for us to be sure. Anyway, with the overcast sky it made things less discernible. Then, at last, they did come into view, having advanced two or three hundred yards under cover of the dunes. Then we could hear small arms fire and observed figures running about firing their weapons into the sandbanks, advancing diagonally from one side to the other, keeping up with their bursts of fire against an imaginary enemy.

When the advancing men were only a matter of a few hundred yards away, I expected the exercise to have run its course (after all live ammunition was being used and we were standing on their line of advance). Then the scene we had been watching changed with dramatic suddenness. We observed to our consternation a line of tracer bullets arcing their way towards us, into what could be our positions on the bank. It all happened swiftly, taking us by surprise, giving no one any chance of avoidance but drop onto the ground and hope.

The firing had ceased, so we could now hear a brave voice from the flank ordering us to stand up, but for some, crying out in anguish at their wounds, would not find it possible to obey. We were hurried away from the accident and formed up ready to march back to camp.

The men were fast regaining their composure from the shock, but it was evident they were furious at the turn of events and realisation of such a catastrophe having taken place. Before leaving the ill-fated spot, we watched one of the blood-soaked men being carried away on an old wooden door they had found, being the best they could do for the wounded man. We were marched back to camp, a sullen body of men, each with their own thoughts about the accident that should never have taken place.

That evening, back in the camp, the word had done its round with the rest of the men about the tragedy back in the desert. This, in turn, started a rebellious kind of talk against the camp authority who in the first case refused to inform us of the extent of the casualties. Instead, they told us the most unlikely story, or fable, of how the accident had taken place. It was this: "One of the men taking part in the demonstration had unfortunately tripped over when firing his Thompson submachine gun." We, who were standing on the bank, knew that was never the truth of the matter. The damaging fire had come from somewhere at the head of the valley with fire from a machine gun, with a mixture of tracer rounds making the projectiles visible in flight.

The next day, the men in the camp found it hard to cope with the rigid discipline imposed on us, especially after hearing the dishonest account of the accident that only made conditions worse. The murmuring voices in the camp soon reached the captain's ear. He then decided, for our trouble, to take us out that very night on a march down into the desert. He was in charge, so he wished the disrespectful talk going around the camp to cease forthwith, otherwise other ways of discipline would be introduced in the running of the camp.

It was dark when we started our trek into the desert. It was still warm and would remain so for several hours. The only light provided was from a number of oil lamps carried by members of the camp staff, spaced out down the length of the marching column of men, creating a weird scene from the poor lights from the lamps and made worse with the rising dust.

Some of the men in the ranks used the cover of darkness to make remarks about the injustice of the punishment we were being made to suffer, in trying to establish the truth about the accident. This, in turn, had the captain doing his best with the aid of his lamp in trying to locate the dissenters in the punishment march. This, he failed to do, but not before he had threatened us all with more of the same.

We marched on, into the night, surrounded by the inky-blackness of the desert. Then I saw in the distance a tracery of tracer rounds being fired at what must have been a night manoeuvre for some troops in training, and seemed to be taking place on a high plateau above the desert floor, too far away to hear their private battle.

On we marched, tired and flagging now, urged on by the ever-present voice of Captain Montgomery who still thought he had the justifiable right to impose his own cruel brand of authority on us, who so far had travelled over eight thousand miles to fight against the enemy, not him.

It must have been early morning with the men slowed down with fatigue after many hours in the foot-dragging sand. Even the robust captain looked the worse-for-wear and was now mercifully almost silent. I, alone with my own thoughts, had gone over many times the events since we had left the ship just a few short days before, but in that time had seen the most inhumane acts I would never have thought possible, making our own survival less sure. But deep within me, activated no doubt by the unpredictable events of the past few days, I said to myself, "Mother."

The march, to our relief, finally came to an end, but not before the captain had reminded us once again why the march had taken place.

All of the men were completely exhausted by the supposedly corrective march, only having the remaining strength left to crawl into their beds.

With the new day, reveille came too soon for our tired bodies. However, it also brought the good news that we were moving on with the next stage of our journey taking us to Bizerte in Tunisia. I think we were all pleased in escaping from the clutches of this officer who had come very close at one stage to losing control of his command.

Early the next morning with our kit, we boarded a line of 3-ton lorries with their tarpaulin covers on, no doubt a good way of controlling the excess of hot sun and dust on the journey that would take all day. It was most unpleasant in the back of the lorry, but after our ordeal in the last camp, a little more suffering could do us no harm. On the way, we were never far from the sea, but not all of it was desert. There was high ground in places where battles had been fought with the evidence still lying around in the form of rusting vehicles and the flotsam of war – a grim reminder that's where we were heading for.

At last, we came to a camp on a hillside with walk-in tents for our accommodation, a great improvement on the last place. Here at the camp, we were expected to work on the construction of a road with rubble that arrived in open-sided trucks. The reason for our work was for the provision of a good road into the camp in the winter months ahead. This was obviously going to be a large staging camp for reinforcements for the Italian campaign, and the jumping-off place for this was the port of Bizerte.

We stayed at the camp for a few days, and then were told about our move over to the Italian mainland. We left the camp in transports for our short journey down to the docks, stopping at a row of American LC-I (landing craft – infantry) ships. They were going to take us to the mainland of Italy, a distance of around 360 sea miles and at times infested with enemy naval craft supported by the Luftwaffe.

Going onboard the flat-bottomed ships, we were each given a lifejacket and a tin of bully beef. This was to be our haversack ration for the journey. Once onboard, we were soon heading out to the open sea where a small convoy was forming up and backed up by a number of destroyers. Our ship didn't ride very well in the swell of the Mediterranean with that flat-bottom, but we managed in the uncomfortable conditions of our lot. Thankfully, we had a very uneventful journey, not the kind of voyage you would link with the rich of the day, but quite adequate for our needs.

Arriving in the bay of Salerno, at the port of the same name, our ship ran up onto the sandy beach and we stepped ashore onto mainland Europe. We were then marched off in the direction of the town. I was well aware of the landings made here only a few short weeks before with a terrible loss of life on both sides. Now the enemy had been pushed back to the port of Naples, over thirty miles away with severe fighting still going on there.

We marched through the streets, seeing hastily dug graves by the roadside – wooden crosses denoting who was laid to rest there. One such cross was that of a young lieutenant who had fallen and this would register in my mind forever.

At last, we arrived at our billet and of all places it was the Salerno opera house; a most magnificent building with its ornate façade that continued throughout the entire building. We were told to bed down on the stage, which was vast and not in the auditorium. At the back, I could see, by evidence of the props standing there, that in the recent past they had performed a production of Verdi's Aida on that very stage. For me it gave a moment of wonderment in this hostile land at war. I can say, with complete honesty, that I made an appearance on the stage at the opera house in Salerno.

We still had part of our bully beef ration left and that would have to sustain us till the next day, and by then we should be receiving hot food. Next day, we did get the meal promised and my friends and I decided to eat outside in the sun where we very soon attracted the attention of a small boy who was just skin and bone. He approached us and asked in Italian for food, which we gave him from our own rations and were pleased to do so.

From that day on, he followed us about whenever we left the opera house. We gave him food, which he always needed in this impoverished land, and one day an Italian asked if we would like our picture taken with him. And so we did. I have a copy to this day.

Soon after, we received orders that sent us on to the next staging camp, in a place called Castellammare, this being just a short journey away and there finding ourselves in a large railway wagon repair yard.

Our billets were now in some of the wagons in the yard, just a few of us in each. The former workers here, I should think, used the mess hall. It had a beautiful tiled floor that became one of our everyday fatigues, of washing it with seawater (the sandy beach only being about twenty yards away). Afterwards, we would wash the floor over with clear water from a vast well in the complex.

On several evenings, while there, some very fine Italian singers treated us to a concert of musical entertainment with the help of a few musicians. The soldiers in the audience always greeted the singers with rapturous applause, and to show appreciation of their fine efforts, a collection was taken up for the artists of many thousands of lire at each performance. This would supplement the fact that none of the artists were in work.

The vast machine shop at the plant had been subjected to an act of vandalism, but by whom? With the country being in a state of turmoil, things were very bad indeed. I purchased a walnut jewel box in Castellammare that I then sent home to my mother.

Our stay here soon ended with us moving on to another staging camp, this time in Naples. The fighting had then moved on to the north. This was the next step towards joining our battalion in the line. We were found billets in a most ruinous part of the city, but we were going to be fed here, there being cooking facilities available to us. The camp commandant here told us to "Sleep on the floor, even if unclean and covered in white dust. Just don't sleep on old doors or wooden frames because they are full of lice!"

While here, we seemed to be on perpetual fatigues everyday of washing up and cleaning in the cookhouse. In the evening, after the work was over for the day, we all sat on the ground and would sing all the favourite songs of the day, the most popular among us being *'Home on the Range'*. The singing was good for us and a lift to a higher moral feeling within us.

A few of us not on duty decided to go into the city for a sightseeing tour. It would have been better to have stayed away. Once there, we were confronted by a host of irate women with empty shopping baskets who swallowed us up in their midst with them all chanting together just one word, "Pane, Pane, Pane (Bread)," as if we were responsible for their shortage of the staff of life. After extracting ourselves from the Neapolitan horde, we decided to move on, not that we were unsympathetic to their needs; we just didn't have the power to help them.

Later, we came across a similar situation of a very old man lying on the ground with his neck on a tram rail, uttering the same word, "Pane, Pane!" He would not budge from his position on the rail, even with the tram making small movements towards him. A large crowd had gathered and in the end, still complaining, he was dragged very forcefully away from the rail. After our tour, we were glad to return to *'Home on the Range'*.

We had a few night visits from the Luftwaffe, dropping bombs in and around the port. Time came to leave the city, making way for the men coming along behind.

Our next move was to tented accommodation just a few miles north of Naples. On our journey, we came across a most disquieting sight by the side of the road, of a German soldier who had been killed whilst driving his vehicle with his hands still stretched out to the steering wheel and his knees bent as they would have been. The poor man was frozen in death. Some callous brutes had placed him on the grass verge at the roadside. This was a show of downright cruelty on someone's part and was the true face of the brutality of war.

We didn't stay very long in our new campsite, moving next to a place called Teano. This was no great distance from our former position, making it seem that we couldn't tarry for long in any one place. Teano turned out, for us, just a place to bivouac with a small tent between two. I could see no habitation from our camp, but right in front of us was a large slab of rock around two hundred feet long by a hundred high. It was the only feature I was ever to see there.

Teano was our first link with the battalion and the headquarters of B Echelon, where all the stores were held for distribution to all the companies in the line. The captain quartermaster was in charge here. We found out from the staff that the battalion was at this time fighting at a place called Calabritto, underneath the mountain mass of the enemy defence line running through a place called Cassino and beyond.

8. The frontline.

We were now officially in the 10th Battalion The Royal Berkshire Regiment, and in the 56 London Division with its emblem of a black cat on a red background; also in the 10th Corps serving in the American 5th Army under its commander, General Mark Clark.

There was nothing for us to do here except keep our equipment in good order. The laundry was another matter of keeping our clothing clean and only with cold water, it being a mercy that we were not invaded by lice and other forms of life. My own mother would have had a fit if she had known of our predicament.

One morning, when on parade, they asked for volunteers to make up a carrying party for the battalion fighting in the line. We were told it was no easy task to do, but men were urgently needed to carry supplies up to our beleaguered battalion. About twenty of us volunteered for this, some of them my friends who had the same thoughts as me of finding out at firsthand what it was like at the sharp end.

The next morning, the volunteers, myself included, boarded onto a 3-ton lorry and we were on our way into the unknown. Had I done the right thing? After travelling some way on our journey, we could hear a rumble that sounded like thunder in the distance, but our conclusion was wrong and as the journey progressed it became apparent it was the roar of gunfire that could be heard.

At last, we came abreast of the gun-line and could see our 25-pounder guns blazing away at targets miles away from here. The noise had been bearable, but now it was thunderous as we passed by the gun muzzles and were glad when we had gone well passed. The guns had been sited both sides of the road and were in extended line across the fields. In the past, I had talked about sitting in a safe cinema seat back home, watching the war newsreels, but this was now entirely different. I was of the opinion that I was about to leave it. I had known, from when the war started, I would be in the conflict someday and it turned out to be now.

We arrived at our destination, in the village of Roccamonfina, with its high ground behind the village and its slopes covered with edible chestnut trees. Here, we found we had arrived at A Echelon, the forward post of the battalion not in the line. It was a staging place for reinforcements or replacements for the battalion as well as being a forward stores for the needs of the companies in the line, of ammunition, food and water. That's where we came in, to supply the rifle companies without them leaving their positions.

We left Roccamonfina immediately on our way into the frontline, along a tree-lined road till we came to a Bailey bridge across a rock gorge at the same time as an air battle was going on overhead. I suspect the enemy were trying to destroy the bridge there. We crossed over without harm and continued on our way to a village called Saraceri, nestling under some mountains that looked very close and were occupied by the enemy.

The village was empty of its inhabitants; whether by order or self-preservation, I had no way of knowing. We found our own billets in the deserted village. All of us had been warned not to make any noise or have fires (due to the smoke) and, above all, to keep a low profile in the daylight hours.

Stores for the battalion were packed and ready for dispatch. Most of the things would have to be carried in a large webbing valise (every soldier had one with his kit and was carried on the back). The carrying party could only operate under the cover of darkness and in complete silence. The sergeant in charge of the party told us, "When you get to where you are going, you will find most of the men in their slit trenches. Unfortunately, you will be on open ground, and in the event of trouble there, you must find whatever cover is available to you. Don't run away!"

That night, with the aid of the light of the moon, we started off on our journey from the village and walked on down the main road where there was a ban on all types of vehicles owing to enemy shelling there. The moon cast its light through the tree-lined road, as we struggled along with our load of supplies, with a tracery of leaves forming a pattern on the road and moving about in the gentle breeze.

After a time, we came to a wall running along the side of us and must have been about seven feet high. Further along still, we came to a niche in the wall which held a statue of the Madonna, looking down on us, and I had the feeling her face was full of compassion. The Madonna was a most familiar sight throughout this land and found in the most unexpected places.

We now came to a hole in the wall, knocked through for us so that we had a different approach to the battalion positions without using the road. I had to stoop to get through the wall, where now I found myself in a sunken lane covered over with the foliage of trees and shrubs. Here, the sergeant warned us again about complete silence. We moved on under cover of the leafy glade till we came into a clearing from where you were able to see the mountains.

A few men appeared out of the gloom and, at last, we had arrived at the 10th Battalion at Calabritto. We didn't see any evidence of the village for we were soon on our way back. Our journey back to the village of Saraceri was uneventful, and those not on guard duty turned in for some sleep.

We went on a carrying party every night, some of them being more hazardous than others. One night, we had almost reached our destination when we could hear fighting up ahead and it sounded like a real skirmish, which in fact it was. The enemy had made their attack from their positions under the foot of the mountain and almost succeeded in their effort to overrun the battalion.

Mortar bombs had fallen in and around the village, and when we arrived there, you could see plumes of smoke and steam rising up from the ground where the bombs had impacted. During the enemy attack, they constantly called out each others' Christian names in German, making sure each other were safe from injury or death. This, we were told on hearing it, was a most bizarre experience for the men of the battalion. The carrying party didn't dally there and made off with some haste for we had no cover from attack.

One night on a carrying party, we had just passed by the Madonna statue and through the hole in the wall into the sunken lane. Moving on, we could hear the unmistakeable sounds of mortar bombs coming our way. We all dived onto the ground and tensed ourselves for the inevitable. But we were most fortunate in that the bombs landed the other side of the lane, and a second salvo fell in the same area, showering us with twigs and leaves from trees above us, cut down by the vicious shrapnel flying around. No one was injured in this episode and we soon moved on.

The 10th Battalion had a bad time at Calabritto with a mounting casualty list. One young officer, who had been placed on our overseas draft, was killed the very same evening he joined the battalion. Calabritto was a bad position to be in, so 5th Army decided to pull the battalion back out and wait for the major attack on Mount Camino.

The carrying party was used to bring the battalion back out and to give help where needed, and it was in some cases. Some of the men came out on stretchers, too weak to walk out. If the enemy had known of our intentions of withdrawal, he would have given us a very bad time. But all went well and the battalion was able to extricate itself from a serious position.

We had transport waiting for us along the road, but had no idea where we were heading for. The trucks started off on their journey, but to where? We passed by Saraceri that had been our base for over a week, and from here, we had started out on the carrying parties every night we were there.

Two incidents in Saraceri spring to mind. One of finding an Italian-American passport on a sideboard in our billet and he, by chance, had served in the American Marines. There was also a windup gramophone on the sideboard with a record of a Marine band playing Sousa Marches. I wound up the gramophone and started it, then placed the arm onto the record, and to my complete surprise the sound of the band blasted out of the speaker, giving me a shock. I acted swiftly and turned it off, embarrassed by the commotion I had caused, thinking of the sergeant's words of "No noise."

The other incident being we had a man in the carrying party by the name of Minter, and was far too old to be in the infantry with a large family back home. One day the enemy fired two shells into the village, though we being most fortunate that no one was hurt. But Minter, at the time, had come out of a door from his billet and was walking by a stone-built wall of some five or six feet in height. One shell hit the wall, causing it to collapse, some of it on Minter. A few moments later, Minter emerged, staggering out of the acrid smoke and dust. Although unharmed, the explosion had blackened his face and the words he used to express his thoughts are unprintable.

With the transports having passed Saraceri, it began to rain, cold slanting rain, and before we had gone a mile or so, we had arrived at our destination in the middle of nowhere.

We climbed out of the transports into the rain swept night and followed the men in front, not easy in the darkness and the atrocious conditions that were abroad that night. We came to a track leading up into the inevitable chestnut woods. The track was steep in places and the men of the battalion, who had little or no sleep in a very long time, were now dead on their feet.

After making it to the crest of the hill, we came to a halt having arrived at our billet in the great outdoors with the elements being so unkind. The men tried to find a place to rest their weary bodies on the wet ground. They put their gas-capes, which were waterproof, over themselves and tried to rest. No hot drink or food was provided for us and it seemed like a bad dream with the water cascading off the trees onto us. It was a case of complete privation with the roots of the trees making fine bedding for us.

Later, I could hear the sound of an engine coming up the track that turned out to be the battalion ambulance that stopped, and from the cab appeared the medical officer and the padre. Not for them to sleep in the open with the men, but in the ambulance holding a stretcher on each side.

The men didn't begrudge the medical officer his berth; he had been in Calabritto tending to the dying and the badly wounded of the battalion. But the padre, that was very different. He was known throughout the battalion as 'Snip'; the reason for this was of his cutting off of the bottom dog tag of a deceased soldier. The padre should have been outside with his flock, suffering with them the tribulations they had been put through.

It was now starting to thunder and lightning, making it a most miserable time for the tired and weary infantry. Encouragement from the padre would have helped, if sincere.

Come the morning, and the rain having ceased, the battalion cooks at last managed to serve us up some hot food and tea to support our flagging spirits. We were told at this stage that we were in a blocking position and that only.

While here, we had some Russian top brass visit our front, looking from the crest of our hill through binoculars mounted on tripods across the valley at our old positions and the mountains beyond. They were the guests of 5th Army and paying us a visit.

We stayed in the position here for a few days longer. Then came the good news that we would be pulling back to Roccamonfina for a short rest, where we were found good billets in the village while our carrying party was disbanded. We, in turn, were sent to our own company in the battalion. This was joining the battalion proper with the destination for our mail now to: The 10th Battalion Royal Berkshire Regiment, Mortar Platoon, Specialist Company, Central Mediterranean Forces (CMF). The platoon commander was Captain Blake and my detachment commander was Sergeant Pullman. The detachment was made up of Lance Corporal Mason, Cherry, Good, Taylor the carrier driver and myself, being by far the youngster of the detachment.

We had a visit from the commanding officer who liked to welcome his new men in person. His name was Lieutenant Colonel Baird, and he had led the battalion since its inception in 1940. He was a good commanding officer, always being at the sharp end with his men. Other men, who had come from England on the same draft as me, were absorbed into the battalion who were very short of men after Calabritto. Bob Manley, my best friend, was a trained mortar-man but finished up in the signal platoon.

Roccamonfina seemed a strange place to me. The women of the village doing their washing at a communal washing place in, I might add, cold water. It was a large brick-built type of bath, sloping on all sides down into the water, so the ladies could thump their washing on in the process of cleaning it. I must say, after it was hung out to dry, the washing looked most successful.

I have two lasting memories of the village. Firstly, just outside was a cemetery with the remains of men who had fallen in the 56 Division. Someone had lovingly built up the graves and placed white stones around the perimeters of each grave, with a small white wooden cross placed on top. The cemetery was covered with an inch or two of water from the recent rain and, with mud everywhere, it looked the most forlorn of places. The hopelessness of it all was very hard to endure.

For the last memory, being somewhat different in manner, we were told one evening that a cinema show had been laid on for us, but the only place they could show it was in a monastery on the hillside above Roccamonfina. Transport would be available to take us there. That night, we piled into the trucks and were soon off up the hill that was very steep in places. On arrival, we walked into the courtyard, or cloisters, that was very large with pillars all the way round, linked up with an ornate marble surround on top, but was open to the sky. We would have to stand during the show, but that was a small price to pay for so much pleasure.

The show started with its flickering light passing over the courtyard and signifying it was a film starring Cary Grant and Ginger Rogers in *Once Upon a Honeymoon*. The film, a mixture of comedy and drama, was the kind of medicine we all needed. All was going well when a thunderous roar sounded from below, in the valley, and moments later you could hear the passage of shells roaring overhead, into the night sky, and falling on enemy positions miles away. Going back to the screen, you could see them speaking but not hear a sound spoken due to the artillery barrage going on. Our attention was sadly removed from the screen by the flashes of gunfire we could see between the pillars, with the film now appearing more like a silent movie of long ago.

It was some time before we realised there was another event taking place in our view between the pillars, of an eruption of Vesuvius in Naples, 60 miles away, and we could see fire coming from its crest. Back to the film again, the barrage had eased off somewhat, but I'm afraid by now everyone had lost the thread of the story with the gunfire only ending just before the film. To sum it all up, it was a most bizarre evening.

In the meantime, while we were resting at Roccamonfina, the Queens Brigade of 56 Division had retaken Calabritto and Mount Camino beyond. It was our battalion's turn now to take over from the Queens on the many peaks of the mountain mass. It is well worth reflecting on the amount of ammunition expended against the enemy and their fortification on the mountainside – the Americans aptly called it 'The Million Dollar Hill'.

The battalion moved back in by the same way we had moved out, but this time we had a mountain to climb. This we did, assisted by the aid of an old mule track winding up the steep mountain slopes. We had to carry all the things the battalion would need in the defence of the mountaintop. The enemy would very soon move back into their old positions given half a chance. They were masters of infiltration.

In climbing the mountain, we found German dead in many places where they had died in defending the mountain. Even to us, it was a shocking sight seeing a fellow human being in this grotesque condition with black hands and face owing to their exposure to the elements. In the sangars (slit trenches) they occupied, you would invariably find a loaf of black bread – their staple diet when in the line – not a great deal to have to die for.

After climbing the mountain, we were most fortunate in being allocated a position where we could find some shelter, in the form of an old building standing in our sector. It was now December and was very cold at night in the mountain air.

This front had gone very quiet with not a lot taking place, but one morning we were watching a Lysander aircraft being used for spotting by the artillery, flying up and down the valley several times looking for a target. We, on the mountaintop, were looking down on the plane and the enemy side of the valley when a Messerschmitt fighter came into view, chasing the spotter plane with its guns blazing away. By this time, the Lysander had become aware of the danger and started to weave and bob about in an effort to shake off the fighter. But it was soon lost to our view by a turn in the mountain mass. I was never able to discover the fate of the Lysander – or its crew.

A rumour was circulating round the battalion that we were about to be relieved and moved out of the line for a rest period. This was good news and turned out to be true. On the day in question, we were relieved by other troops who had made an indenture for all of our stores we had carried up the mountain with us and, for once, was a most sensible idea.

After wishing our relief good luck, along with the rest of the battalion, we started off on our journey back down the mule track. It felt a lot steeper going down than when we climbed up. The view was fantastic, you could see for miles with the village of Calabritto at the bottom. We, after all, were moving out of the line, so we had to be in good spirits and furthermore were looking at things in a different light. The downward path, we were on, would hopefully lead us to some peace. The other way surely led to some kind of hell.

After what seemed a very long time, we eventually came to the foot of the mountain, but before being released from its shadow, a dogfight developed thousands of feet above our heads. It ended with one of the planes being shot down (of what origin I had no idea) and nose-dived into, or near, the mule track on the side of the mountain. Its debris, along with fuel it carried, showering over a large area. The pilot of the doomed aircraft didn't bale out. For us, who had been at the bottom of the mountain and safe from harm, it came as another grim reminder that death was always just around the corner and could never be avoided. We left the mountain behind and soon arrived at our waiting transports, climbing thankfully aboard.

After a journey, we finally came to our destination at a village called Casanova, where once again we were found reasonable billets at our disposal. It was now more than halfway through December and our thoughts turned to Christmas, and what it would mean for us.

We did see a film show, given by an Army film unit that had its own generator, but the best show was without a doubt the pantomime of *Snow White and the 7 Dwarfs*, produced and acted by the 56 Divisional Concert Party. The hall where it was staged could only hold part of the battalion at a time. I think we could have been the first to see it because at the end of the show they came very near to burning the stage down.

They had a row of candles burning at the front of the stage, on the wooden boards, there being no mains electricity anywhere at this time in the war with the populace having to suffer for it. The concert party had had several dress rehearsals before first-night, but they had not taken into account the extra time the encores would take. One of the 7 dwarfs played a piano-accordion and he was very good, so with everything he played, the audience demanded an encore.

This had put the calculations for the burning time of the candles sadly amiss with the result at the conclusion of the show, with all the cast on stage and a draft fanning the candle flames till most of them melted right down onto the boards, leaving the wicks still burning away. The cast, who had been watching all this, had alarm written all over their faces. With the last notes fading away, they dived onto the boards, frantically working to extinguish the flames. However, we gave them a cheer for all their efforts and a most wonderful evening.

We had a good Christmas dinner, of roast pork with all the trimmings, though not like home but as much as you could expect under the circumstances of war. Some of us would remember this day being special – Christmas 1943, Casanova, Italy.

It became apparent now that we would very soon be returning to the line, what with the platoon officer and sergeant leaving for a reconnaissance with other members of the battalion looking over a different sector for us to occupy on our return.

Soon after Christmas, news got round that we would be relieving the London Scottish on New Year's Eve, and take over their front on the Garigliano River line.

The front was very quiet at the moment, but the enemy were actively patrolling on our side of the river under cover of darkness. We were told to be on our guard, for they had spirited many of our men away in the past on their incursions into our territory. Sergeant Pullman told us, "Even challenge a shadow. Call out the first part of the password and if you have no reply – fire!" The enemy were very keen on their patrolling. The reason being to gain information about the strength of our forces for a river crossing which they knew was inevitable.

The battalion formed up in the main square, in Casanova, at dusk on New Year's Eve, where we could see the mountains in the far distance and realised we were on our way back. With a new set of problems now facing us, *Snow White and the 7 Dwarfs* paled into insignificance at the thought of what might be in store. I could see that the men had rather grim faces on returning to the front, mine must have looked similar. The infantry were riding in the battalion transports and we in the mortars were riding in the carriers.

It was not a long journey, arriving in the village of Lauro at dark. We moved into and out of the village and came to a single house, which was to be the detachment's billet. The other carriers moved on to their own positions. We climbed out of the carrier onto frosted ground and a guard was placed in position just in case, after making sure the carrier was safe by the side of the house, well away from enemy eyes over in the mountains. The sergeant, who had posted the guard with the strict instructions about the severity of the situation, gave the day's password of New Year's (and the answer was 'resolution').

The civilian population had by and large moved away from the war zone, but not them in Lauro. We were most vigilant by night and kept a low profile by day. What would this New Year bring for us? I think it was just enough to ask for our survival at the end of each day.

By the light of New Year's Day, we could see what the ground was like between the river and us. A flat plain was there that sloped right the way down to where we thought the river could be. The ground was lightly covered in trees and bushes with houses scattered around at irregular intervals over the area.

One night our detachment was asked to fire our mortar in support of the battalion. They were going to flush out a pocket of enemy infantry, still on our side of the river. We mounted the mortar in a hedgerow that would in part eliminate the flash of the gun when fired. The enemy would respond in kind if they happened to see the flash from the muzzle. The attack was successful, leaving the infantry a clear run up to the river line. I might add that the platoon officer was present at the shoot.

After we had stayed in our present position for about a week or so, we moved down into the valley and were now about a 1,000 yards from the river, but still had a farmhouse to billet in. While we were here, another mortar detachment joined us to increase our firepower in readiness for the river crossing. Pits had to be dug for the mortars, which had to be done in the half-light to stop prying eyes from looking on over in the mountains. When the pits were finished, we removed the ammunition from the carriers and placed it in them ready for firing.

Alongside the farmhouse ran a track, or footpath, that went on to the river and back to Lauro. The night for the river crossing was set for the 17th of January 1944. The battalion was to be used in a deception plan, in making the enemy think they were about to cross there. If they could create a diversion with the sounds of boats being placed into the water, they would have little time to move away from the riverbank before it received a deluge of shell and mortar fire. They hoped this would enable the attacking force farther down river to make a surprise crossing and would need all the help that could be given. Our job that night was to fire in support of the units making the crossing and fire on all suspected targets. The barrage was to start when a single Bofors tracer round was fired over towards the enemy lines.

Our section was waiting inside the house for the barrage to commence, when we were alerted to what sounded like an explosion outside and within seconds a much larger one. We grabbed for our rifles and went outside, only to find our mortar pit ablaze. The bombs were exploding from the heat of the bomb propellant, nitrocellulose yellow, which was a highly inflammable material and there were nearly 500 capsules with the bombs in the pit at the time.

It was a mercy that none of us were in the pit when it happened, but what had caused it? An enemy patrol could have come down from the high ground on the side of us and thrown a stick grenade into the pit, and would account for the first explosion? We would never know. One good thing with the bombs exploding, they were below ground level so the shrapnel would be contained in most cases and be directed upwards.

The pit being only a short distance from the footpath made it necessary for us to post a guard further up the path, to warn the assault troops coming down of the danger there. Responsibility for this job fell to me, so I slipped out of the door and ran like a thing possessed, passed the pit and up the path till I thought it was a safe distance.

I had not been waiting long when a file of men approached from out of the darkness. They were men of the Marine Commando who would be making the crossing of the river. After warning them of the danger ahead, they somewhat quickened their pace then ran passed the burning pit from where, at times, loud explosions occurred. Hundreds of men passed by on the path and they all received the same warning.

Later, out on the path, I saw the single Bofors tracer round fired, arcing its way across the dark night sky, signalling the commencement of the barrage by the artillery. A ring of bright lights were flashing like lightning, running along the horizon from the direction of Lauro, then the thunder of the guns with the shells shrieking overhead to add to the confusion of a living nightmare. It was war in its bitterest form. Hundreds of tons of shells would rain down on the hapless enemy, even making the most hardened of soldiers on both sides shiver at the enormity of it all.

After the barrage had lifted, the Marines, with boats taken to the riverbank by the Royal Engineers, would cross the river and consolidate on the other side before attempting Mount Damiano beyond.

Our other detachment, who had been firing in support of the battalion's deception plan, had been more successful than us, what with our own pit destroyed. So when I came off the footpath duty, after the last troops had passed by, I went to help the other detachment and immediately found they had a misfire on their hands. The springs retaining the charges of nitrocellulose yellow had broken away from the tailfins, from their last bomb fired. When the next round was placed in the barrel, it was caught up in a tangled length of wire and unable to reach the firing pin at the bottom of the barrel.

We tried for some time to release the bomb, but failed. It would take special tools to extricate the bomb from the barrel. What we had tried was a dangerous exercise in trying to shake the bomb out of the barrel, it still being very hot from its recent firing and could have ignited the propellant charges held in the tailfins. This was done in total darkness and if it had gone wrong, the battalion would have needed a new mortar detachment. It was a bad night for the section, having a most unsuccessful time, whereas the Marine Commandos were very successful, crossing the river and moving onto the slopes of Mount Damiano.

We, after our lamentable performance of the evening, waited at the farmhouse for our orders, but in the meantime the enemy was to take a hand. Firstly, we were shelled. The enemy may have seen movement around the house, of the mortar crew trying to dislodge the bomb in the barrel, so the section moved out to a ditch by the side of the lane. A few more shells came over, and then the fight was joined by a Messerschmitt fighter who flying parallel with the lane raked the side of us with cannon fire that left the ground with furrows in. Fortunately, for us, he didn't return to the fray and the shelling ceased.

Later, we returned into the house, when word came through that we would be moving back to Lauro that evening under cover of darkness.

9. A place called Anzio.

The detachment was billeted in a house where the Italian family still lived. I recall the place well owing to the father there keeping an open fireplace going with charcoal. And it was most fascinating and delightful for us, sitting around the fire watching the clear blue flames and the warmth it generated into the room.

Our idyllic way of life ended very abruptly one night later. The platoon sergeant came into the house in the early hours of the morning and told us that we had to return back into the line. Our destination was the slopes of Mount Damiano, with two mortar detachments forward with the battalion. The rest of the company would have to porter for them with food, water and ammunition (all of it done under cover of darkness).

So, with sleep in our eyes, the battalion wound its way back down the dark lane towards the river. The carriers were left back in Lauro, along with the drivers. They would not be in demand where we were going. Later, we halted a few hundred yards from the river where there was good cover for us with trees and shrubs everywhere.

It was not long before dawn with the mist rolling in from the river, an eerie place to be, when we were startled by a flash of light and simultaneous bang. It was obvious that some unfortunate soldier had trodden on a mine, for they had been planted everywhere by the enemy.

After some time had elapsed, an authoritative voice called out of the morning gloom, "Who was it killed?" And a voice, full of meekness, answered back with, "Smith—42, sir!" The '42' being the last service numbers of the unfortunate man. I personally didn't know Smith, but I would remember him by name and number for the rest of my days, it being emblazoned on my very soul. Who was 'Smith—42'?

About midday, we moved off towards the river and were glad to hear that Damiano on this side of the mountain was now in our hands. Before reaching the Garigliano, we passed by a field where I could see many men of the Marine Commando laid out there in death, their bodies covered in frost. It was a tragic sight, remembering they had passed me in the lane two nights ago. There were warnings everywhere about the danger of mines, but you can't read them in the dark. They had stumbled into the minefield with terrible consequences.

We came to the river and crossed over on a pontoon, finding it quite wide and deep. Moving on, we reached our destination, not far from the mountain, and were told to dig in. We needed no encouragement to do so when it could be a matter of life and death.

From where we were digging in, we could see the town of Castelforte to the right of Damiano with another mountain the other side. Castelforte sat between the two mountains and it would have been the best plan to pass through Castelforte, into the plain beyond, without being embroiled in tackling the mountains. There was just one problem with the town of Castelforte, that being it was packed with top quality enemy troops, some of the best in the German Army. American 5th Army had already tried taking the town, but had received a sharp rebuff with severe losses inflicted by the defenders. Now if we could see the town, they in turn could surely see us milling around here?

About 200 yards from us, on the other side of the footpath, was a unit of Italian soldiers employed with mules carrying essential supplies to the troops here. They were well dug in, having made caves into the bank there and would be in comparative safety in the event of being shelled.

Most of us were brewing up a mess tin full of tea on the side of our slit trenches with the aid of a heating tablet. At this point, we paused in our tracks as we could hear the most ominous of sound to an infantryman's ears, of a shell coming our way from over the mountaintop. We didn't stand around and jumped into our newly dug slit trenches, forcing our bodies into the soil.

Crash! It landed no more than 30 yards beyond us, throwing up a tower of earth and rock. By the sound and impact, it was a 210mm shell. It had spoilt my tea, and I suppose others, finding mine was now a mess tin full of dirt! If that was their ranging shot, we were going to be in for a bad time. The next time, it was two or three landing together, showering us again with lumps of dirt and small pieces of rock. This went on for some time till during a lull in the shelling we put our heads out and called to our colleagues to see if they were safe, and thank god they were.

On the other side of the footpath panic was taking place. The Italian muleteers were all running like the wind back down the track towards Lauro leaving the mules, some of them badly wounded from the flying shrapnel and braying harshly in pain. One of my close friends, Norman Sadler, a farmer's son, pulled his rifle out of his slit trench and, without orders, stalked off to the other side of the track and shot the mules that were badly wounded and suffering, putting them out of further misery. The shelling by now had ceased, but we kept a low profile just in case.

At dusk, we moved out and came to a house that was close by the mountain and would be our new billet, while the battalion would have to sleep on the bare mountain.

If any member of our platoon were under the illusion that we would be putting our heads down that night, they would be sadly mistaken. With the two mortars supporting the battalion, up on the mountain, they would need all the ammunition we could carry. Our loads that night would consist of a case of three bombs and a sandbag full of rations or a container of water. Your load, with your rifle, would be in the region of around 60lbs in weight. The needs of the battalion were great and supplies they must have, or be overrun and pushed off the mountain.

We started out that night without any kind of knowledge of what the mountain was like to climb. We left the house and soon reached the base of the climb where we found a rock-walled terrace to ascend, no easy task with a load and in the dark. Upwards we went, meeting the obstacle of a terrace every so often.

At last, they finished at the mountain proper where at times we had been forced to use our hands and knees in making progress of any kind. Someone had said back at base that it would take all night to climb and return down. Not a very good prospect for us in regard to sleep, and we were all now desperately short of it.

We could hear guns firing a long way off and, within seconds, you could hear the sounds of incoming shells, the enemy being aware they would be landing on our supply route up the mountain. I pushed myself onto the rocky ground, closed my eyes and waited for the detonation, which was rather too close for comfort, showering us with loose shale but not shards of shrapnel. After a while, the shelling lifted as they concentrated their fire on lower targets of the route.

After what seemed an eternity, we bumped into an outpost of the battalion who directed us to an unloading place. They were pleased to see us, being very short on supplies. Most of the battalion were in their sangars built up of rocks that were in good supply, for no one could dig a slit trench in the rocky ground on the mountain. It was the only way the battalion could protect itself from the enemy guns and small arms fire when they mounted counterattacks against their positions.

From the mountain, I could look over into the enemy held territory where flashes of light appeared and disappeared; it could have been gunfire or shells exploding. Castelforte was also down there in the dark, making it a most eerie and unreal situation. By now, we were all totally exhausted from our labours. My body was wet with perspiration from the effort in hauling the load up here.

We thought that returning back down the mountain would be simple for us, but alas that was not so. The main problem was that you were unable to see where you were placing your feet in the murky darkness. After what seemed like another eternity, we stumbled our way to the bottom, more like drunken men than soldiers, and thankfully came at last to the billet. We were then able to place our heads on the floor for an hour or two before returning to duty.

We were very soon back on our feet to carry stores from a dump along the road. Once again, we were to see a most disquieting sight of a jeep with its driver lying dead in the back, and no one around had even bothered to move or cover the poor man. When we returned later with the stores, he was still there, left for everyone to gaze on.

That night, we had a repeat of the night before, but without the shelling this time. However, when I came down the terraces at the bottom, I was unfortunate and slipped and sprained an ankle, so had to limp painfully back to our base. It was obvious to me, seeing the swollen foot, I should not be asked to carry that night. After a word with the detachment sergeant, he asked to see the damaged foot, and after examining it said, "You will have to stay here tonight, but you will have to do a guard duty."

On the third carrying party that night, they left without my company. While the carrying party were on the mountain, our own 25-pounder guns had some of their rounds drop short, supposedly a miscalculation in range for nighttime firing. The sad result was that the shells fell in and around the carrying party. Some were wounded, but the worst catastrophe of all was a sergeant who, in the confusion at the time, was decapitated.

Without any prior warning, the battalion was pulled off the mountain and out of the line for a rest. This turned out to be in open fields under canvas in two-man tents. It was nothing special, but at least we were far away from the tumult of war, and in that alone we were truly thankful.

While the battalion was on the mountain, the American 5th Army, who we were a part of, had launched an attack on the port of Anzio to try and outflank the German defences on the Cassino front. However, after a few days, the enemy counterattacked in an attempt to push the Allies off the beachhead and into the sea.

Meanwhile the engineers had erected some showers for us, made out of sacking to keep out the cold winds of January. Some of us went to the showers, but inside found the water rather tepid and with snow on the ground outside it was 'move quickly or freeze!' Even the second in command, Major Heal, found the potent deluge more than he could take and walked out more smartly than he walked in. It was our first contact with water since our stay in Casanova, a month ago, other than our daily ablutions in a biscuit tin of murky looking water that we shared with others in the detachment. This, of course, was not afforded to the foot soldier. Whereas we could carry the biscuit tin on the carrier, they could not.

Our sojourn away from the strife soon ended when we were briefed about our next role – the struggle for Mount Damiano and beyond. Division had come up with a plan involving the whole brigade, comprising of the London Scottish, London Irish and us, the Royal Berkshires. The scheme was for each battalion to leapfrog through each other and advance over and down the other side of the mountain into the valley beyond, isolating Castelforte at the same time. The plan looked good on paper but?

We would be out of our carriers (no biscuit tin) and have to lug and haul our piece of mortar, case of bombs, rifle and kit, up and hopefully down the other side. There had to be a flaw in the plan somewhere. After our two or three days out of the line, we had to return to where we had left off. The fighting at the Garigliano River and the heights of Mount Damiano had been very costly in the casualty rate of dead and wounded. But then the fighting had been very bitter with the German Army not willing to give us his main defence line, especially after the landings at Anzio.

Once again the transports collected us, and later on, we arrived at Lauro where we were unloaded from our vehicles. After we had managed to get our kit together, we started off down the lane towards the river and what lay beyond. The possibility was that the assault on the mountain could take place that night.

Before we had started out, I could see the grim faces of my comrades with no one smiling. Mine must have looked the same at the task we were about to undertake. After marching for what seemed a long time with our respective loads, we reached the river and waited to cross over.

While here a very strange thing happened, when out of the blue we were halted in our tracks and told we had been pulled out of the impending battle, and now marched back the way we had come to Lauro. Why had they pulled us out of this major engagement, and to go where? So, we retraced our steps and on our arrival back at the village, the infantry climbed into the 3-ton transports and we in the mortars repacked our carriers.

The convoy started off on its journey with no one having any idea where we were bound for, or any kind of inkling of what we were going to do at the end of it. The convoy travelled slowly through the night.

And in the cold light of a new day, we saw a volcano with its telltale plume of smoke that could only be Vesuvius, establishing the fact to us that we had arrived in Naples.

The convoy moved on into the harbour and left us in no doubt that we were about to take a sea journey. Shortly after, I saw my good friend, Bob Manley, from the signal platoon standing on the quay. He told me without hesitation where we were bound for. Having seen the maps, when taking them round to each company, it was Anzio.

On the quayside, waiting for us with its bow doors open, was an American LC-T (landing craft – tank). After a very short time, the landing craft swallowed up the entire battalion of eight hundred men and transports within its hold. Only hours after our arrival at the port, we moved out into the bay to join a small convoy waiting for us there. Now that we had sailed, we were told officially of our destination over the intercom. Bob was right.

The Anzio beachhead of some two weeks was now in jeopardy of being overrun by numerically superior forces. The Germans were attacking the whole perimeter with great ferocity, after a direct order from Hitler himself to throw us back into the sea. If he could manage it here, it would be a bad omen for our forces later in the invasion of France.

Sailing up the enemy held coastline under cover of darkness, daylight found us standing off the beachhead waiting our turn to dock in the harbour. From the deck of the ship, standing about a mile offshore, we had our first view of Anzio – the very name that would loom so large in our lives.

The town looked like the most inhospitable place to land. Antiaircraft guns onshore and in ships in the harbour were putting up a curtain of fire, trying to stop enemy aircraft from bombing targets in and around the port. At times, a column of water would erupt out of the sea. This was from the enemy long-range guns trying for the shipping in the bay. They were getting close when you could hear the rattle of shrapnel on the ship's hull.

One of the most distressing features of the Anzio beachhead was the constant enemy shelling. With the congestion of the Allied effort there, this meant that any shell landing in the perimeter would find a target, whether a combatant, tank, gun, ammunition dump or medical unit – it was all the same. And when the front was quiet (which wasn't often), you could hear a dull boom coming from the Albani Hills, then seconds afterwards have a shell tear overhead to land in the harbour or bay after the Allied shipping. The long-range guns were called 'Anzio Annie' and 'Anzio Express', both possessing a calibre of 280mm (11"), and they were mounted on reinforced railway wagons and kept hidden in a railway tunnel till fired, then moved back inside to minimise the risk of being spotted by Allied aircraft. Between them, they caused a great deal of devastation. It was estimated that almost 75% of the Allied casualties on the beachhead were due to enemy artillery and mortar fire.

Later, we came safely into the harbour and the ship unloaded its cargo with great dispatch. The battalion moved in and out of the town, now standing in ruins. Leaving the town way behind, we eventually came to a small wood or spinney, and here we would wait for further orders for our move into the frontline.

After digging ourselves in before darkness fell, we prepared to get some sleep while we had the chance. None of us had had a proper rest in the last few days. Anyway, it would be difficult to sleep with the knowledge that we were 60 miles behind the enemy lines, virtually cut off from our main forces in the Cassino line.

During the night, sixty shells were to fall amongst us in the battalion area. This mercifully killed just two men, a company commander and his runner, in the act of delivering a message to him. Next morning, when moving out from this position, we could see two blanket-covered forms laid out on the grass. The only indication that they were human beings was from their boots protruding out from the folds of the blankets. This grim scene was a stark reminder to the rest of us that we could be in for a very hard time, having our first casualties without us yet being committed to the line.

The battalion was now moving into the line to plug a gap made by inadequate forces there and we arrived without trouble of any kind. Fortunately, for us, the sounds of battle on this front had died away for the moment. This gave the men in the rifle companies now deployed a good opportunity to dig in which they would do without being urged in any way, it being a task to safeguard your very life.

We, in the mortar platoon, would first have to dig a sizeable pit to take each gun and ammunition with room for the three men of the gun crew. Each pit would be in the region of 6' by 4' by 3' feet deep or more and had to be accomplished before starting on your own individual slit trench.

Having completed this task, after a lot of physical effort on our part, it was time to take stock of our own surroundings. Our position here did not afford us a very clear view of our immediate front – the landscape here being of small trees and bushes. In a small clearing within yards of our position, we found a great deal of discarded British Army equipment scattered around, clear evidence that fighting had taken place here. Then finding in an abandoned kit a forage cap with a badge of the Loyals Regiment in it established who had been the former occupants of this position.

Later in the afternoon, after all of our strenuous efforts of digging in, word came via the company runner that we were moving out. After reloading our equipment, we moved out onto a crossroads and waited for the rifle companies to come in.

This then was the position we found ourselves in on the evening of the 5th of February, with our orders for supporting the Guards Battalion. In the fading light of day, the men of the rifle companies started walking passed us in single file down the road towards the front. The men, with gloomy faces, were loaded down with their accoutrements of war. The mortar detachments were more fortunate in that we would be riding towards the battle in the carriers, bringing up the rear.

After the front had remained quiet for most of the day, we could now hear the noise of shelling in the distance. Moving about a mile up the road, the sound of enemy shelling had now become almost incessant. Our own guns, sited in some cases miles away, started up a counter barrage with their shells tearing overhead in the night sky. Some time later, we were able, by the light of the fires up ahead, to see a bridge set on high embankments. By now the men of the rifle companies had deployed, disappearing into the night, while we in our two mortar detachments could go no further along the road without running into enemy shellfire at the bridge.

Now we were close enough to observe that the fires burning were vehicles of all descriptions, among them was an ambulance with flames licking at the Red Cross sign painted on its side. This was a sight that made me feel very insecure, in seeing the very symbol of our civilisation being treated in this way. With the petrol and rubber tyres blazing away, the Germans would know by now that they were ranged onto a prime target and would continue fuelling the flames with more shells. It was a place of general confusion and disorder, and had become untenable.

We were too close for comfort, giving me the notion that the scene I was witnessing, with the bridge and embankments on either side, was like a stage set with illuminations from the flames for an act out of *Dante's Inferno.*

After a short reconnaissance, the two detachment commanders returned having found a suitable position for the two mortars, this being a bomb crater on top of the railway embankment. It would take both of the mortars, so we should be spared the task of digging them in; an almost impossible job with the shelling going on. Unfortunately for us, we could not reach this isolated position in the carriers. They would have to stay back on the road.

What we had to do was manhandle the three-part mortars and ammunition a distance of around 200 yards, swept by shellfire, and having to make more than one journey. Each man in the crew would make the first trip carrying his own mortar part along with a case of bombs and rifle, a load of over eighty pounds, and carried for the most part in the dark and over wet, slippery ground. It would prove most difficult, but it had to be done if we were going to support the companies in the likely event of German counterattacks taking place. The mortars in position with a plentiful supply of ammunition available would be vital in breaking up an attack.

Removing my piece of mortar (the barrel) from the back of the carrier, fixing on the carrying harness and taking a case of bombs out of the rack, I started out. I was stumbling rather than walking over the uneven ground, in darkness but for the light coming from the fires. Keeping away from the bridge at the start, I then moved over to what I thought would be safety under the high embankment, but that was the wrong impression we all had at the time.

The shells that were a danger to us were coming in from the German held side of the beachhead and not over the embankment, a big mistake on our part. I had not gone far when above, with the sounds of battle going on, I could hear the sounds of approaching shells. And with that clear warning, I dashed myself onto the ground in time to escape the lethal, vicious shrapnel flying from the shell bursts while your whole body is made to cringe at the thought of being hit by a piece of this hot, jagged metal. With the strong smell of spent cordite in the air, and very shaken by the event, I picked up the equipment from the muddy ground and got underway again.

After reaching the mortar position and climbing up the embankment, I found myself in the bomb crater. You could well feel that you had come to a place of sanctuary from the violent night outside. It was an eerie sight, looking out into the misty darkness of the enemy side with flashes of light from their own guns firing away in the distance.

Looking back along the tracks to the bridge, the fires that had been raging were now dying down. The rest of the mortar crews were now coming in, so were able to mount the guns; a difficult task with the large lumps of soil and water in the bottom. That now accomplished, we were ready to fire in support of the battalion if needed.

With the mortars only having a dozen rounds each, I was detailed along with my friend, Stan Abbey (one man from each detachment), to return to the carriers for more ammunition. Reluctantly, we left the safety of the crater to run the gauntlet back to the road. Keeping close under the cover of the embankment, we found that we could hurry along without the load of our last journey. Also, the barrage had all but lifted with now just the occasional shell to worry us. This was enough to always keep your senses alert for sounds of danger, otherwise you would never survive the main intention of your adversary – to try and dispose of you in one way or another.

Before reaching the bridge, we moved away from the embankment. Then we could see that most of the vehicles were now burnt out, just derelict objects still glowing red from the intense heat. We had seen no sign of any living person since leaving the mortar position. Coming back onto the road and finding the carriers and drivers, who were pleased at our return, it was comforting to know that the rest of the section were safe.

Taking two cases of bombs each, we soon started on our way back. Struggling over the uneven ground, with the ammunition cases swinging like pendulums in our hands and helped only by the remaining light from the fires to guide us through the undergrowth, we finally came back to the embankment. I was hopeful of a rest after the completion of this trip. Both of us by now were feeling the effects of not having had proper food or rest since leaving the ship.

Above the noise of distant gunfire, we could hear a voice calling out into the night for a "Stretcher!" very soon repeated, but in a more urgent tone. Both of us stopped to listen and look around in the gloomy darkness to try and locate the source of the call. When it came again, we could see that it was coming from behind a tarpaulin screen at the bottom of the bank, admitting small chinks of light to escape from round the edge. What we could also see, what the voice was calling out for, were two or three of them lying under the bank.

Without any hesitation on our part, we started by laying the cases of ammunition in a pile on the ground and then moved towards the bank for a stretcher. Bending down to lift one up, we were astounded and taken aback with the discovery of finding men in slit trenches, in comparative safety from the recent shelling, dug in under the bank there.

After getting over the initial shock, we asked them, in a language bordering on contempt, why had they refused to answer the call? It was obvious to us that they were in fact official battalion stretcher-bearers. None of them would respond to our coaxing or threatening tones to get them to help. They would not budge out of their safe trenches, whatever the need of the caller. We were wasting valuable time with them, so taking a stretcher, but filled with disgust and dismay at their attitude, we moved away towards the long-neglected voice.

Both of us still carried our rifles, being unwilling to leave them behind with the ammunition. Reaching the tarpaulin, we cautiously lifted up the flap, causing light from the hurricane lamp inside to stream out into the darkness. We quickly moved inside with the stretcher, blinking like a pair of owls at the brightness inside, into what must have been a platelayer's hut built into the embankment, and now we could see turned into the regimental aid post.

The man who had been calling out was now revealed to us in the shape of Captain Zangen, the battalion medical officer. He was working on his own, attending to a seriously wounded sergeant, lying unconscious on a table and trestles. We recognised it was Sergeant Scott, and could see at a glance why the MO had been unable to leave the man's side. He was holding the unfortunate sergeant's head by the neck and trying to stem the flow of blood from the head with a large red-stained swab.

Looking up, the captain was very surprised at not finding his own medical team, but two unknown soldiers with their rifles standing there with his stretcher. "We could hear you calling for a stretcher, sir." The captain was most grateful for our participation on his behalf, and then asked if we could help him further by transferring the sergeant from the table into the stretcher where he could then work to better advantage.

The MO, with great care, held the head while he gave us instructions on how to move the unconscious man. After doing this, Stan and I held the sergeant while the MO dressed the terrible wound on the back of his head. It was a gory sight to behold to make even us, now hardened by such sights, to feel great pity for Sergeant Scott in his plight.

Taking our leave from the regimental aid post, Captain Zangen expressed his thanks for our help. We made no mention to him of our encounter with the men outside in the trenches and their total failure to answer his call, or ever did we to anyone else. We would always feel a personal satisfaction in knowing we had made an effort towards trying to save a man's life, when in extreme danger of our own and with other pressing duties to attend to.

Outside the regimental aid post, it was some time before our eyes became adjusted to the dark again after being in the brightness of the lamp. Finding the ammunition, the two of us were very soon on our way back to the mortar position. Having arrived back, we had a visit from the company runner who warned us that we were to move out immediately. The battalion would be moving into a more urgent position than the one we held now, but first the move would be a reserve position a mile back down the road.

After all our endeavours carried out that night, we now had to move it all back to the carriers again with all the physical effort needed to return it, even with the shelling almost ceased and the promise of a hot meal waiting for us at the other end. After our task was completed, the carriers moved back down the road leaving the bridge behind us, now in darkness, waiting for the next act to take place there.

In the small hours of the 6th of February, waiting in the dark for our promised meal, we were all feeling very tired and hungry. The meal was still over the cook's burners and we, with nothing better to do, were watching the tins of steaming pudding bobbing up and down in the boiling water of the container. After our food, we tried to get some rest except the ground was very wet, but we were all past caring. Just to close one's eyes and sleep – and hopefully cut the bad visions out.

10. The mortar reserve. Time of crisis.

The outcome of the battalion's withdrawal from the battle at the bridge was that a new role had been found in this drama, now being played out in a grim struggle for our very survival on the beachhead. We had come out under cover of darkness, back to our new harbour that concealed us within the thickets and scrubland that the beachhead abounded in, from prying eyes of the Germans in the Albani Hills.

We found some German propaganda leaflets scattered around with pictures of Allied forces pushed back into the sea and floundering off the beachhead. This was not the kind of picture to reassure us when our backs really were to the sea and in big trouble.

We remained at this place during the hours of daylight; getting some much needed rest as well as cleaning up our muddy equipment and ourselves. When darkness fell, we started moving out to our new sector of the line, and by the middle of the night our new positions.

The rifle companies up ahead deployed themselves astride a secondary road in an area called the flatlands where farms had been built on reclaimed marshland. The rifleman, performing his first task of digging in, found water seeping into the trench, not the best of conditions to live under in mid-winter. By daylight, they would find themselves facing the distant Albani Hills. These hills should have been taken on the first day of the landing, but had not been made possible due to the circumstances of a shortage of forces made available for the venture.

Inadvertently, the place was fast becoming a death trap for all the troops engaged here.

The farms here had been built on alternate sides of the road, spaced about 250 yards apart and just set back off the road. Detachments of the mortars positioned themselves around each farm. We, who had been in the forefront at the bridge, now found ourselves more or less in a reserve position in the last farm, a short distance from a culvert and a spinney. My friend's detachment, that was with us at the bridge, now occupied the farm to our immediate front.

The Italian family were still in residence at the farm we now occupied, but they were going to be evacuated from the beachhead along with their cattle at the same time and taken by ship to the port of Naples. For the military authority to go to this kind of trouble, they must have concluded that the civilian population were in mortal danger in staying on here. One could reason with this action that it did not look too good for us either!

Our mortar was sited about 35 yards from the farm building, so placed that it gave cover from the German eyes scanning us from the hills. It would very soon draw fire from the Germans if they thought the military now occupied the place. Being outside of the main battle area, we had not dug the mortar in but had placed some discarded parts of farm implements and fencing around it, giving it cover from low flying aircraft that put in an appearance now and then. Normally the ammunition would have been removed from the carrier and placed in the mortar pit, but this time only one case each of high explosive and smoke were taken off and left at the mortar for any emergency.

The carrier was now standing in an open-ended barn attached to the house. We had to move the farm equipment outside to fit it in. This turned out to be most fortunate for us in the events that befell later on.

Not far from the mortar but near the road, a flock of sheep (visible to the enemy eyes in the hills) were milling around in a pen. They had been fed and watered by the farmer, but were still very uneasy. Sheep, along with other animals, have a natural instinct for signs of danger and they were obviously showing it now. I, for one, would be glad when they were gone.

During the day some very rundown looking Italian vehicles appeared, coming down the road and turning around in the yard to face back the way they had come. The Italian drivers, without wasting any time, soon had the sheep and other farm animals loaded onto one of the vehicles. I could see that they did not wish to be there and were in a hurry to leave the place.

Soon after, the Italian family, who till now had remained in their upstairs quarters concealed from the rest of us, made an appearance by way of an uncovered staircase at the back of the house that faced towards the enemy. We could not help them with their few belongings without exposing ourselves to view. They were only able to take their bedding and clothes with them. The rest of their property would have to be left behind to the possible ravages of war.

Judging by the number of Italians here, there must have been more than one family. I suppose they had come in from the other farms in the neighbourhood and were now in the battle zone. They crowded into the open-sided transports, sitting on top of their bedding. The young children looked rather bewildered, the elderly totally dejected. Without delay, the vehicles moved off down the road, over the culvert and were lost to view.

For the Italian families, their troubles were not over yet. They would have to brave the dangers of shells falling in and around the port of Anzio. When they arrived at the town, they would have to wait before going onboard ship. They could not evade going into the port, that being the only way to reach Naples and safety. The long-range guns would even shell them when they left the harbour till they reached the open sea. Only then could they breathe freely again.

Six months before, the Italians had been our enemy till their separate peace made with the Allies. Italy was now a ruined nation with a devastating war waged on its soil. Now having seen the abandonment of the Italian farms to a possible battlefield and the obvious plight the Italians were living under, I felt it had been a most unfortunate remark made at the time of the Italian surrender by the British Prime Minister. Well knowing of the terrible predicament they were suffering under, Churchill said the following: "The Italians can stew in their own juice!" Having spent the last six months on the peninsula and seen the people at firsthand, I knew that they had come very near to starvation in the winter. So, I found it a most uncharitable statement to have made.

After the departure of the Italian families, we made ourselves as comfortable as possible, not in the house but in the cattle stalls on the ground floor of the building. We were prepared to suffer the smell for the privilege of sleeping in the warm, dry conditions of the manger.

The front, on the whole, remained very quiet. There was just the occasional exchange of artillery fire to remind us that the enemy still surrounded us and confident that we were not going anywhere. Our main duty was for a twenty-four hour guard, being most vigilant in the hours of darkness, having no wish to be picked up by a German patrol in this isolated position.

Soon after dark that night, we could hear a jeep coming down the road. They were looking for us, having our rations. I did not envy them of their task in getting round the rest of the company, locating all the outlying positions our men were in and carried out in total darkness under very difficult conditions. The jeep was soon on its way, disappearing into the blackness of the night, leaving us who were not on duty a chance to write home or mend and clean our kit.

Our mail had not caught up with us yet, but that did not stop some of us from writing home even a few lines. It was no easy task trying to write on thin airmail paper with cold hands, using one of your mess tins on your knee for lack of a tabletop, and at times undertaken by the yellow light of a small, smoky paraffin lamp or a candle. Being very restricted in what you could write about in letters back home, one could only state that you were fit and well or otherwise. No other information could be given like as to where you were or what you were doing. All in all, it just added up to a series of very boring letters with no substance in them. If it did convey a message home to our families, it showed that we were still in the land of the living.

During the hours of darkness, we could hear the sounds of small arms fire up ahead, the result of increased patrol activity on both sides of the line. What we did know was that the Germans were preparing for a large-scale counteroffensive. Where and when it would come, no one could tell. Our own offensive had run its course, now we must wait and see where the blow would fall.

None of us in the detachment had a lot of rest that night; we all expected something to happen. One thing we were very aware of was the shortage of our own forces on the beachhead, being very thin on the ground and very exposed to any large-scale attack.

By first light and the start of another day, we carried on with our normal routine of guard duty and other fatigues necessary for the running of the detachment. In the yard outside, I found a dirty, torn out page of a book, which must have been carried by a British soldier and lost by him in some unknown engagement here. During the course of it lying there, it had been trampled on by all and sundry, but I could still see that it contained a religious text with words like 'Taking the sword of justice into battle'. In all probability, some German soldier on the other side of the line would be carrying around a similar text with the only difference being the text would be in German.

I don't think anyone of us had given much thought to the fact that just over the hills, to the north, lay the Eternal City – Rome. How many of us would survive to gaze on its splendour?

Unfortunately, the new day brought about more artillery exchanges on both sides and continued intermittently throughout the daylight hours.

With the coming of darkness, we could hear the sounds of small arms fire join in. After the company jeep had come and gone on its nightly visit around the company, we settled down for another night of vigilance and disturbed rest.

Later in the evening, Detachment Sergeant Pullman had reason to leave the farm, and later returned with the news that a man from the signal platoon had been killed while out repairing a battalion line cut by shellfire. He also told us, "The man's name was Bob, that's all I could remember." I was almost too afraid to ask, but I had to. "Was it Bob Manley, Sergeant?" "Yes ... that's it!" My reply came in a weak, stunned voice. "He was my friend." The rest of the detachment remained silent. None of them would have known Bob, but even then, they were still shocked at a fellow soldier's death.

I left the warmth of the manger and the comradeship of my colleagues, and went outside into the cold, dark night air. Standing there alone, tears ran down my cheeks at the thought of my friend.

I had last spoken with Bob while taking shelter in a barn from the cold, the night we moved into our present position. In the dark of the barn's interior, I could hear someone whistling between his teeth. It could only be my friend Bob. So having called out his name, the two of us groped our way through the dark till we reached one another. We shook hands before talking about our perilous position we now found ourselves in on the beachhead. We talked mostly about our own chance of survival here, both of us being in some agreement that we could very well be in for a bad time.

In parting, he left me with the words of his own brand of homespun humour, "You die if you worry; You die if you don't!" How many times had he quoted this to me since I had first met him? Now he was gone.

We had made a pact with the exchange of our addresses with each other, that if one of us were killed the other, if at all possible, would make contact with the bereaved parents. From the start, I had carried it around in my battledress pocket. Just a small scrap of paper torn out of Bob's notebook with his name and address. Eventually, I hoped that I would be able to carry out my friend's wish, with the scrap of paper to act as a form of talisman for my own safe conduct in the times ahead.

The night wore on and none of us were getting much rest, even when off duty with the increase in activity up ahead. The Germans were desperate to find a weak spot in our defences, so they could start their own offensive and push us back into the sea. We could hear more than usual amounts of vehicles on the road. With the battle going on, some would be Red Cross ambulances bringing back the casualties from the struggle to hold the line.

By daylight, we could see smoke coming from the front – a clear indication that the battalion was having a bad time. With the light to help them, the forward artillery observers started to bring fire down onto suspected enemy concentrations. Standing off the beachhead our warships joined in, firing salvo after salvo into the enemy positions, their large calibre shells roaring overhead with a sound very different from land based gunfire.

Later in the morning, the volume of fire gradually died away. Later still, we received information that our rifle companies had thrown back several enemy counterattacks, still trying to infiltrate and overrun their positions. The battalion had taken severe causalities, but had displayed great resolution in holding back the enemy. The thin red line of the infantry still held fast.

Reinforcements were desperately needed for the badly depleted companies, but there were none. Even if we were in reserve, I could never understand why we were never called on to fire in support of the battalion in some way or other. This, of course, rested in the hands of the platoon commander, back down the road at Battalion HQ. This officer, a captain, never enjoyed the warmth of his men in the platoon and never praised it for work well done. He was a standoffish person, keeping out of the way most of the time, leaving most of the day-to-day running of the platoon to his platoon sergeant.

Three weeks before, when one night we were firing on a possible enemy target at the Garigliano River, the officer paid us a surprise visit. I might add that we were not in any real danger of retaliation in firing from this position. If any trouble came it would be from very active German patrolling in the area.

After firing the first round, the mortar baseplate had sunk into the soft ground. This was making the bombs go astray from their original line of fire. The problem came about when they increased the maximum range of the mortar, from one thousand and seven hundred to two thousand and eight hundred yards, with a greater charge of propellant agent nitrocellulose yellow. I made a general remark for the crew's benefit in saying, "It would be a good idea if they fixed steel ribs on the bottom of the baseplate, giving it more resistance to entering the ground." On hearing my remark, the officer gave me a sharp rebuff with the words, "You don't know what you are talking about!" Within a very short space of time this became standard on all mortar baseplates, the ribs welded onto the base.

By this time, the detachment was beginning to wear a rather grim and jaded look, due partly from lack of sleep and knowing what the men in the rifle companies had to endure. By this time, they would be feeling the cruel rigours of their existence out in the wet flatlands with formidable enemy forces that were fresh in the line.

Intelligence on our side had been able to identify new German units brought down from their Army in Northern Italy. Our battle-worn battalion had been in contact with the enemy since Sicily (their first engagement in the summer of 1943), now they were far from being fresh troops. Now in a beleaguered position, the exhausted men were still fighting and holding the line. In support, the artillery were firing a tremendous concentration, well ahead of the infantry who would be well dug in and keeping their heads down.

Back at Battalion HQ, a composite company was formed. This comprised mainly of drivers, cooks and HQ staff, all rushed into the line under the command of the transport officer. They were the only reserves the commanding officer could muster for his depleted battalion and could only hope and plug the gaps made by the German infantry, infiltrating in and around their positions.

The weather had turned very inclement with icy rain lashing the beachhead, giving the dogged infantryman a bad time in his slit trench. Just one more problem to come to terms with.

With the ending of the day and the coming of the night, the time had now lost its meaning for us. The night was, of course, the time to get the news on what was going on with the vehicles now running on the road under cover of darkness.

In the cosy conditions of our manger, we were all wondering what could happen next. Then the most disturbing news came in that one of our mortar detachments had taken a direct hit on their gun-pit, killing all three men instantly. They, at the time, had been supporting the battalion with covering fire. The crew were killed in full view of the detachment commander, a corporal who had been standing in the doorway of the farmhouse sending out his instructions over the telephone to his crew. After the completion of the shoot, he had given them orders to stop firing and to return into the building.

There was some enemy shelling going on at the time and they could have made a dash back into the comparative safety of the farmhouse. But here, fate was to take a hand. Not disobeying the order but being the good soldier he was, Lance Corporal William Lawrence, along with his crew, stayed on in the mortar pit to relay the mortar back onto its aiming post with slight corrections, ready to fire again without delay if called back out. However, their time had come. They had done their best only to be killed for doing it.

William Lawrence, a bachelor in his late thirties, was rather old for the infantry. He came from my hometown and, by coincidence, had also worked with my father before the war. He was a quiet and unassuming man, never making a lot of conversation, but on our last short rest out of the line, he told me of two events that had happened to him recently. Both had taken place over the Garigliano River the week before.

William told me, "I was standing near two slit trenches and could hear a shell coming that would be landing very close, so I jumped into one. The shell landed in the other!" He went on. "And then, when we were climbing Mount Damiano, it happened again with a shell going to land very close, dropping down into the rocky ground. It rushed overhead, bursting not more than ten yards away!" He had no reason for telling me, having in no way a boastful nature. I think he just wanted to tell me about his two brushes with death coming together like that and it had unnerved him, of that I had no doubt.

The last time I spoke to him was on the quayside at Naples, while waiting our turn to move into an American LC-T. We had just found out where we were going from my friend, Bob Manley, who was going round the battalion with maps of our destination after the voyage – the town of Anzio. On seeing William, I said to him, "Do you think the Pope will have a bed ready for you, Bill?" He made no reply to my remark, but he did have a big smile on his face.

One other member of this ill-fated detachment had carried an extra burden around with him. When the battalion came down off Mount Camino to spend Christmas 1943 out of the line, in the village of Casanova, the mortar platoon was billeted in some good Italian homes in the main street of the village. Being wintertime, we needed to keep ourselves reasonably warm when off duty in our rooms. This we did with the aid of any old tin can, which was filled with petrol and placed in the capacious Italian fireplace, promptly igniting. This would provide us with heat and light in the room in the long winter evenings. It was strictly unofficial, the burning of petrol for the reason given, but the method was used throughout the British Army and was called a 'Benghazi'.

Coming back to the ill-fated person, the men in the detachment, myself included, had noticed that this man spent all of his free time in his billet, sitting near the fire with his head held in his hands, staring into the flaming petrol. He never went out with his friends or take part in any platoon activity whatsoever; he had lost all interest in what was going on around him.

We all found out later that he had received a letter from his parents warning him that, in his absence abroad, his wife was being unfaithful to him. I didn't think it a very wise decision for his parents to have made for him. Even in telling him the truth, they should have known that he could do nothing about it. He would have been better served in being told nothing at this stage. His parents should have thought, at the time, that their son was on active service in an infantry battalion where the quality and expectancy of life are not very high. They had given their son a mind-shattering piece of news when he could well do without it.

What would happen when the wife received the letter, back in England, from the War Department informing her of her husband's death, killed in action? She would eventually have to go and face her husband's parents. After writing the incriminating letter to their son, what would the parents' reaction be when informed of his death?

William Lawrence's wristwatch was removed from his body, miraculously it was undamaged and still ticking away. It was the only thing left of the ill-fated detachment.

One other very close friend in the detachment was Norman Sadler, always a very brave man. At this particular time, he happened to be reserve gun-number but, just like the detachment commander, he had seen the men killed and later on cried like a baby at the death of his friends. This would always remain a most unpleasant memory for him to carry through life.

An air of gloom settled over our detachment with the thought that it could have been us in the gun-pit. No one could think about sleep that night. Sleep we needed, but sleep we could not.

Outside, looking towards the front, you could see Verylight flares arcing into the night sky signalling back a message – red over green, two reds, two greens, or green over red – they all had a meaning for someone to take action on.

The long night came to an end with both sides exhausted from their struggles. The battalion, like other formations on their flanks, were very near to breaking point. The enemy were winning the war of attrition by their ability to feed fresh troops into the battle, while our members were fast becoming depleted with no hope of replacements for the battalion. The whole front was on the verge of collapse.

Again in the course of the day, the Allied artillery were able to control the situation from their advanced observation posts, right up with the infantry, bringing down fire on seen or suspected targets. But in the hours of darkness that was another matter with the enemy, who were masters of infiltration, working their way into our weakened positions and overrunning them at will.

The day passed, and the return of another uncertain night for the remainder of the battalion to carry on. The faces of the detachment were now grim and hollow, formed by lack of sleep and the eventual outcome of it all. Along with the others, I prepared for the worst to happen with a German breakthrough at some point in the line. This view was confirmed when later in the evening, with the arrival of the rations, a message was sent around the brigade by the commander, Brigadier Davidson.

He had seen his three fine battalions gradually and remorselessly worn away by continuous attacks without him being able to offer them any form of help. At his headquarters, now a very worried man, he had drafted a message to go out to his men that night, the only thing he could do under the circumstances left to him. The gist of it being that he hoped we would very soon be relieved, but we must first go on making that extra effort till it happened. His message ended with the words 'Good Luck, and may God's blessing be on you all'.

The message went round to the men who were fighting in a 'backs-to-the-wall' situation. They could do nothing but comply with the order. But carried out it was, in full measure. All the detachment could do was watch and wait – and hope.

In the semi-darkness of our manger stalls, with the feeble light of the oil lamp casting shadows where animals should have been, we lay sprawled in the hay, resting but not closing our eyes. None of us could foresee the events that would evolve around our position here at the farm within the space of the next twenty-four hours.

The final chapter in the epic struggle started sometime in the late evening with a massive concentration of enemy fire falling on the forward positions of the companies. Watching outside, we could see the extent of the barrage falling on the battalion front, with eruptions of great showers of sparks and flames leaping from the ground, making one wonder if any living soul could survive such an onslaught. The night sky over the battlefield was turned into a hazy red glow, with fires started by the bombardment of haystacks and buildings in the path of destruction laid by the enemy guns.

This was undoubtedly the prelude to the enemy's long-awaited counteroffensive. I had never seen a German barrage of such intensity and it could only mean their infantry would be advancing in strength when it lifted.

After the ruthless pounding had ended, we waited to hear the crackle of rifle fire and the splutter of the Bren against the ripping sound of the enemy Spandau (MG42), telling us the front still held fast. We stood there listening in vain. The sounds of war had all but ceased with the sounds of gunfire coming from other parts of the front. A very ominous silence settled over the battlefield, an indication that all was not well. It must have been around or near one o'clock in the morning with a complete absence of traffic on the road. It was too quiet.

We had no idea what was happening; us not being in direct contact with HQ or receiving any form of information from them, or orders. Sergeant Pullman thought it would be best to increase the guard outside, from single to double. I noticed my hand on my rifle had taken on a firmness that had not been there before. Also, I had been half asleep, now I was fully alert to our new dangers.

Enemy infantry could, at this very moment, be exploiting a breakthrough with their axis of advance, most likely down the road passed our farm. Out there under cover of darkness, the men in field-grey uniforms would stealthily be feeling their way forward over ground recently held by the battalion. Off duty inside the manger, waiting for something to happen or to hear news from some quarter, we were startled into action by one of the guards who hurried in saying, "I think the farm up ahead is being attacked, Sergeant!"

We moved outside and could see and hear that was so with the flashing and thump of exploding grenades and short bursts of Schmeisser fire, leaving us in no doubt now that there had been a German breakthrough at the front. I asked the sergeant, "Are we going to help them?" He replied, "No, there is nothing we can do about it!"

He was, of course, right, but our friends were in that farm. What had happened to them?

The fight was soon over, the countryside around us going quiet again. After that, would it be our turn next to feel the enemy assault? They were only 250 yards or so away from us and we were the only opposition between them and our Battalion HQ, back down the road.

The sergeant now placed a cordon round the farm, expecting the worst, but after some time had elapsed, and when no attack materialised, he had us back inside and just leaving the double guard outside. Keeping vigil inside the manger, the old saying of 'sitting on a powder keg' readily came to mind. We were now in deep trouble, finding that we were the frontline with no hope of support of any kind. The enemy could well have bypassed our farm and be well on their way towards Battalion HQ by now?

From outside we could hear the guards calling out. They were challenging a figure, emerging from out of the darkness towards them. The figure called out, "Don't shoot!" It was not the password for the day but it was spoken in good English as the man came staggering forward. Meanwhile, back inside the manger, we stood clutching our weapons with some anxiety as to what the voices outside could mean.

The door swung open, revealing one of the guards supporting a man in a very distressed condition. His uniform and sleeveless leather jerkin over it was in a sorry state, covered in slimy mud. We helped him down onto the hay-strewn floor of the manger, while the sergeant lifted the oil lamp off its hook and turned up the wick for a closer examination of the man 'out of the night'.

By the yellow light revealed 'Sergeant' stripes, then a face to go with them of Sergeant Hamilton. The last time I had seen this man was in the square at Casanova, on New Year's Eve, with the return of the battalion back into the line on the Garigliano River sector. Back then he had looked a well turned out soldier, but now in the manger he looked in a pitiful state. Sergeant Hamilton drew attention to his back, and on being turned over we were able to see that the leather jerkin he was wearing had been shredded at the back with holes.

From the information the sergeant could tell us, it appeared that he had been sheltering in the farm in front of us when it came under attack. After a short skirmish there, the Germans forced them to surrender.

They had no other choice but to comply with the order. Herded outside into the dark night, Sergeant Hamilton made up his mind to make a break for it. Seeing his chance he slipped off into the night, though not getting far before the Germans noticed him with the result that several bursts of Schmeisser fire followed him into the darkness.

One such burst had passed between his jerkin and uniform. He dived to the ground, avoiding the fatal bursts of fire. With the Germans seeing him go down must, with good reason, have thought him to be killed. I don't think, even at this time, they would have been too keen to go looking for him with the chance of bumping into a hostile unit. The sergeant stayed down, having the presence of mind to play possum with the enemy who were not that far away. The enemy were not to know we had no other forces in front of them other than a mortar detachment 250 yards or so along the line of their advance.

After some time had passed, the sergeant decided to crawl away from the danger around the farm, getting himself into a terrible state on the cold, muddy ground. When he thought it to be safe, he managed to get back onto his feet, then staggering over the dark uneven ground, he came at last to our farm and indeed to him a form of sanctuary.

The evidence of the bullet holes in his jerkin made us realise just how close he had come to death. For all that, we had been witness to one of the strange events that happen from time to time in war and are at best unexplainable.

After a short rest, the dishevelled sergeant made his way back towards Battalion HQ and the long-awaited attention of the regimental aid post. Sergeant Pullman now found himself in the most awkward dilemma, from being the mortar platoon reserve to the apex of the battalion effort. He had received no message or order from Platoon HQ (now stationed at Battalion HQ) who by now must have been well aware of the fate of the battalion.

Out here, at the farm, the detachment was now out on a limb, and no one in their right mind would expect us to function as a mortar detachment without a screen of riflemen in front of us. By the same token, if attacked like the farm up ahead, we could end up the same way. Rifles are no match for grenades or automatic weapons like the Schmeisser (MP40). At worst, we could be killed or become prisoners of war.

After some time had elapsed, the sergeant told us he had come to a decision to try and get back to HQ for further instructions. He gave strict instructions to his lance corporal, who would now be in charge, not to leave the position, and he would return unless something unforeseen happened to him.

11. "Give us this day!"

Sergeant Pullman slipped away into the dark night, leaving our small garrison at the farm in a much-depleted state. Right or wrong, I had always been under the impression that a commander of a unit should never leave his post for any reason, in that he had a choice. He could have given a message for Sergeant Hamilton to hand to the platoon commander, Captain Blake, or detail one of his crewmembers to go back with a message about our present predicament.

At this time, we did know that there were some members of the platoon who had been ousted from their positions by the German advance. Surely, they would have been better employed in strengthening our position.

The platoon commander, along with his platoon sergeant, had not been near us when it was their duty, by rank, to give us guidance and support if needed. They never stirred from Battalion HQ, or gave us help in any form. In fact, we were left to our own devices. We did know that there were men out there in field-grey uniforms who could be members of the Hermann Goering Division, or a Panzer Grenadier Division. Our intelligence told us they were now on the beachhead and two of the most formidable units in the German Army.

The night wore on and the strain of waiting with the danger around us was most nerve-racking. Where was the sergeant? It was time he returned after being away so long. We were beginning to feel that something had happened to him out on the road. There was the possibility that the enemy, who could by this time have bypassed our position without us knowing, had confronted him. If the sergeant had failed to get through, HQ could still be unaware that we were still holding our original position or they could already have written us off.

The lance corporal now in charge of the detachment was a family man. He was getting very worried by the sergeant's continued absence. He could only think the worst had happened and he would have to make the decisions now.

We had been most fortunate till now, in that we had not followed the same kind of fate as our friends. They could possibly be dead or hopefully on their way to a prisoner of war compound.

After a reasonable amount of time had elapsed, the corporal asked all four of us for opinions on what he should do. It was agreed by all to wait till a certain time, or deadline, and only then if the sergeant still failed to turn up, we should move out and hope we had done the right thing. After all, the other detachments that had survived had found a refuge back at Battalion HQ.

The agreed deadline came around without the appearance of the sergeant to give us a morale boost. So, the three of us not on guard duty started to load the carrier with the minimum of noise, having no wish to attract attention to ourselves at this crucial time. We left the mortar till last, strapping the parts in position on the back of the carrier without clanking the parts together in the dark. The driver moved the carrier out of the lean-to barn and onto the road without advertising our departure. The guards were brought in and we climbed into our positions with our rifles at the ready.

Keeping it in low gear, the driver moved off, but before his tracks had moved more than one or two revolutions over the sprockets, the carrier came to an abrupt halt. It was Sergeant Pullman. He came out of nowhere, or so it seemed, and putting his head over the side of the carrier, told the driver in a quiet voice to "Turn back."

After the carrier returned to the barn and the guard restored, we placed the mortar back into its original position. The sergeant and the rest of us moved back into the manger, where the lamp was rekindled to reveal the stern face of the sergeant who said, "I have been given orders to defend this position against attack, and here we will stay till relieved."

The sergeant was not pleased with his orders to stay, thinking they were rather foolhardy in the extreme in keeping us here without support, but there, we had to make the best of it.

A council of war was held in the manger, by the shadowy light of the oil lamp, on how best the place could be defended. The sergeant suggested we could best do this from upstairs. Move into the rooms there and take with us an unopened box full of Mills 36 hand grenades left here by former occupants of the farm.

Without delay, the light was put out again and we, being in a hurry to get the work finished, started with the transfer of all of our kit into the upstairs rooms of the farm by way of the outside staircase. Once we were sure that the shutters were over the windows, the lamp was relit, showing us cold and austere rooms recently vacated by the Italian family.

The sergeant asked me to help him in priming the grenades with their detonators, making them ready for use, leaving me in no doubt that he would use them if the situation so demanded. With the oil lamp on the floor between us, we opened the base and started to prime them, first by unscrewing the base plug and inserting the detonator with due care into the body of the bomb and then replacing the plug. The evil looking things were now armed, ready for use if we had callers come in the night.

The remainder of the night dragged on in an atmosphere of suspense. After what seemed an eternity, the dark night started to change into the cold light of a new dawn. This brought with it a sense of relief for all of us that we had come through the crisis of the night unscathed. So far, we had been most fortunate in having escaped the attention of the enemy. But what would the new day bring us, in the light of what had befallen our friends in the battalion?

The Germans were very good at exploiting success, but here they had failed to take advantage after having made the big effort of breaking through the main defences. With the coming of dawn, we were able, from the safety of our windows, to discern objects outside and thankfully, above all, we could see no sign of the enemy around.

The sergeant had made up his mind to use the vantage point of the upstairs window as an observation post. He would have a good, clear field of view from the window provided he was not seen up there;

otherwise they would soon make the place untenable for us. The sergeant was going to man the position on his own during the hours of daylight. There was just one snag with this idea, in that he would be unable to get back down by way of the outside stairs. Unfortunately, they were facing towards the enemy. He would have to wait up there till the return of darkness, or try and jump from the rear window if made necessary by some unforeseen event. The rest of us wished him well with his daylight vigil and we returned by way of the stairs before it became too light.

We kept up the guard around the farm, keeping well out of sight from any prying eyes. By daylight, the landscape up ahead looked empty and forbidding, but we were not deceived by the lack of movement. They were out there in force. The ominous sounds of war were, for the moment, stilled. We could be the last combat unit of the battalion still left in the line. A sobering thought if you then think who will get to us first – friend or foe?

The morning was well advanced before we picked up the sound of gunfire from some other sector of the beachhead. From time to time, the sergeant would come to the rear window and have a few words with us, but he had nothing of any significance to report, which was just as well.

It was now early afternoon, when one of the guards called out that he could see figures in the distance that seemed to be converging on the farm from our left rear. All eyes were turned in that direction, trying to identify who they could be. They were coming towards us in extended order, but keeping a very low profile over the rough ground. We could see them now and were very glad to see they were wearing British steel helmets, a great relief for us all. It could only be an act of deliverance that none of us had ever expected.

They came on, using whatever cover they could find on their approach, not wishing to reveal themselves unduly to any enemy eyes in the vicinity or in the distant hills. On reaching us, one group of about platoon strength broke away and hurriedly crossed the road. This group deployed in line with the farm, setting out their rifle sections and merging into the rough terrain. The rest of the men were deployed on the farm side of the road and, seeing them start to dig in, left us in no doubt they were here to stay.

I was very grateful for their presence here and it had taken the pressure away from our detachment. Our own assessment of the situation made twelve hours before, in that we must now be the only ones left from the battalion still in the line with the new frontline pushed back to the farm here, had turned out to be regrettably true. This was born out by the events now taking place around us.

The newly arrived men were a company of the London Scottish, one of the battalions in the brigade and could very well have been brigade reserve. The company commander was a Major Will. He wanted to know, "Who's in charge of this detachment?" So, we called the sergeant to the window who then started to relate what had happened here and at the farm up ahead. After listening to the sergeant, the major said to him, "I shall need this building for my headquarters." The sergeant moved back from the window, out of our view, and returned to his post at the front window.

I asked one of the Scottish company if he could tell us any news, but he was very vague about it so I gave it up. The major could have briefed us on the situation, but didn't volunteer to do so. He would have been fully briefed before moving into this position. Nevertheless, we were pleased at their timely arrival on the scene. I, at once, had a feeling that the major did not appreciate the value of us being here and looked on us as being in the way.

He used a room on the ground floor for his headquarters, but he and his staff would have to climb in by the window. Access by the door was impossible as that faced the enemy side of the house. The major now detailed one of his men to dig him a slit trench, right under the window of all places. No other member of his company staff, or our detachment for that matter, went to the trouble of digging a trench for ourselves. My only concern now was that the enemy might have seen the increased activity around the farm. If they had, they would soon let us know. After some time had passed by, it was obvious we had not drawn attention to the farm.

The major's slit trench was soon completed and, within a short space of time, some of his men started to deposit their cigarette packets and other paper oddments into the bottom of the trench. On coming to the window to examine his trench, he got most indignant at the contents at the bottom and wanted to know, "Who's responsible for this?" Nobody volunteered to come forward to answer his childish demand. Here we were, in a life and death struggle and all he could do was find fault with a few pieces of paper in his personal trench.

Our own artillery still remained silent. This could very well be due to the forward observation post having been overrun by the enemy advance during the night. No forward artillery observer officer had come up with the London Scottish, so they were without the crucial support of the guns.

Sergeant Pullman came to the window in a hurry, calling down to us, "I can see a column of men coming towards us on the road and they look like Germans!" That stirred things up no end with the major trying to clamber out of his window, with the hazard of the trench to negotiate first. After dropping down into his hole and climbing out again, the major wanted to speak with the sergeant, but he had returned to his front window. Minutes later, he appeared at the window, calling down to the detachment (the major included), "They are Germans, but they appear to be carrying a white flag or cloth." The major called up to the sergeant, "Are you sure, and what strength are they in?" The sergeant replied, "I am sure, and I would say about company strength or more. They are still a good distance away."

The sergeant returned to his lookout only to immediately reappear at the window. He called down, "They have moved off the road, just disappeared from view!" A surrendering force would have stayed on the road, being only too keen to be seen by the opposing force in that they had no wish to fight on. They had been very bold in using the road. It was a good way of exploiting their success with a quick advance. They must have been confident at the time of not bumping into any great opposition and were taking a chance at not being challenged. If they were, they could soon lose themselves in the shelter of the rough ground by the side of the road. This, they had done, was most likely brought about by spotting the London Scottish moving about up ahead.

It was now obvious that the German display of a flag of surrender had been nothing more than a deceptive ruse, then hastily digging in close to the farm. I had a strong suspicion, since the Germans left the road, that they were now about to give us their undivided attention.

The situation had turned very menacing. They were out there, somewhere within striking distance with a far superior force. This then was the situation that February the 10th, with an under-strength company of the London Scottish, depleted by a week's fighting, and one 3" mortar detachment of the 10th Battalion Royal Berkshire Regiment. Our detachment were still standing under the upstairs window, waiting for instructions from the sergeant, if he had any to give, in what our own role would be in this new development. But he was still observing the new turn of events from his front window.

The sound of a single shot rang out. We looked at each other expectantly, for we had no idea which side had fired the shot. Some time afterwards, a man came running in from the platoon that had crossed the road. He was bent double in an effort to make himself less of a target to the enemy, only straightening up on reaching the cover of the farm building. He walked up to the major and, in a breathless voice full of emotion, said, "Sir, a corporal has been killed. Shot through the head by a sniper!" The man killed had only walked across this yard just a short time ago. Now he was dead, just becoming one further casualty in the battle of the beachhead.

Our sergeant was back at the rear window, calling down to us, but at the same time seeming to address himself to the major, informing him of the changing events. "They are forming up about 200 yards away on a bank in a gully and they look well armed!" I was feeling rather worried about the sergeant, for without a shadow of doubt if they caught sight of him at the window he would suffer the same fate as the unfortunate corporal.

Speaking directly to us now, the sergeant said, "We can't use the mortar in its present position, it's far too exposed out there. So if we are going to use it, could it stand down there in the corner between the barn and the house?" The sergeant didn't give us a direct order to bring the mortar in, but we were aware of what we had to do. We would be exposed to the enemy the moment we left the cover of the farm. I was as much concerned for my own safety as the next man, but if we had to bring it in, I was not going to wait around getting cold feet. I looked at the other crewmembers and could see that they were not going anywhere. They just needed a push.

I gave it to them by starting off at a good pace, out to the mortar, with the other two falling some way behind. Reaching the mortar, I pulled off the leather muzzle cover and had released the barrel retaining spring from the bipod yoke before the others joined me. We had slipped the yoke off the barrel when the first bullet arrived with a sound of a cracking whip.

The sniper had spotted us the moment we had broken the cover of the farm, and would soon have made a correction on his rifle sight for his second round. I gave the barrel a quarter-turn and pulled it out from the baseplate, then turned to run back with it when the 'crack-of-the-whip' sounded for the second time. The bullet had missed one of us by inches and was too close to think about it.

I started to run back with the cumbersome barrel, making sure I made myself a difficult target for the sniper by running out to the side, to cut off his vision of me, before turning directly back to the farm. Having reached there, I turned to watch my two colleagues struggle to bring their parts in, no easy matter without the carrying harness on.

Crack! The 'whip' sounded again, but like before he was unsuccessful with his aim, though this time he was firing at a moving target. The two came in at the gallop, panting from their efforts, and on arrival, we looked at each other in a kind of awe that we had survived the sniper's fire.

We had left the two cases of bombs out there. Nobody being so foolhardy, to risk their lives again bringing them in, when we still had eighty bombs on the carrier in the barn.

Still breathing hard from our recent exertions, we mounted the mortar in the general direction indicated by the sergeant, angled in-between barn and house, and as close in as we could get it. The barn would give us some protection from enemy fire if they did break through. Now the mortar sight, which had been kept on the carrier, was placed onto its spigot with a range of 200 yards set on its scale. We were too close to the house to use the aiming post, so we did the next best thing by scratching a datum line, in the shape of a cross, onto the brickwork of the house and finished off by centralising the longitudinal and cross-levelling bubbles on the sight.

It was at this stage, we found another problem to surmount, in that the third member of the crew, if he worked in his correct position, would be standing in the major's slit trench. We decided on the spot that two of us could work the mortar. It was very irregular, but it was the best we could do in the circumstances. Number Three of the crew started to remove the bombs from off the carrier with the help of the driver, placing them in a pile behind me, and also prepared the ammunition by removing the safety cap and waterproof bag from the tailfins. We were now ready to fire.

This had only taken minutes to retrieve and remount the mortar. Now, while waiting, I had time to think about what we were about to do. In the past, I had fired off many rounds into suspected enemy positions with supporting or harassing fire for the battalion. But this was different with a visual target of very brave men about to match themselves against us (the enemy).

The old saying that 'A soldier must kill, or be killed!' was, unfortunately, about to become a grim reality. We had to try and stop the London Scottish, and indeed ourselves, from being overrun after having seen an illustration of their intentions with the death of the corporal and our own near-fatal encounter with the sniper. If their attack did get underway, there was a good chance we would be overwhelmed with consequences we could not even contemplate.

The sergeant came back to the window and asked the major, "Have I clearance and permission to proceed, sir?" The major replied, "Carry on, Sergeant!" The major must have seen the advantage in breaking up the attacking force before they came to grips with his own men and, for that matter, us. We each needed each other in this kind of situation.

Sergeant Pullman gave the order. "Fire just one round of HE, at range 200 yards, at charge-one, but wait for me to get back to the front window before you fire." I picked up one of the bombs and removed half of the charges from around the tailfins. They were not required for charge-one at a very short range. I looked at the lance corporal and awaited his order to fire but none came, he just remained silent.

I was very aware of what I was about to do and hesitated before placing the bomb in the barrel. With the tailfins clanking on the metal tube, I released the bomb and turned my head to the right to escape the blast. Thump—, the bomb sped away over the roof while we waited, with some trepidation, for the inevitable explosion up ahead. When it did come, it surprised us by the loudness of the detonation, it being so close. Others may not have shared my own feelings about what we were doing, but after the first bomb, there was no turning back.

The sergeant was now back at the window with more instructions for us. "Down 25, left 5 degrees! The first round was close." The barrel of the mortar now looked almost vertical after the 25-yard correction, giving the impression that the bomb could fall back onto the detachment. The sergeant called out, "Fire three rounds this time." I prepared the rounds by removing the unwanted charges from the tailfins, placing one round under my left arm with one in each hand. Having fired the three rounds off, we waited for the explosions. They came in rapid succession, falling in and around the gully after the first ranging round. "The same range, left 10 degrees, three more rounds!" the sergeant called down.

While carrying out the order, we were approached by the company sergeant major who had been observing the extent of our fire from the cover of the side of the farm. He was in a very excitable mood and started jumping about like someone demented. "Fire more rounds, fire a hundred!" he cried out. Speaking in a very sober voice to the senior rank, the lance corporal replied, "We can only take orders from our own Sergeant and no one else." The sergeant major left us, by climbing back through the headquarters window, never to bother us again.

Our sergeant was doing his best to conserve the limited supply of ammunition we had at our disposal, with the controlled firing of the three rounds each time for maximum effect in his effort to break up the enemy concentration in the gully. We carried on with the firing, with small changes in range and deflection, and never more than three rounds at a time.

During a lull in the firing, the lance corporal leaned towards me and in a quiet voice said, "Do you know, Dave, that if the 'brass hats' at the War Department could see the way you are working this mortar, not strictly by the book, they would have you up on a court-martial charge. Never mind the fact that we are trying to stop the enemy from advancing any further here."

One of the soldiers from the company had unfortunately lost his nerve after the events of the past few days. He was wandering about smoking a cigarette, and we at the mortar were standing near a pile of charges of nitrocellulose yellow. What if his cigarette, when finished with, came into contact with the charges? He was fast becoming a danger to us all and started crying and calling out in a voice full of anguish, "We shall all be killed! We shall all be killed!" Of course, one of his own comrades should have been responsible for his welfare. In the end, he started to worry our men preparing the ammunition from off the carrier.

I certainly had no authority, but decided to take a hand. And by going to him and showing more courage than I felt, by taking his webbing straps and giving him a gentle shake, I said, "Shut up! No one here will get killed if you let us get on, just keep quiet." To my surprise, and relief, he calmed down at once and made no further mention to 'our imminent demise at the hands of the enemy'.

Returning to my position at the mortar, we decided to check on the number of rounds we had left and found we had already expended more than half our bombs. So, when Sergeant Pullman next came to the window, we informed him of the situation, who then passed the problem over to Major Will. He, in turn, soon had a message relayed back through Brigade to our Battalion HQ for a carrier-load of 3" mortar bombs. This message would, most certainly, have surprised our intelligence section at Battalion HQ to receive such a request for more ammunition, showing them that someone was still in the struggle to stay on the beachhead.

The afternoon was well advanced with about an hour of good daylight left, when the sergeant came back to his window and said, with a note of excitement in his voice, "I can see that sniper! He's hiding in some bushes at the top of the gully." He gave us a new range and deflection, and we were to fire a single round. It was while carrying out the change in range with a further lowering of the barrel that it was obvious that the path of the bomb was going to be too close to the guttering, and roof for that matter.

There was one way of making sure, so I laid down on the ground and looked along the barrel to make sure it would clear, and was satisfied it was safe to fire by a very small margin. The bomb was fired without mishap and, after hearing the explosion, the sergeant was soon back at the window with a further correction (thankfully not of extra range). "This time two rounds," he said. Having carried out the order, he came back to the window and said, "The bombs were close. The sniper just fell out of the bushes. He must have been killed?"

More rounds were fired at intervals, keeping up the pressure on the enemy with more changes in range and deflection, containing the force in the gully from mounting an attack against us.

At last, a carrier was seen coming down the road, moving at a good pace. It would now be in our own interest to get it unloaded and away before the enemy came to the conclusion that we occupied the farm. It turned off the road and ground to a halt, the driver keeping the engine running. He was on his own and looked very apprehensive from his journey down this ominous looking road that was now, in part, in the hands of the enemy. It had taken a lot of nerve on his part and he was keen to get away.

They had sent a standard Bren carrier that had no ammunition racks for the bombs and had just piled the cases by the sides of the engine. The detachment set to work in the unloading, and then the carrier was soon on its way back over the culvert and out of sight. If the enemy had seen it arrive, I hoped they would have seen it leave and think it had just been here on a reconnaissance.

We were soon using the new ammunition, but our rate of fire had slowed down to just the occasional round, and eventually the gun fell silent. The light of day was gradually fading when the sergeant came to the window for the last time with a few words for Major Will. "I can see no sign of enemy activity in the gully. The whole force has been dispersed, sir."

I could tell that the major was very relieved at the sergeant's words, but the major, at no time, said a word of encouragement to the detachment for the way we had handled the situation here. Without the mortar, they would have been overrun in this under-strength company.

In their defence of the farm, the Scottish company showed no form of retaliation in anyway, they just left it to us. The detachment on the other hand had made a real effort. Firstly, in exposing ourselves to the sniper in collecting the mortar from its original position, then showing some initiative when remounting the mortar, we were unable to use the aiming post so used a datum line on the wall. Lastly, we could not use the Number Three of the crew because of the major's slit trench outside his headquarters window.

In the meantime, Sergeant Pullman decided to come down from his self-imposed exile in the upstairs room, but how? It was still too light to use the outside staircase that faced towards the enemy and, after looking, we could not find a ladder. There was only one thing for it – he would have to jump. So, after throwing his kit down to us, he gingerly crawled over the window ledge, letting his boots feel their way down the wall till he was hanging at arms length, still a long way from the ground. When he did jump, he would have to avoid the major's slit trench. When he could hang on no longer, he swung his legs out and jumped.

He came down in a rush, but we did manage to break his fall before he hit the ground. He scrambled to his feet with a smile on his face and decided on the spot to have a brew-up, having had no hot drink for about fourteen hours during his vigil at the window.

Standing around in small groups behind the farm, we were waiting and discussing the events of the past few days, when our attention was drawn towards the roar of many engines. The noise was coming from a column of grey Sherman tanks, trundling their way out of the murky light that still remained, over the culvert and down the road towards us. We had no idea what they intended to achieve, or what roll had been found for them.

They came on with the hatches on the turrets closed down, passed our farm with its thinly held screen of infantry, possibly completely unaware that they had gone through the frontline, and were now advancing into enemy held territory.

The lead Sherman had barely travelled a hundred yards or so passed the farm when disaster struck with a direct hit from an enemy antitank gun, possibly an 88mm (with its lethal solid-shot projectile), sited somewhere along the road behind one of the farms. The tank ground to a halt, black smoke billowing out from its interior, causing the rest of the column to halt. No other Sherman could pass on the narrow road, now blocked by the unfortunate tank. They were all reluctant to leave the road for fear of becoming bogged down in the soft ground.

Before the column could make any kind of move, a barrage of solid-shots struck the front tanks, fired now from many guns with the same catastrophic results inflicted on the first one, leaving many burning. Some of the shells, while hitting their targets, would ricochet from off the armour with terrifying force, making them thrash their way through the air and making the most awesome noise. Some narrowly missed the farm and gouged out large clods of soil. And every time a shell struck the ground, it made a steaming furrow along its vicious path with the violence of its passing.

The spinney in the distance, on our side of the road and ending at the culvert, was now feeling the impact of this deluge of shellfire falling on the Shermans. The near misses, or ricochets from off the armour, were scything into the trees, lopping off the trunks and branches with the sheer speed of the missiles. You could see the tracery of the trees on the darkening skyline suddenly disappear from view, caught up in the frenzy of the shelling.

This had been too easy a target for the enemy to fail with, in this straight column of tanks in their gun sights. Fortunately, for the tanks in the rear, the guns turned against them were only firing along the axis of the road and not from the flanks; otherwise they would have lost many more of their number. Several of the Shermans, which had taken the full brunt of the attack, were totally immobilised. Some of them were burning, and most of the crews in them were dead.

The tanks in the rear were at last able to extricate themselves from this awkward position by doing the only thing now possible – reversing as fast as the gear would allow them, back down the road, over the culvert and out of sight to safety.

One or two of the American crews managed to get clear of the vehicles and had crawled back over the rough ground to the farm. They had had a very close call, and were most fortunate to have survived the fury of the enemy fire. Even then, one of the crew seemed to show little concern, or remorse, at the loss of his comrades. He could only lament over the loss of packets of cigarettes, left behind in the turret along with the dead.

The few who had survived this horrific experience refused to stay with us at the farm and would not wait for the cover of darkness before leaving. They decided to make a dash for it across the field towards the spinney. The enemy gunners were still firing the odd round into the knocked out tanks, possibly making them irreparable against any future use. The Americans found it hard work trying to run over the rough terrain in their tank clothes. They stumbled and fell many times on their journey to the spinney, propelled on their way by the fear of being hit by one of the ricochets that flew passed them with such vicious force. In the end, they reached the trees, disappearing into the undergrowth.

That was the end of an effort by the American tank crews to regain the initiative on this broken front. The truth could be that they should never have been sent along this road in the first place. They had been too vulnerable from the start to attempt such a task. The tanks were replaceable, but not the men. We, after all, could count our good fortune in that none of the shells or ricochets or otherwise had damaged the farm. That in itself was a miracle considering we were in direct line of the enemy gunfire.

This was, unfortunately, not the end of the bloodshed for the day. We still had one more episode to witness before the cloak of darkness descended on the battlefield. Once again, our attention was drawn to an ever-increasing drone, but this time of a large number of aircraft. They soon came into view, flying very low and in close formation, even in the bad light of this winters day. The aircraft involved turned out to be several squadrons of Mitchells, flying parallel and just left of the road.

Their target was a factory about a mile directly to our front, from which the London Scottish had been involved in bitter fighting there. Now it would be reduced to rubble in a series of enormous explosions that shook us at the farm. It was over before you could think about it. The aircraft turned, flying out to the safety of the sea, away from the enemy gunfire.

Darkness at last cast itself over the land, and with it a hope we would get some much needed rest now we had the protection of the London Scottish company with us. Apart from the air raid, the whole front had remained quiet since the destruction of the Shermans, but this could very soon change.

One good aspect, I noticed with our relationship with the London Scottish, was the friendliness shown towards us by the company, being very appreciative at what our detachment had done in warding off the enemy attack. Some of them had seen us run out from the safety of the farm for the mortar and our subsequent trouble with the sniper. They were fully aware that our presence here had turned the tide in their favour.

Going back over the events of the afternoon, I could not remember hearing any small arms fire other than from the sniper. The only weapon used against the enemy being the mortar. Credit was due to the sergeant for his control of the gun throughout this critical time.

Later that evening, the major sent out a patrol to gather information on the enemy positions in the near vicinity, and investigate the site of the recent action in the gully. Upon their return, they were able to report to the major they had seen no sign of the enemy; but going down into the gully, they had been able to locate the enemy dead that lay in its dark interior. Coming back, by way of the road, they passed by the destroyed Shermans, most of them containing American dead. That made the patrol glad to return back to the safety of the farm and away from the silent and eerie battlefield.

The detachment was resting in the manger when news came through that we had been relieved from our position and would return to Battalion HQ. The sergeant had been instructed to leave our mortar in position, still sited on the gully in case of the enemy infiltrating back into its old position. The London Scottish would send in a mortar crew to man the gun.

We started packing our equipment together, and I looked around the place where so many events had taken place over the past week. The flickering lamp was blown out for the last time and we moved out of the manger into the dark outside, packing our things into the carrier. Having wished the men who would be left behind the very best of luck, we mounted into our positions on the carrier.

The sergeant gave the word to start with a wise reminder to the driver to keep the noise down. With the driver starting the engine, the carrier started to pull out of the barn and into the yard with very little noise. The carrier rolled out of the yard and moved up onto the road with the tracks making very little noise in the turn. (They must have been made of rubber!) We moved along the dark road at no more than a walking pace, over the culvert by the spinney and away from the battlefront.

We had been most fortunate in having survived the day, most probably being the last of the battalion to come out of the line. I could feel no elation for what we had done. The events were never talked about in the detachment or with any other person. Sergeant Pullman was asked to write a report about the action at the farm, but he never got round to it.

My best friend was dead, along with him many others who were close. And what had happened to my other friends, among them Stanley Abbey? It was good to be going back, but what of the rest of the battalion?

Top and above. Front and back of Allied military currency, printed specially prior to the invasion of Italy – September 1943.

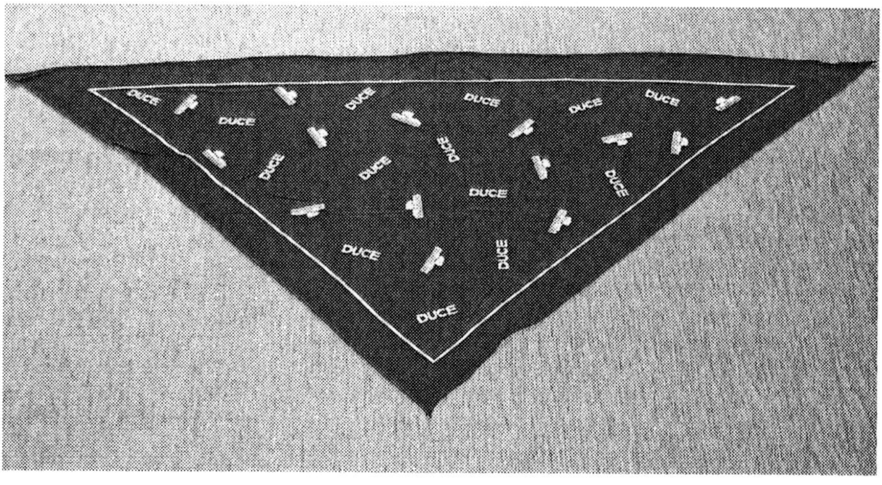

Top and above. Emblems that started the war. German Nazi flag & Italian Fascist neckpiece.

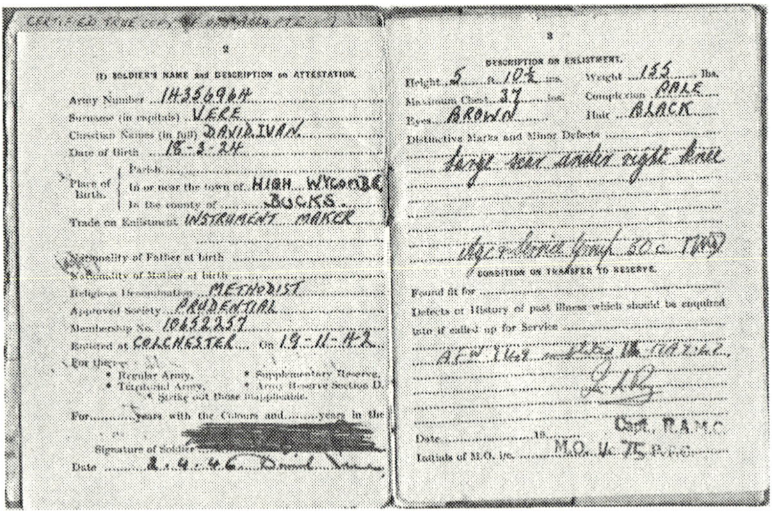

2

(1) SOLDIER'S NAME and DESCRIPTION on ATTESTATION.

Army Number 14356964

Surname (in capitals) VERE

Christian Names (in full) DAVID IVAN

Date of Birth 18-3-24

Place of Birth: Parish ... In or near the town of HIGH WYCOMBE ... In the county of BUCKS.

Trade on Enlistment INSTRUMENT MAKER

Nationality of Father at birth ...

Nationality of Mother at birth ...

Religious Denomination METHODIST

Approved Society PRUDENTIAL

Membership No. 10652257

Enlisted at COLCHESTER on 19-11-42

For the: * Regular Army. * Supplementary Reserve. * Territorial Army. * Army Reserve Section D.
* Strike out those inapplicable.

For ... years with the Colours and ... years in the

Signature of Soldier [redacted]

Date 2.4.46

3

DESCRIPTION ON ENLISTMENT.

Height 5 ft. 10½ ins. Weight 155 lbs.

Maximum Chest 37 ins. Complexion PALE

Eyes BROWN Hair BLACK

Distinctive Marks and Minor Defects

large scar under right knee

CONDITION ON TRANSFER TO RESERVE.

Found fit for ...

Defects or History of past illness which should be enquired into if called up for Service ...

Capt. R.A.M.C.

Date ... 19...

Initials of M.O. i/c. M.O. i/c

Soldier's Army Pay Book 64 – part 1. This gave full description and details on enlistment in 1942, and replaced the Civilian Identity Card.

Picture of Author. Taken on insistence of mother before going abroad. June 1943.

Picture taken by Italian, at Salerno, Italy. September 1943.
From left to right: Robert Manley, Peter Dorset, George Govey, Author. We used to share our rations with this starving Italian boy. Whatever happened to him? Robert Manley and Peter Dorset were killed in action. George Govey was injured three times and sent home.

With friends. Esbecar gardens, Cairo, Egypt. May 1944. Norman Sadler is on the end left.

3" Mortar Platoon, 10th Battalion The Royal Berkshire Regiment, taken before its disbandment, 15th May 1944.
Back row, from left: Cherry, Good, Sadler, Bowering, Abbey, The Author, Banks, Petchley.
Middle row, from left: Taylor, Newbury, Corporal Bovington, Mort, Lance Corporal Sherman, ?, ?, ?, ?
Front row, from left: Govey, Sergeants' Simmons, Church and Luxton, Captain Blake, Sergeants' Pullman and Rudd, Godfrey.

Leaflet given out by Papal Guard (Swiss) on a visit to Saint Peters, 1944, where we had an audience with the Pope, Pius the XII, who blessed us British and American Soldiers of the American 5th Army. He told us he had blessed German soldiers just weeks before. A very memorable occasion that's lasted a lifetime.

Saint Peters 'By Night', Circa 1940.

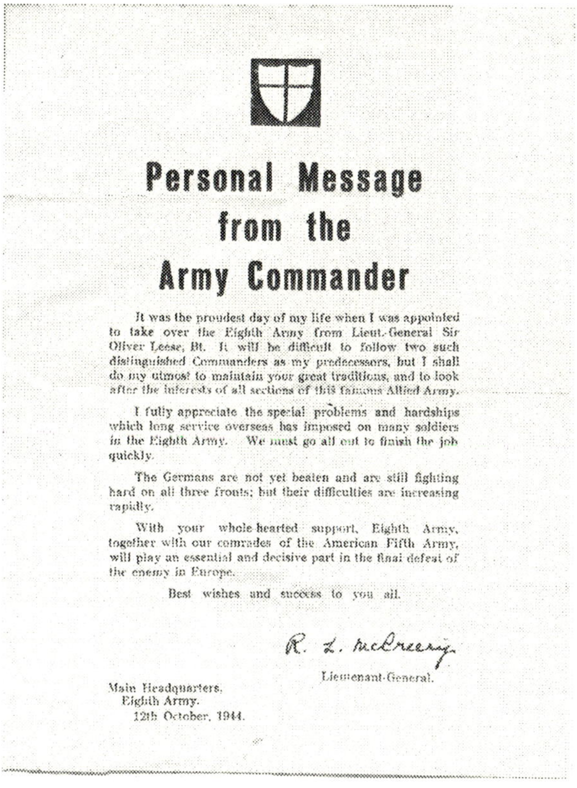

Personal Message from the Army Commander

It was the proudest day of my life when I was appointed to take over the Eighth Army from Lieut.-General Sir Oliver Leese, Bt. It will be difficult to follow two such distinguished Commanders as my predecessors, but I shall do my utmost to maintain your great traditions, and to look after the interests of all sections of this famous Allied Army.

I fully appreciate the special problems and hardships which long service overseas has imposed on many soldiers in the Eighth Army. We must go all out to finish the job quickly.

The Germans are not yet beaten and are still fighting hard on all three fronts; but their difficulties are increasing rapidly.

With your whole-hearted support, Eighth Army, together with our comrades of the American Fifth Army, will play an essential and decisive part in the final defeat of the enemy in Europe.

Best wishes and success to you all.

R. L. McCreery

Lieutenant-General.

Main Headquarters,
Eighth Army.
12th October, 1944.

Message from the 8th Army commander, General McCreery.

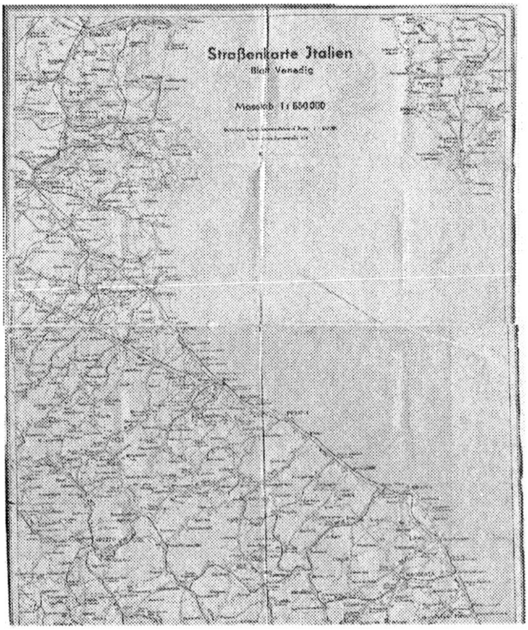

German map from 'The Gothic Line' campaign. Autumn 1944.

3" mortar platoon section, 9th Battalion Royal Fusiliers, taken on the banks of the Senio River line - 23rd or 24th January 1945.
Back row, from left: Sergeant Chambers,
Raymond (carrier driver), Author, Lance Corporal Morgan.
Front row, from left: Solomons, Corporal Vairian, Jarmin, Fletcher, Ellis.

Other members of 3" mortar platoon, taken on the Senio River line, at a battered farmhouse. January 1945.

German propaganda leaflet found on the battlefield in April 1945, before we reached the Po River, showing, when closed, in vivid colour a picture of the bountiful life …

... But when you open it, you are given a stark warning of sudden death if you attempt its crossing. Notice that the Grim Reaper holds both an American and British steel helmet

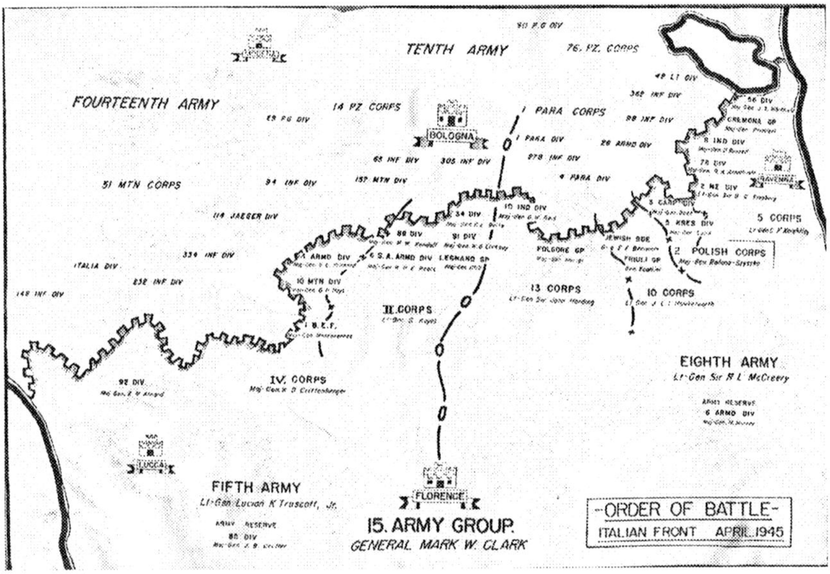

The final battle – the advance to the Po River with the 15th Army Group. General Mark W. Clark commanding.

In pensive mood. General Mark W. Clark, commander of the American 5th Army, who also had British divisions under his control.

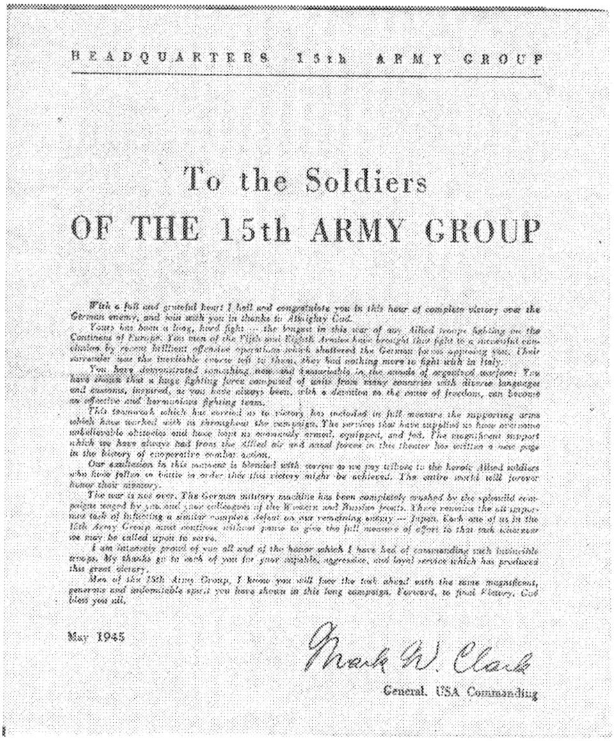

HEADQUARTERS 15th ARMY GROUP

To the Soldiers OF THE 15th ARMY GROUP

With a full and grateful heart I hail and congratulate you in this hour of complete victory over the German enemy, and join with you in thanks to Almighty God.

Yours has been a long, hard fight — the longest in this war of any Allied troops fighting on the Continent of Europe. You men of the Fifth and Eighth Armies have brought that fight to a successful conclusion by recent brilliant offensive operations which shattered the German forces opposing you. Their surrender was the inevitable course left to them, they had nothing more to fight with in Italy.

You have demonstrated something new and remarkable in the annals of organized warfare: You have shown that a huge fighting force composed of units from many countries with diverse languages and customs, inspired, as you have always been, with a devotion to the cause of freedom, can become an effective and harmonious fighting team.

This teamwork which has carried us to victory has included in full measure the supporting arms which have worked with us throughout the campaign. The services that have supplied us have overcome unbelievable obstacles and have kept us constantly armed, equipped, and fed. The magnificent support which we have always had from the Allied air and naval forces in this theater has written a new page in the history of cooperative combat action.

Our exultation in this moment is blended with sorrow as we pay tribute to the heroic Allied soldiers who have fallen in battle in order that this victory might be achieved. The entire world will forever honor their memory.

The war is not over. The German military machine has been completely crushed by the splendid campaigns waged by you and your colleagues of the Western and Russian fronts. There remains the all important task of inflicting a similar complete defeat on our remaining enemy — Japan. Each one of us in the 15th Army Group must continue without pause to give the full measure of effort to that task wherever we may be called upon to serve.

I am intensely proud of you all and of the honor which I have had of commanding such invincible troops. My thanks go to each of you for your capable, aggressive, and loyal service which has produced this great victory.

Men of the 15th Army Group, I know you will face the task ahead with the same magnificent, generous and indomitable spirit you have shown in this long campaign. Forward, to final Victory. God bless you all.

May 1945

Mark W. Clark

General, USA Commanding

Message from the 15th Army group commander, General Mark Clark.

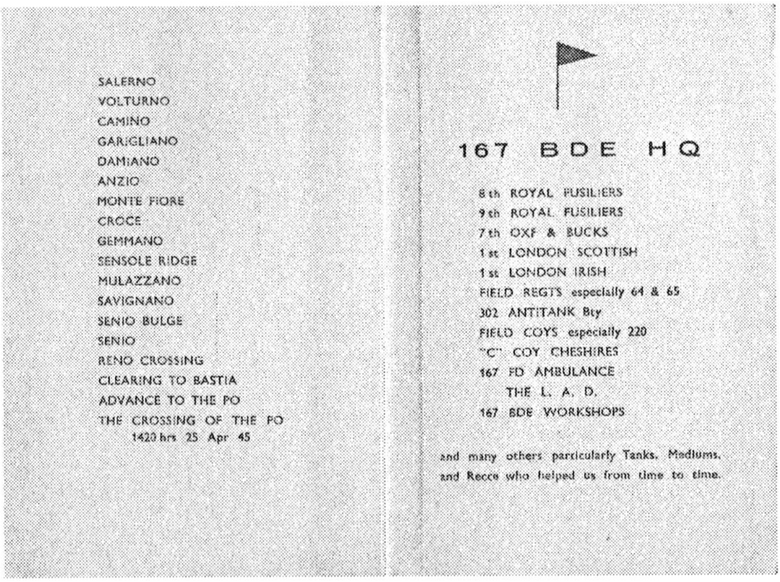
SALERNO
VOLTURNO
CAMINO
GARIGLIANO
DAMIANO
ANZIO
MONTE FIORE
CROCE
GEMMANO
SENSOLE RIDGE
MULAZZANO
SAVIGNANO
SENIO BULGE
SENIO
RENO CROSSING
CLEARING TO BASTIA
ADVANCE TO THE PO
THE CROSSING OF THE PO
1420 hrs 25 Apr 45

167 BDE HQ

8th ROYAL FUSILIERS
9th ROYAL FUSILIERS
7th OXF & BUCKS
1st LONDON SCOTTISH
1st LONDON IRISH
FIELD REGTS especially 64 & 65
302 ANTITANK Bty
FIELD COYS especially 220
"C" COY CHESHIRES
167 FD AMBULANCE
THE L. A. D.
167 BDE WORKSHOPS

and many others particularly Tanks, Mediums, and Recce who helped us from time to time.

Top and above. Commemorative leaflet from 167 Brigade HQ at end of the war, showing the list of battles fought by the brigade in the 56 London Division, The Black Cats.

The 3" mortar platoon, 9th Battalion Royal Fusiliers, taken in the school grounds at Pola. Author not in picture – on escort duty to Klagenfurt, in Austria. Sergeant Pepperell, front row, far left of picture with small dog at his feet.

The amphitheatre at Pola, where the 9th Battalion Royal Fusiliers were on garrison duty for 8 months after the war.

3" mortar platoon, 9th Battalion Royal Fusiliers, before its disbandment – March 1946. With Captain Sherlock sitting in middle, front row, Author and Stanley Abbey on left and right ends of picture, before we left for the 1st Battalion London Scottish Regiment in Trieste.

Out training in the 3" mortar platoon around Trieste. Author is 2nd from right.

Author standing in carrier with background of old Italian barracks in Trieste.

Out training in the 3" mortar platoon around Trieste. Author is on the far left.

Fascist headquarters, Padova 1941.

Former Fascist headquarters that was turned into GHQ Central Mediterranean Forces in 1946. Notice the awning covering the word FASCISTA (Fascist). Taken by Author.

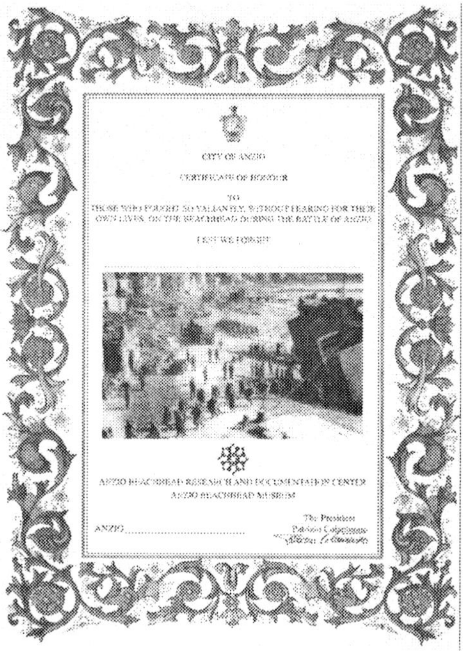

Copy of the Certificate of Honour awarded by the citizens of Anzio to commemorate the 60th Anniversary of the Allied landings on the beachhead in 1944.

Picture taken at the 10th Battalion The Royal Berkshire Regiment reunion, 2003. Author is on the end left, front row.

12. The struggle goes on.

Just before we came up to the crossroads, we could just make out in the dark two columns of men in single file walking on opposite sides of the road. They loomed up out of the darkness and were American infantrymen moving up into the frontline, taking over our old position. There was no talking amongst them, and all you could hear was the sound of their boots on the road and the occasional clank of metal against metal. They must have known what they were in for up ahead. I was moving out, but I could still feel pity for them at what they must face in the days ahead.

The carrier moved on, over the crossroads, and soon found by a guard that we had arrived at Battalion HQ. Turning off the road, the carrier came to a halt by the side of a large building.

I, along with the others, was about to find out what had befallen the battalion and our friends. Climbing out of the carrier, I was within seconds of making a wonderful discovery in that my friend, who I thought to be dead or missing, was talking away to a fellow guard only yards away from us. With that voice, it could only be my friend and calling out, "Stan!" into the dark night, a reply came back immediately. "Is that you, Dave?" And there we were with our arms around each other in disbelief that we could both be standing there.

We were both under the illusion that something ill-fated had happened – he not expecting to see me again or I of him – each thinking the other dead, such is the uncertainty of war. The rest of the crew were going inside the building, so I left him there, saying I would see him the next day.

There was only one thing we must do and that's sleep, which overcame us when we laid on the floor, casting out all thoughts and memory of the farm.

The next morning was far advanced when we came round from our slumber and, after having hot food and a drink, I sort out my friend who told me his story. He said, "I was on guard, that would be two nights ago, at this farm and it was getting dark, when I was hit in the chin with a piece of shrapnel and the sergeant sent me back to the regimental aid post to get it dressed. The strange thing is," he went on, "when I returned later in the night, I found the farmhouse deserted with no sign of life there or a light inside. I can tell you, Dave, I left in rather a hurry, back passed your farm to Battalion HQ where I told them of my experience."

After my friend had finished his story, I told him of the German attack on the farm while he was away and how we were unable to help. "Did you know, Stan, that Bob Manley was killed on the 6th of February, while out laying a signals cable?" I could tell by Stan's face he had no idea of the tragedy. Afterwards, he asked me how we had managed at our farmhouse. I told him, "We were most fortunate in that a company of London Scottish had moved in around our position and made the place secure." I never told my friend of our engagement with the enemy and the consequence in life at the result, nor would I ever tell any other person of the time there. It was best left unsaid.

What now remained of the battalion, now down to just 40-strong, moved out of the old Battalion HQ to a spinney that the beachhead abounded in, and south of the town of Anzio. Our campsite was beside a sandy track. The sand was very hard to walk in, but we had excellent cover for the carriers in among the undergrowth and trees, a good place to be away from the eyes of the enemy aircraft. We soon made our slit trenches that we could jump into at the first sign of trouble, which was always present.

Now I am one who believes in strict discipline because war demands it, but the powers that be (in this case the platoon officer) decided we needed some. And this after the battalion had all but been destroyed in conflict with a handful of men remaining. The platoon was called on parade by the platoon sergeant, a good advocate for his master who then informed us that we needed smartening up with some saluting drill. This would be fit and proper on a parade ground, but not here in a war zone.

The officer was responsible for this fiasco, possibly after some poor swine had failed to salute him. This was discipline turned into a farce by the spectacle that we made of the drill on this sandy track.

After the command of "Quick—march," the platoon found it a struggle just to move along without stumbling after every step in the loose sand. Then the commands came. "To the right salute; To the left salute; To the front salute," and this carried on till we were nigh exhausted from the effort. This could only have happened to us and would have been laughable to every soldier on the beachhead. Here we were, 60 miles behind the enemy lines, swept by gunfire by day and night with the enemy wishing to push us back into the sea, and we were engaged in this worthless exercise. The officer was no doubt a martinet.

Next day, a large shell, which we could tell by instinct would land two or three hundred yards away, passed over our heads and landed with a large detonation. At this time, a small group of the platoon were standing, talking with one another, when a scream of pain made us aware that one of the men had been wounded.

We closed in on the injured man to see if we could help, but there was nothing any of us could do except keep him warm while we waited for an ambulance that had been called for over the field telephone. A piece of shrapnel had travelled all the way back from the detonation, ploughing its way into the flesh of the man's face and taking out his eye and socket. He laid in a pool of his own blood until the battalion ambulance arrived and whisked him away to one of the numerous hospitals on the beachhead, and later evacuated by ship back to Naples.

Our next move was to a place about a mile north of Anzio, into some accommodation there on top of the cliffs overlooking the sea. It was nothing much, but better than being out in the open at this time of year. The battalion was in a depleted state and unready at this stage to return into the line. Men who had been sick and wounded before Anzio now rejoined the battalion. Also, a fresh intake of men from England helped swell the numbers.

While staying here, we were entertained by the 56 Divisional Concert Party in a large hut with a small stage they could perform on. Also, there were folding chairs down each side, making it most commendable to us all.

Before the show started, the commanding officer came in the door behind us and we were called to attention. After sitting down again, the brigadier made his appearance so we came to attention again. Having sat down with the show about to start, we had the final interruption when the Army commander came in. General Mark Clark of the American 5th Army, who we were a part of, walked down between the chairs while we were once again called to our feet.

I could see that he must have been 6 feet 3 inches tall and slim, with a large revolver swinging from his hip. On reaching the stage, he exchanged salutes with the officers and had a word with the brigadier before turning round to face us. "I have come here today to congratulate your Battalion on the stand you made against the enemy, till you were overwhelmed by the sheer weight of numbers. I do feel very proud of you all." Clark continued. "I don't suppose you will be committed to the line again while you are here?" At this stage, Brigadier Davidson whispered in the Army commander's ear who then said, "I hope the Battalion will be well rested before returning into the line!" He ended by wishing us good luck. And with that, he stalked out of the hut with his aide-de-camp.

At long last, the show started and it did make us smile again, the first in a long time. When it was over, we found we had another celebrity with us in the hut, in the shape of Wynford Vaughan-Thomas, war correspondent for the BBC who said, "I am making a recording for the folk back home." Then speaking again to the assembly here, "This recording will be played over the BBC Home Service within the next few days, and what I want you to do is to give three cheers to show them, after this, that we are not downhearted here on the beachhead. Right then, hip hip ..." "Hooray," came the muffled chorus back from the hall.

This was repeated several times without any real enthusiasm on our part. "That's no good!" Thomas called out. "Shall we try again?" But once more, he had rather a negative response. None of us here expected a flourish of trumpets on our behalf, but in the light of past events it would have been more appropriate had he arranged for someone to give us three cheers and not the other way round. The whole thing, in the main, was somewhat resented by the survivors of the battalion. In the end, Thomas called a halt to his recording, saying, "What I have here will have to do."

A day or so later, we were marched to a secluded place to parade before the brigadier. When he arrived, we were standing in three ranks, and when called to attention, he saluted and said, "Break ranks and stand round me," which we did. Brigadier Davidson spoke to us, saying, "In my lifetime, I have seen and taken part in many battles, but never have I seen a Battalion fighting it out to the very last and holding the enemy at bay in stemming their tide of advance. You may all feel very proud of yourselves as I do of you, so it only remains for me to wish you well in the times ahead and I salute you all." The brigadier saluted the group of men and turned away to his jeep.

Within a few days, the battalion, with a new intake from England and the wounded from past engagements, was formed into two rifle companies instead of the usual four. The rest of us, for the time being, would be going on carrying parties with supplies to keep them there.

Two evenings later, we assembled by the side of the main road which ran into Anzio, and the other way, the perimeter of the beachhead where our party were bound for along the coast road. I noticed that no vehicles were moving to the front, but only to the port of Anzio.

I must have been standing very near to the roadside when someone in our party shouted, "Watch Out!" and I jumped back from the roadside as a 3-ton lorry swept by. It was carrying a reel of barbed wire and steel stanchions at the rear of the cab, but one had fallen down and was protruding out of the side of the cab by several feet, and it would have scythed me down if I had ignored the call from my protector. Whoever he was saved my life, and stopped my parents from receiving a cable from the War Office, of 'killed in action'.

The transports arrived, being 3-ton lorries, and we climbed onboard with our various loads, mine being Mills 36 hand grenades in a large bag-pack, and I sat down on one of the wheel-covers that was raised a few inches above the floor level. It was not my seat for very long, as another man climbed up, over the tailboard, and I had to vacate my seat for him. His name was Peter Lipman who worked on the HQ staff, and was a professional dancer in his civilian life. We all settled down and the transports moved off up the coast road in the gathering darkness.

After a few miles, it was totally dark as we came up to the crossroads with an obstruction across the road, stopping any vehicle from going straight on into the hands of the enemy. This was the extremity of the beachhead and our transports turned right, then stopped at the side of some houses there.

Word came down that the road had been shelled shortly before we arrived, and here we were sitting around on the most likely target of the shelling – the crossroads. We were feeling very uneasy at the prospect of us being rather like the sitting duck. Then there was an almighty bang. A shell had landed at the back of our vehicle and I found myself pushed out, over the top of the tailboard, and onto the road by the surge of humanity trying to find cover.

There was just one casualty and he had been sitting on the wheel-cover I had vacated, and now unable to move with his ankle nearly severed from the leg by a shell splinter. He was removed from off the vehicle and made as comfortable as possible by the side of the road. Someone waited with him for transport to take him back into Anzio.

We all returned to the transports and soon got underway. This time, I steered clear of the wheel-cover and found myself sitting next to a young officer, straight out from England, who started up a conversation by asking me what it was like in the frontline and what happened there. I must admit that I was mystified at the question coming from an officer, but had to answer him. I spoke into his ear, above the roar of the engine. "Well, sir, it's always the unexpected that happens at the front, like this carrying party. It's never an easy thing to do, being exposed most of the time. Even when you find the battalion, you are still at risk in returning to the safety of the jumping-off place, but you will soon learn the ropes, sir, for your own preservation." He was satisfied with my comments and sat quietly on the bumpy floor, no doubt pondering over what I was able to tell him.

At last, we arrived at our destination and the tailboard was dropped as we climbed down in good order this time. We soon got organised and moved off the road into what looked like a depression in the ground, but turned out to be like a wadi that criss-crossed this part of the beachhead. Some of them being quite deep in places, their sides covered for the most part in bushes, and several of them with very sharp thorns or prickles that you bumped into from time to time in the dark at the bottom of the wadi.

The enemy was good at infiltrating into our positions in the wadis, and a patrol could be bumped into at any time, day or night. It was a most unhealthy place to tarry in. We staggered along the narrow footpath at the bottom, occasionally lit up by the flickering light of a Verylight flare, and whether by friend or foe I had no idea. At last, we climbed out of this dark, overgrown trench-in-the-ground, onto what seemed to be like a field with an undulating nature to it.

Later, we were to find it was indeed grazing land by what we found there. We started off in loose order, trying to keep up with each other in the darkness, being a time of great caution for all concerned in this walk into the unknown territory. No talking, no noise, just walking along I hoped on a compass bearing. This wasn't the kind of place to get lost in.

The carrying party was getting rather strung out when our first Verylight flare confronted us. We froze in our tracks, keeping our faces to the ground, thereby minimising the light of the flare on our faces. I could see out of the corner of my eye a picture of dozens of men standing absolutely still, with the flickering light of the flare casting our dark shadows onto the ground, as the sizzling flare descended in the cold, damp atmosphere. Then it was gone. We paused to adjust our eyes to the darkness, and then moved off again with our nerves a little shaken by the events of the night. Before proceeding very far, there was another flare hanging in the sky, making it as light as day and making us follow the same procedure as before till it died away.

It was a wonder to me that the enemy, who were always most vigilant, had been unable to see a party of about sixty men milling around in no man's land. At the time, I was unaware that the officer, who had asked my opinion of life in the frontline, was in sole command of the carrying party, he being the only officer present. After a while, we came to the conclusion that we were well and truly lost. The whole horizon seemed to be encircled by gun flashes and we had no idea about where our own lines were.

The enemy, amazingly, still did not see us after more flares had arced up overhead, enabling us to see that we were passing through a flock of dead sheep that must have been killed by the intense exchange of gunfire on the beachhead. At this stage, I had some doubt about getting out of this and felt sure others shared it.

The order came that we must hold hands and walk in extended line in the hope of bumping into someone on our side, but with a 50-50 chance it could be our enemy. What would happen if we were still wandering about by first light? This is a time when an attack could be mounted by one side or the other and is appropriately called stand-to – when every eye on both sides would be looking for something out of the ordinary and then takes action against it. We could be cut down like the sheep.

Taking the hand nearest to me, I found it was the hand of Company Sergeant Major Clark who was baffled like the rest of us by the lack of leadership shown. Things were going from bad to worse now with the number of flares increasing. It was only a matter of time before being spotted.

One of the sergeants in the mortar platoon, Sergeant Rudd said, "I'm not staying here to get killed. I'm going to find my own way out of this mess!" And he was gone, swallowed up in the darkness. He was ordered to stay by someone but he wouldn't listen.

Then, by shear chance, we thankfully stumbled into some trenches occupied by a section of the Oxfordshire & Buckinghamshire Light Infantry, where a full corporal was in charge there. Our officer came forward and said, "Could you lead us to the Royal Berkshire positions, they must be somewhere near?" The corporal, standing up in his slit trench, answered, "I can't leave my post here, even if I did know the way." Our officer answered him in a most pathetic tone of voice, "Corporal, I ... implore you ... to take us to our Battalion." But the corporal would not budge from his statement.

So the officer moved us through the Oxfordshire & Buckinghamshire lines, back down into the wadis and eventually back to our transports. Summing up the whole dreadful night's episode, you could say it was an act of deliverance to come away unscathed from it all. Sergeant Rudd also found his way back. But we, having spent the night trying to find our battalion's two rifle companies, had failed miserably.

Returning back to our base on the cliff-top, we managed to get some much needed sleep, away from the riggers of the past night. Its conclusion could well have been entirely different to what did happen, and I feel sure that all of the men involved in that ghastly carry would remember it in detail forever. With the day well advanced, we paraded to find that the mortar platoon would be returning to the line.

That same evening, the platoon moved out with our carriers once again going up the coast road under cover of darkness, but this time when we reached the barrier across the road and turned right, we carried straight on without stopping. After a mile or two more, we moved off the road into grassland and thickets where a halt was called. The carriers were then concealed in the undergrowth with the camouflage nets draped over them, and then, by the flickering lights of the gunfire on the beachhead, we dug ourselves shallow slit trenches that would suffice till daylight when we could finish them off.

Come daylight, we were roused by the standing guard, and after warming our compo breakfast rations through, we soon devoured it and returned to increase the depth of our respective slit trenches. The mortars were still on the carriers as we had still not been designated the positions they would occupy when they were operational. Here, we were only in a holding position waiting for orders from above.

I was sharing a slit trench with the detachment commander, Sergeant Pullman. It was now an Army order to dig two-man slit trenches. This was due to a psychiatric problem of lone men in slit trenches going out of their minds in continuous combat.

Nightfall came and lying there in the dark, surrounded by walls of dank-smelling earth and talking about nothing in particular, both of us dropped off into a kind of half sleep in keeping one eye open and your ears cocked for any sound of trouble. After a while, I was under the impression the sergeant had fallen asleep when his voice spoke out of the darkness, "Do you know, Dave, that by the book we are dead. We can't keep getting away with it like we have done in the past." I made no reply for sometime, and then all I could say was, "I guess so, Sergeant." A nice inducement for sleep I thought. But sleep I did eventually when the need of the body overcomes the mind.

I awakened with a start, along with the sergeant, both of us hearing some kind of commotion going on above our heads. Being fully clothed with boots and steel helmets still on our heads, we jumped out of the trench and could just see a group of people standing there talking away, at what I had no idea. A flashlight was switched on and the talking turned to sounds of alarm at what the light had revealed to the onlookers. The occupants of one of the trenches had received a direct hit from a shell that fortunately had failed to explode, but damage had been done.

They in the trench had placed an old wooden door over their dugout, making for a more agreeable place for sleeping in. By the light of the torch, we could see that a hole had been punched in the door, and when removed could see two men still lying there. One being badly dazed, the other badly wounded. My friend, Norman Sadler, was the one who was dazed – the man who had put the mules out of their misery back at the Garigliano River a few short weeks before. After pulling Norman free of the trench, they turned their attentions to getting the wounded man out.

His name was Albert Luck, a carrier driver who had just come out from England, this being his first encounter with the enemy. At this moment, German aircraft were flying around looking for a target and someone called out, "Watch that light!" whereas the man holding the light made his reply with, "Bugger the light!" and carried on with what he was doing, of trying to save a man's life. They carefully lifted Albert out and he was in a bad way, the shell having passed between his legs, damaging the thighs. The battalion ambulance had been alerted and was soon on the spot, making Albert as comfortable as possible before leaving for one of the field hospitals on the beachhead.

Albert died in the ambulance before reaching a hospital. He had married on his overseas leave prior to going aboard, and one failed to think what his bride of just a few weeks would do when she received the fatal communication from the War Department.

After having talked about the incident, we returned to our trenches with our morale at a very low ebb. It would do well to mention the man with the torch and his complete disregard for the enemy planes overhead, in his efforts to bring some relief to the trapped man in the trench. His name was Lance Corporal Sherman, and he played his part to the full that night.

By daylight, our detachment moved out of our holding position to become operational and support the two rifle companies again. Each of the six detachments were allocated firing positions, ours being in the back of beyond in tangled woodland, but good cover from the enemy with the carrier tucked away out of sight in the bushes.

We removed the mortar and mounted it on good firm ground, only to find we had a problem. Looking along the length of the barrel, we could clearly see that if the mortar were fired it would be like committing suicide. The detonator cap on the bomb was formed out of soft brass that only had to touch a twig to explode above our heads. We couldn't go any farther with the mortar owing to the ground dropping away to a stream, and the enemy would most likely see us, especially if the mortar were fired. By the same token, we couldn't go back deeper into the wood; it would only make matters worse.

There was one way to overcome our trouble – fell the trees in the bomb's flight path. There seemed to be two trees to cut down. They were like our silver birch back home, thirty to forty feet tall with trunks around five inches in diameter. All we had in the carrier toolbox was a machete. This would do well in the jungle, cutting a path through succulent growth, but not here. We need not have worried for I had found an axe on Mount Camino way back in December and had returned with it from the mountain, placing it in the well on my side of the carrier.

Going there now, I rummaged around in the well and found the axe. The sergeant soon had me working on the two trees and before long, with the help of the detachment pushing, the first tree was felled and likewise the second. The mortar now had a clear field of fire and was operational.

We had now dug ourselves slit trenches and started to clear the site from the debris of the trees, when we stopped what we were doing and listened. We could hear the sound of an aeroplane flying very low. It must be one of ours, we thought, the enemy only making an appearance after dark and not during daylight. As it flew out from the cover of the trees, we were very surprised at its closeness to us, even more so at it being a Messerschmitt fighter and I could plainly see the helmeted pilot sitting at the controls. The sergeant shouted, "Get under the bridge!" which we did without any encouragement from him.

We waded into the cold water of the stream that came up to our knees. The pilot was so close, you felt you could put your hand out and touch him. He was moving so slow it was a wonder he did not stall the engine, no doubt looking for a target or any glimpse of any kind of movement in that dormant landscape. Of all things it was a Messerschmitt, with a black German cross on the fuselage, passing us less than a hundred feet away and just skimming the tops of the trees. Under the arched bridge that was no higher than my head, the six of us crouched down as he made a tight turn and came back to have another look.

It was most fortunate for us that he didn't fly the length of the stream; otherwise he would have seen us cowering there. He made just one more pass over us when he came back out of the trees, then fortunately flew away. It was a very near thing for us. If he had seen us there, he would have strafed us with cannon fire and that would have been very disastrous for the whole detachment.

After things had calmed down again and we had taken stock of the situation, all of the detachment were rather wet and in need of drying out, but how? The building of a fire was out of the question with the smoke by day and flames by night. The enemy would react to this with a few well-placed rounds.

Later, I removed my boots and gaiters, tipped the water out of my boots, removed my trousers and wrung the water out of them, then felt quite belligerent to our own side in that we had no greatcoats. They had been handed into the stores when we had come to the beachhead. The Army authority had decided, in their wisdom, to take away our greatcoats in the middle of winter so not to impede our fighting quality, and replaced them with sleeveless leather jerkins. The greatcoats would have kept our legs warm now while we tried to dry ourselves. We always carried a spare pair of Army grey socks that we changed into after drying our feet, which now looked rather white after standing in the cold water.

After drying out, we then used our towels to dry our boots. It was the only way. You cease to be a gentleman after this, when the thin veneer of civilisation wears off and become anything but what you were originally. In fact, we were on the Anzio beachhead for 6 weeks and never had a bath or shower in that time, but did shave when we could. Some of the men shaved in their cups of tea. You had to do the best you could under the circumstances at your disposal at the time.

After spending a cold, wet night in our soggy clothes, we felt thoroughly miserable at our misfortunes. Later in the morning, we were told that we would be leaving this position to a new one near the main road.

Our new position was an old house, standing on its own but badly damaged by the presence of war all around us. We had a second detachment with us, under Corporal Church, and included my friend, Sadler. They decided to move for safety into a brick-built bakery that looked very secure. When they had mounted the mortar and parked their carrier with ours by the house, their crew all crawled into where the fire for the oven used to be with a large slab of stone over their heads, many inches thick, where the bread used to stand and bake.

Our detachment moved into the battered building. All of the rooms were untenable, just shells of what they were originally. There was only one place in the house that afforded us any kind of protection and reasonable security, and that was under the stairs.

Out in the yard was a considerable heap of Army compo rations, each box containing the rations of fourteen men for one day. There were four different kinds of contents, but every box held a large tin of Army biscuits that were very hard. The boxes were in the order of around 18"x12"x12" in size. They must have been placed there by the Army Corps at the start of the offensive, back in January, but now looked in a wet and bedraggled state.

The sergeant, with this in mind, suggested that we move the boxes around to make a mortar pit, it being more than useless in trying to dig one in the waterlogged ground. We rearranged the boxes to suit our needs, interlocking the boxes together like brickwork several boxes deep. At best, it would stop small arms fire. It would have to suffice, as we had no alternative.

We now waited for orders from Platoon HQ over the radio transmitting set after having sent the message, "Ready to fire." After our midday meal had been cobbled together and a guard posted, we settled down in the stairwell and talked about the position we were in. We would be more or less in the dry if it rained, and all the timbers in the joists and roof looked very substantial to me, even after the battering the house had received.

Without any warning or hearing the shell fired, it hit the roof with a crash, smashing the tiles into small fragments or shards of a lethal nature, sped on by the explosion, showering the inside rooms with the debris from the ceilings overhead. We crouched there, under the stairs, now looking more like ghosts than soldiers, choked by the fine white dust that hung in the air.

The second shell hit the building and caught us unaware once again with the same result as the first, starting with a nerve shattering explosion and crash (that must play havoc with the nervous system), and a further rain of debris over us. We all looked ghostly from the experience and, after a while, all was quiet. All of us later came to the conclusion that it must have been a tank firing along open sights to register such accurate hits like that. We called out to our friends in the bakery to see if all was well with them and a few heads came poking out from under the slab telling us it was, but soon retired under it, a wise decision and us to our stairwell.

Next day, Corporal Church and his detachment were moved out to a place that afforded more protection from the eyes of the enemy, for they must have seen us milling around here. And our detachment too would be moving out when a suitable site was found for us to operate from.

We cleaned ourselves up the best we could, but badly needed a bath. The continuous wearing of our steel helmets, since coming to the beachhead, had formed unnatural waves in our hair, formed by the bands of protective webbing inside. A clean face could be kept by shaving, but that was as far as our cleanliness went. I had no idea what my mother would say if she could see the kind of conditions we were living under. And knowing mother, she would have been very rebellious towards our predicament, and the condition of her son, had she known. Mercifully, she had no idea of where or what I was doing.

It was at this time I was feeling a weariness of body, in that everything I did it seemed more difficult to carry out, not that I didn't play my part in the detachment and would never shirk from my moral duties. However, it was I who felt that something was wrong, but not made obvious to others being able to perceive the change in me. Could they have all been the same, but had been unable to grasp it? All of us were now very tired from lack of sleep and hygiene conditions, like washing and clean clothing, along with the absence of keeping warm in winter and good hot food you must have in sustaining bodily strength. A form of malaise had found its way into our lives. The battalion was tired before we came to the beachhead, but now after almost six weeks here where there was no hiding place or safety, we were slowly grinding to a halt in this perpetual state of uncertainty, and where death was a daily visitor.

We thankfully left our last refuge, under the stairs, along with the most costly mortar position ever constructed with about a hundred compo ration boxes. After leaving our old position, we travelled about two road miles distance to our new position with plenty of good cover around and the inevitable wadis.

13. Good news and deliverance. Egypt.

The position to which we had come was also Battalion HQ, not that anyone would know. There was soldiering in and out of the wadis, coming and going it seemed every minute of the day to this hallowed place in the thickets, when it was normally a grand building with double guards posted at the entrance. Indeed, Anzio was a great leveller of such notions.

My good friend, Norman Sadler, had been told to select a good dry spot for our position, and he had done just that in finding us a suitable site for the mortar, which was mounted under a rim in a wadi, giving us some four feet of protection and room to take our carrier-load of ammunition. The enemy could fire on us from every angle of the beachhead, but not the sea, and the wadi being about thirty feet deeper than the mortar position, it was wise to keep away from the edge; otherwise you would be walking in space.

It wasn't long before we were brought into action, firing in support of the battalion. This went on throughout the day with the enemy trying to probe its way into our positions in the wadis. Norman Sadler came from his own detachment position to see how we were fairing at the site he had chosen for us. He was amazed to find that our baseplate had not sunk into the ground like all the rest had, forcing them to dig it out and re-site the mortar after every few rounds fired.

Most of the ground in and around the wadi country looked like swampland, and had been until Mussolini had the land drained before having the farms built, never knowing it would one day become a battlefield for the nations to fight over and destroy.

Anzio should never have taken place with the small number of troops committed to the venture, 60 miles behind the enemy lines, on the false premise that Hitler would quell the landings with forces from the Cassino battlefront. Hitler had other ideas.

While on the beachhead, I saw two types of a natural phenomenon (though this time caused by man). In the first instance, I saw ripples or waves in straight lines zooming along in the sky, and secondly a whirlwind or twister sucking up things on the ground in the funnel. Both of them were created by massive and incessant gunfire by both sides, the noise reverberating round the few square miles of hostility that was the Anzio beachhead of 1944.

A day or so later, we were to hear a small whisper of a rumour running around, but we felt unable to believe in its authenticity having heard it so many times before to have our hopes dashed later on. Even the regimental sergeant major had a smile on his face, whereas it was always a perpetual frown when he was looking out for any infringement of Army rules and regulations in his domain. The RSM, even in this godforsaken place of slimy mud, always had his boots highly polished. A contradiction to the boots of us lesser mortals who were finding it hard to even have a wash.

We did find out later, to our relief, that it was no rumour but a fact. Our positions would be taken over by a fresh battalion to the beachhead (unfortunately for them), with us leaving our carriers, mortars and ammunition behind for them, and I hoped it would serve them well. All we would be taking out were our own personal weapons with containers of spare ·303" ammunition. We made doubly sure that the mortar was clean and in good working order. Also, me sadly having to leave my trusty axe behind as there was no room for excess baggage, for we were going to walk out a distance of several miles till we met the transports to take us to the docks.

There was just one other thing to remember, that as darkness fell on the beachhead, they were going to test a new antiaircraft system with a barrage that would entail the entire naval force of the American and British ships in the harbour there. We were advised to seek some form of cover when it started. This was a way of combating the enemy aircraft during the hours of darkness over the docks where they did a great deal of damage to the unloading ships.

When we were relieved in the afternoon, we left our old positions to the new battalion. Having wished them well, the remnants of us left, marching gratefully away, feeling sure that we had met the devil at close hand.

I, of course, was carrying an extra burden of a case of ·303" ammunition, but was under the impression of the rules of common decency that I would be relieved of the duty after a satisfactory distance had been travelled, and hand it over to the man marching beside me. So, when my physical senses started to flag, I asked my immediate colleague if he would take a turn. His answer back to my request was a shake of the head and the same from those around me. All of them only had their rifle and small kit to carry, but I had the extra ammunition to handle which they allowed me to carry all the way to the transports where I was very near to a state of exhaustion, and I don't remember boarding the truck. My colleagues could have justifiably felt the same as myself, but at the time it was a bitter pill for me to swallow.

We came to the town of Anzio and went straight to the docks, stopping at the gaping doors of an American LC-T. We climbed out of the trucks and straight up inside the ship where it soon pulled out into the open sea for safety, and out of the range of the large guns in the hills.

We had our first hot food served to us in ages on the mess deck, and it was just fine. Later, I went up on deck to have a last look at the place where we had been captive for so long, with Anzio fading away in the half-light. It should have been a time for celebration, but all was quiet with everyone wrapped up in their own thoughts and memories of this most terrible of places. A few of us had managed to evade the enemy's intentions, but most were not so fortunate in that they would stay there forever.

I can't for the life of me remember our journey back to the port of Naples, even being in a most dangerous shipping lane. I have no recollection of what went on, but would like to think it was the sleep of the just. Waking up to the world of reality again, I found it was time to vacate the ship that in a sense had brought us home.

We walked out of the vast doors onto the quayside where here, just a few weeks before, my friend, Bob Manley, had told us of our destination of Anzio and the crumbling beachhead there. Transports were waiting for us and we were soon on our way, but where? Looking round the occupants in the lorry, I recognised the signal platoon sergeant who sat nearby, so I said to him, "Excuse me, Sergeant, can you tell me anything about Bob Manley? He was my friend." In a voice with some feeling, he said, "Bob was out laying a signals cable when a shell landed close by, and he was hit by a small fragment of shrapnel in the back and it penetrated through his chest. They were taking him back in the ambulance to the field hospital, when he asked one Orderly, 'Am I going to be alright?' and the Orderly replied, 'Yes, of course you are, son,' and Bob closed his eyes and was gone." The sergeant was very moved by what he had told me and finished with, "He was a very good man."

I thanked him for telling me and remembered Bob's slip of paper with his name and address on, which I always carried in my pocket. I had promised him that if I survived I would contact his parents after the war, and Bob would have done the same for me if necessary.

We must have travelled around ten miles or so when we arrived at a small town where we would be staying for a while. This turned out to be like 'heaven on earth' after the privation and horror we had endured on the beachhead which we still had to come to terms with. There, we had been forced into a condition that you could call an act of brutish behaviour just to survive and fight on, and would take a long time to erase from our minds if ever.

Where we were now was a pleasant little town with fine buildings and small shops, though with nothing inside them except the odd thing or two. To us it was like home from home and dare I say it, the sight of women of the town, of any age, gave you the impression of coming back to civilisation and out of the jungle where we had stayed too long for our own good.

There was going to be a film show put on for us in the town and we awaited this in great anticipation, as this would be a rare treat. None of us were disappointed at the kind of fare we received that night. All of the men not on duty attended the show. The lights in the auditorium dipped and went out, then the flickering silvery light came up on the screen and announced Fred Astaire and Rita Hayworth in *You Were*

Never Lovelier. It's a film that I shall always remember, being so light-hearted and helped in transforming us back into normal human beings. This was the kind of tonic that we all needed.

The film ended, but not the show as we were told to stay in our seats while a military band moved onto the stage with their conductor who turned to us and said, "We are the band of The Royal Service Corps. We shall be delighted to be able to play for you music of all kinds with the first half of the concert given over to military band music, whereas the second half will be given over to the dance music section, mostly in the style of the inimitable Glenn Miller, with pieces like *'American Patrol'* (loud cheers). Sit back and enjoy it, thank you." It was a most memorable evening, one that can stay in the back of your mind forever.

This little town was the most delightful place you could imagine. A place of some propriety where we could take stock of ourselves against our past misfortunes, of which there were many. Alas, we did not stay here long enough in this peaceful place, but were going to move on through the mountains of Southern Italy, to a town called Matera.

We left the town that had given us a fair share of happiness and where I attained my 20th birthday. If I survived for another year, I would be eligible to vote. I was allowed to fight and die for my country, but was not allowed to vote in it for being too young. How absurd.

A convoy of trucks carried the battalion through the mountain passes with deep ravines and wooded slopes for most of the journey, a most inhospitable place but with very grand and dramatic scenery at every twist and turn of the road. We passed through small mountain villages with the inhabitants turning out in force, standing at the side of the road, looking on us with awe showing on their faces at the aggressor in their land.

I did feel sympathy for these people in their apparent abject poverty that the war had made for them and not of their own making. They were always dressed in black; the men wearing ankle-length cloaks with a hat to match, being tall with wide brims. It made up the image for us of our idea of what an anarchist would look like – having a round bomb in his hand with a smoking fuse. You could say that you were moving through a place that time forgot. After a long and cold journey, we came at last to the town of Matera and were found billets around the town.

Next day the battalion paraded in the main square, where once again the regimental sergeant major came back into his own with his large mouth and iron discipline to goad us on. After calling the battalion to attention and then at ease, he said, "What the battalion needs now is a lesson in discipline, and that's where I come in. There will be plenty of drill and guards to be mounted, and that means smarting ourselves up till we look the part. Also, the band will be reformed and will be used for ceremonial parades." This had rather a dampening effect on the men with his reminder that we were still in the Army.

Sitting in our billets, a day or so later, someone came in and asked, "Have you seen the company noticeboard yet?" We walked the few yards to Company HQ and there was a notice telling us that in a day or two, we would be moving to Taranto and that was all. However, it did go the rounds that we would be leaving Italy and sailing onto Egypt, where the 56 Division would be reformed. This was very good news for us, and for once in a very long time we would be at peace.

A day or so later and early in the morning, we departed from the town in the transports with a destination of the port of Taranto at the end of our stay in the peninsular. This had been one of Mussolini's naval bases for his large fleet, but it had come to grief in the battle to control the Mediterranean.

Arriving in Taranto, we headed for the docks, and waiting for us was a P&O cruise liner commandeered by the state for the duration of the war. There was plenty of room onboard. The only other occupants of the ship were the remnants of the 168 Brigade of which we were a part, now only numbering a few hundred instead of around two and a half thousand men in total. At the mouth of the harbour was a wonderful piece of Italian engineering in the shape of a swing bridge that closed the harbour off from the open sea.

It wasn't long before I felt the pulse of the engines running through the ship, moving out of our berth, sailing through the now open bridge and back into the open sea and a hostile war zone. The ship being very fast sailed on its own, relying on its speed to evade the enemy. The mess decks looked very spacious with the small number of troops onboard and plenty of room to swing our hammocks. Our food was quite good which we did appreciate after our fast on the beachhead. By the kind of rations seen onboard other ships we had sailed on, ours looked rather derisory by comparison.

The voyage was completed swiftly without any trouble from the enemy, arriving at Port Said at dusk the next day. After disembarkment, we moved into the transports waiting for us dockside and were soon away into a dark desert with destination unknown. Next day, after spending the night journeying in the trucks, we arrived at our camp at a place called Sidi-Bish, which was miles away from anywhere in particular, surrounded by a sea of sand with Cairo about forty miles distance.

The tents at the camp were very good, being square with sloping sides and walls about 3 feet high that ran along the bottom of them and could be removed when the temperature was high. We, of course, had to change into lightweight clothing and had endless talks about Egypt and what to expect here: "When on guard duty, you will walk around the battalion area in pairs. Don't trust the local inhabitants, and if you find one on your rounds at night – shoot them! When your rifles are not in use they must be chained through the trigger guard of each rifle, then chained and padlocked around the two tent poles." We had received no orders to carry out like this in Italy, when they were supposedly our enemy and in Egypt our ally.

One good aspect of the camp was that we would not be sleeping on the floor, or in this case desert sand. All of us were issued with a camp bed made from bamboo and rushes, plaited together to form a strong and supple frame and, above all, they were most comfortable to sleep on. And for the record, never walk on the sand in your bare feet, for the very reason you can get a tiny insect to penetrate the soles of your feet and into your bloodstream with the result of you contracting septicaemia. This comes about from the fact that the desert sand all around here is contaminated. Also, if you were to graze yourself, it must be scrubbed with a brush first before you apply lotion to it.

We very soon got into the routine of the running of the camp, it being quite easy with very little drill owing to the sandy conditions underfoot.

The entertainment provided at the camp was nil, but you could go every night to a film show run by a gentleman called Shafto who owned a string of such places around the Middle East. But don't think you would be going to a theatre like 'The Odeon' back home, otherwise you would be most disappointed. With no grand façade, just the name Shafto's over the entrance, it was of rectangular construction made up of sacking material that looked rather decrepit in the strong desert light. The cost of a ticket was but a few pence (in Egyptian money), but the comforts inside were very frugal with wooden chairs only. As for the delights of the silver screen, they showed black and white films that at the best were very old.

However, you could bank on one thing; you were almost sure to see, in a visit to a Shafto picture house (if you could call it that with its sacking sides in tatters), the World Heavyweight title fight between Joe Louis, the 'Brown Bomber', and Tommy Farr of Wales on the 30th of August 1937. It was indeed a wonderful fight with Louis being the winner on points. I would think that Shafto's must have shown this film at least every other night. His other films were not very good, but it was a case of like-it-or-lump-it.

Leave parties started from the camp for six days leave in Cairo – with a warning. Don't walk about the city on your own. Always be in a group, otherwise you may be very sorry. Stick together at all times and avoid trouble.

Eventually, I went on leave with other members of the platoon, a group of five of us. One of them was my friend, Norman Sadler, who was a trusted companion. On our arrival in Cairo, we went to one of the Army listed hotels which proved to be very decent accommodation with the bed linen looking like mother would have it back home. This was a real treat for us all to be or feel civilised for once in a long time.

No one could ever go to Cairo for the first time without paying a visit to the pyramids and sphinx near Gizeh (Giza), in the Nile Delta. You could reach the site by taking a tram out of the city, but long before reaching the place, I could see the vastness of it all with the pyramids standing around 450 feet high in the stunning sunlight. We moved off the tram at the terminus and were immediately assailed by a group of Arab guides, plying their knowledge of the place at a charge of a few piastres. We picked on one old man to do us the honours, and after a short walk were standing before one of the wonders of the old world.

Standing there in the hot sun, I began to wonder how the pyramids could be made without the equipment we have at our disposal today. How did they lift the blocks of stone? Even with men standing all round a block, it couldn't be lifted for each block must have weighed several tons. I decided to ask the old man how it was done. He told me that the blocks had first been placed in a solid square on a massive foundation. With a ramp of sand built up on one side, this enabled the blocks to be hauled along wide boards, resting on the sand, by teams of men pulling the blocks up with ropes. This process was carried out many times over a period of years till they reached the pinnacle with the last block. Then the sand heaped up on the one side, making it look like a gigantic sand hill, was cleared away leaving the pyramid standing there in all its majesty. A wonderful achievement constructed at the massive cost in human life for a tomb of kings – who were also human.

It was very hot for the end of April, and we still had our serge uniforms on, but that didn't stop us from walking passed the other pyramids to have a look at the sphinx. It looked very strange but very Egyptian in concept, with its nose missing after being struck off by a cannonball fired from a gun of Napoleon's Army. This was during his incursion into Egypt in the early 19th century, in the hope of conquest and the expansion of his empire.

It was time to return back to Cairo, and taking our leave of the old guide, he asked us for more money to buy some wine, it being so hot a day. We gave into him, as none of us wanted any trouble here. In fact, it was a way of life in this land for the inhabitants to live by becoming beggars on the streets, and it was just another way of making a living in an impoverished society.

Back in Cairo, we made a tour of the shops there. We were warned, prior to this, to be on our guard for street urchins who worked in packs with the sole purpose of making your boots dirty by flicking some obnoxious muck onto them with a brush. After this, they had the audacity to tell 'Johnny' (that was the name they called all soldiers) that he had dirty boots, and would he like them cleaned by a shoeshine boy who would then appear as if by magic. They did this to two of our party, mine included, this being the case of juvenile crime that was rampant in Cairo at the time.

We also paid a visit to the Esbecar gardens; a large park that held many botanical specimens in its grounds. Here, the five of us found to our delight something that had been denied to us for many a long year – bananas – and they were wonderful.

We also went to the best picture house in the city, not that we particularly wanted to see the film that was showing there, a war film with the title of *Sahara* starring Humphrey Bogart. This was the story of an American tank crew stranded behind the German lines, in North Africa, and fighting their way back to their own lines. It was sheer escapism, but it had its moments with enough pathos to hold us in our seats. With the interval came a surprise with the dimming of the lights in the auditorium and the quiet running sound of an electric motor above our heads. Looking up at the ceiling, we could see it moving back to reveal the stars shining in a velvet black background. It was a wonderful moment to take in, and remember that here we were marvelling at this innovation in the picture house world when the city in general was utterly impoverished. Also, the audience here were made up strictly of service personnel.

Our leave ended all too quickly and we had to leave our newfound living behind and return back into the desert. The luxury of the clean white sheets, now just a passing memory. Going to Shafto's picture house now was rather a comedown for us after the highlights of Cairo, but endured it would have to be.

It was not very long before I found myself on a guard duty, and on the night in question, I did a stint of duty with a fellow guard of two hours on and four off throughout the night. The time I mentioned was around two o'clock in the morning and as both of us were patrolling around the camp area my colleague decided to slip away, for what reason I had no idea but it could have been for a quiet smoke among other things. So alone, which was strictly forbidden, I patrolled on what I would call the southerly facing side of the camp, hoping that the orderly officer would not be making an appearance, otherwise I would have some explaining to do. My senses were on full alert for the footsteps of anyone other than the other half of the guard.

My attention was drawn upwards into the dark night sky, and at this point saw a light appear. As I watched, I became transfixed with the vision of something that was most unreal and not of this world.

It became a band of light growing in length and was coloured. To be truthful, I stood there in awe at what I was witnessing (the thought of the orderly officer completely removed from my mind). After a minute or two, it stopped growing in length and was straight, but the band of light remained in the sky for about fifteen minutes. Then it began to fade from the end it had started until it was gone. What I had seen was something extraordinary and possibly not in our own solar system. What I saw that night I never related to my friends, but looked on it as a sign for good.

It was about the beginning of May when most of us in the mortar platoon were sent as an advance party up into Palestine to make a camp there for the battalion. We were transported in 3-ton lorries up to the Gaza Strip, and then boarded a train for our journey across the desert, ending up at our campsite about twenty miles south of Tel-Aviv. The journey on the train was rough and one of the men commented that the seats were upholstered in wood. He had a point there, they were!

We all worked very hard at pitching the tents, which had to be geometrically correct. The officer in charge even used a compass to obtain the maximum result. On our second day there, the work was abruptly halted with orders to return to our camp in Egypt. What a waste of endeavour, working away in that heat and with many tents already erected. No reason was given for this about-face.

So, back across the desert by train, then in the transports back into Egypt, till we eventually arrived back at Sidi-Bish feeling somewhat bewildered by the turn of events. We found out soon enough what had happened to call us back from the 'Holy Land'.

On our return, we found that the commanding officer and the company commanders were all on leave in Cairo, leaving our own platoon officer in sole command of the battalion. We didn't have to wait long to know who was in charge. The battalion was called on parade where the platoon officer addressed us. "A Greek Brigade, who were under orders to sail from Alexandria to the Italian mainland to fight, have regretfully mutinied. Now it's fallen to our lot to go and make them change their minds, and I would remind you that 'ours not to reason why, ours is to do and die!'" Everyone on the parade condemned him for his unfeeling attitude to the matter in hand.

That same evening, we left Sidi-Bish for the last time, and even Shafto's picture house looked grand and a haven from our thoughts as to what could happen over this rebellion by the Greeks. By this time, we had been supplied with carriers and mortars that were left behind at Anzio during the battalion handover. The carriers were now driven onto Scammel transports, two on each with the crews sitting in their respective places.

There was no doubt that the time for parley was over, and now it would end with a clash of arms. Riding up in the carrier at that time in the evening, with the sun having just set, you had a job to breathe, even with the airflow of the moving vehicle on your face. It felt like you were sitting in front of a hot oven with the door open.

After a miserable journey, we arrived at our destination on the outskirts of Alexandria. We were then told to stay put, and very much later received news that it was all over (thank God). Unfortunately, there was one fatality; the shooting dead of a major who had been trying to negotiate with them. This is the price of war, paid for in blood.

They decided to hold the battalion where we were and finished up by moving to an oasis about six miles from Alexandria. It was a pleasant enough place except there were no facilities for leisure (no Shafto's). We spent a few days doing nothing in particular except light drill and cleaning our equipment. We even had our platoon picture taken with the oasis in the background.

Then, without any kind of warning, a rumour went round that the battalion was to be disbanded and all the men would be able to transfer to any unit of their choice, however they must remain in the 56 Division. This was a blow to all of us, but I suppose it was inevitable after the battalion had suffered such a disaster. It was official and it would take place on the 15th of May 1944. Most of the younger men in the platoon, myself included, decided to join the 8th Battalion The Royal Fusiliers, while others would go their separate ways in the division.

Firstly, members of the battalion were invited to a farewell dinner with two sittings on the 11th and 12th of May in Alexandria. The platoon went on the 11th. It being a very nice meal; the menu was tomato soup, roast chicken, roast potatoes, vegetables, caramel cream and tea or coffee. After this, we all trooped into a most wonderful picture house in the city to end a most enjoyable evening. This was all paid for by our funds in the battalion that had to be used up. We were soon told that the 8th Royal Fusiliers had accepted us, and when the day came, it was sad for us all at leaving our friends.

Before we said goodbye, each of us were given a commendation paper from the CO which began with:

```
Lieut-Col. W A Heal,
Commanding 10th Battalion,
The Royal Berkshire Regt,
M.E.F
```

With our name, rank and number, it said:

```
I would like to thank you, who are serving in the 10th Battalion The Royal Berkshire Regiment at the time of its disbandment on the 15th May 44, for all you have done for the Regiment.
You know as well as I do what this Battalion has done during its existence, and the name it has made for itself. It is up to us that is left to see that the Battalion is never forgotten. I wish you the very best of luck, and a speedy return to your homes.
W A Heal
Lieut-Col.
```

It was just a small scrap of paper, but which said it all from the well-meaning officer who had lost his command.

All of us transferring to the 8th Royal Fusiliers sadly boarded onto our transports, after shaking hands with our old friends, and waved to them when we moved away. I had mixed feelings about the move, but I need not have worried unduly about it as it turned out at our destination, somewhere in the desert, that we had come to a good purpose built camp with nice wooden huts, each of them holding a full platoon with good wicker beds to sleep on.

All of us from the mortars were taken in, doing what we had done in the old battalion. They seemed a favourable bunch of men in the platoon, doing what they could to settle us in. The camp also had buildings other than quarters for the men, with a grand picture house, small shops and, would you believe it, a large British NAAFI (Navy, Army and Air Force Institutes) where you could get buns with tea or coffee; a nice clean establishment where we would spend many happy hours of our spare time in most congenial surroundings. It was indeed a very large improvement on our previous camps where there were no facilities like this available to us.

We soon got into our training with the other members of the platoon, and all of us worked very well together out in the sand dunes of the desert. The platoon officer was a Captain Waller who if he were to stand sideways, you would almost fail to see him he was so thin. Also, in time, we found he was not very knowledgeable with the mortar and its working roll. That could prove very unhelpful to the rest of us. Other than that, he never overstepped the mark with discipline, which was good. The training in the desert was warm work lugging the mortar around, but that seemed better than sitting in the hot metal of the carriers.

One day out on an exercise, the captain asked one of the men, Private Bowering, to "Paint me a picture of the exercise so far." Bowering turned to the officer and said, "Who do you think I am, bloody Rembrandt?" Captain Waller didn't even blink an eyelid at the reply, but carried on as if nothing had happened. I thought it all very remarkable.

We did guards at the camp, outside Battalion HQ, and there was a wooden awning that you could adjust to keep out the hot sun. It was in the main the most agreeable place and none of us had any kind of complaints.

A group of men were detailed off to make up a party of about company strength who would then represent the battalion, with the band (who were our stretcher-bearers when the battalion was in the line), in the 'King's Birthday Parade'. This would take place in Cairo on the 8th of June. All elements of the 56 Division would be taking part, also with their bands. We were soon knocked into shape and were as ready as anyone could ever be for the event.

One morning, after walking to the NAAFI for our midmorning break, we saw many men talking around the entrance in an excitable manner and with some jubilation showing on their faces. Coming up to them, one of the men turned to us and said, "It's on the BBC News, the second front's started in France with landings over a wide area, and it's going well." The date was the 6th of June 1944, and it would remain a very vivid memory and a talking point for a long time to come.

The morning of the 8th of June saw us on parade bright and early. We were dressed in KD shirts and shorts, with top socks and highly polished boots. We also had to blanco our webbing belts and gaiters, brasses on belt, polish fusilier cap badge and, with rifle and bayonet, we lined up for the CO's inspection who told us it was an excellent turn out, he being well pleased with us. Our shirtsleeves were rolled up uniformly, then the quartermaster sergeant came round with a tin of starch and brush and wetted our rolled up sleeves that soon stiffened up in the hot sun. This was to stop our sleeves unrolling when we were marching in the parade.

The band and troops boarded the transports and started off on our journey to Cairo, a goodly distance away. Later, having arrived at the forming up area, the formations moved into position for the 'march past'.

Major Green (who was unfortunately killed on our return to the Italian conflict) led our contingent of the 8th Royal Fusiliers on the parade.

In the official programme of the event, we were billed as a North London Division and not the 56 Division, which would be a giveaway to the enemy that we were now in Egypt and not Italy. The Queens Regiment would be leading our part of the parade with us being the second formation. The saluting base, holding all the dignitaries, was about half a mile ahead, then after, we would be showing the flag around other parts of Cairo.

We could hear the command of the Queens formation for the march to get underway with their band starting to play. Then our turn came, and off we went with our own band playing away at some piece of martial music. After us, it was the skirl of the bagpipes of first the London Scottish, then the London Irish, and so on back down the line of march.

We had not marched far before we started to break step, and you soon begin to look like a slovenly bunch. This was the fault of the bass drummers in the various bands who were beating out of kilter with the marching troops, and it very soon developed into a shambles, breaking our step more often than we should. Then they decided to have a larger interval between the marching units, so each band would not influence the other with their tempo of the drumbeat.

This was a big improvement, just listening and marching to your own band. We arrived at the saluting base and given an "Eyes—right!" and "Eyes—front!" by the commander of our unit, Major Green, as we marched by the many dignitaries on the stand with the salute taken by Lord Killearn, the British ambassador in Egypt.

The hard part being over, we now marched alongside the cheering crowds, lots of them clinging onto lampposts for a better view. Some were taking photographs of the event and calling out to us where we were able to obtain a copy. Having arrived at our dispersal point, we were given something to eat and drink, and then onto the transports and returned to camp.

About the middle of July, we were told that the battalion would be returning to Italy, the news sending a chill of apprehension through us after our peaceful stay in the desert, away from the trials of war. We had to return to fill the gap made by another division, who like us before needed a rest from the strife after months of active service.

Fighting on the Western Front was now bogged down with stiff opposition from the enemy. While in Italy, the offensive had somewhat stalled many miles north of Rome. So what would our roll be?

14. Return to the peninsular. Rome.

The sad day came to leave the camp for the last time. With transports to take us to Port Said, we had to leave behind our carriers and mortars, but would draw new ones later. At Port Said, we boarded our P&O cruise liner that had been stripped of all its luxurious fittings and left just the decks below for our eating and sleeping accommodation.

It was thankfully an uneventful voyage back across the Mediterranean and into the bay of Taranto. One little event I kept in mind about the journey was that our contingent shared the ship with men of the Queens Regiment. One of them was Stanley Nicholls who had been with us in the 10th Battalion Royal Berks, and was on a course when the rest of us decided on going into the 8th Fusiliers while he, on returning, found that he had been posted into the Queens. This was most unfortunate.

Meeting onboard ship, we told him that if we had known he would have joined us in the Fusiliers. He told us that he'd been promoted to lance corporal in charge of an infantry section, and would I do him a favour by sewing his stripes on for him, saying, "I know you will do it better than me." So sitting on deck, in the sunshine, I started with meticulous care to make a good job for him. After the job was finished to my own satisfaction, I told him to try his battledress blouse on which he did with some embarrassment but also with some pride that he was now an NCO.

Our journey soon ended with us coming into the bay of Taranto, from where we had left more than three months before. Coming into the port, we all said goodbye to Stanley and wished him well.

When we came off the ship, we climbed onto the transports that were waiting for us dockside to take us back in stages to the war we had temporarily left behind. In the next few days, with many short journeys travelling north, sometimes sleeping outside in two-man tents or in buildings that had been specially earmarked for our use, we reached a place called Tivoli, about 20 miles from the Eternal City where at Anzio we had failed to reach.

Here, we were miles from anywhere with fields and small farms for company, but we were under canvas in decent sized tents, so we could spread our mosquito nets over us at night. It was now into August and high summer, and the mosquitoes would bite you to death if given the chance. We also had to take our mepacrine tablets every day, unless you wanted to get malaria, and nobody in their right mind would wish for that. Again, it was an Army order that the issuing and seeing of you take your mepacrine tablet was supposed to be administered by an officer, but that was rarely carried out.

We did light training here, mostly of finding our way back to camp in small sections after walking miles away and then getting back with the aid of a compass. At this stage, we in the mortars were still without carriers or our weapons; they would be picked up later on our journey north.

An Army order had stated (we were now in the 8th Army) that all personnel who had fought in the battle for Rome were to be granted a day's leave there. Our turn came round to visit the city, and in that I must say I was not disappointed. You can't visit Rome without paying a visit to St. Peter's and the Vatican, the most wonderful of sights one could ever imagine. The grandeur of the building outside was more than matched by the splendour inside. With the wonderful paintings and statues that were very lifelike in their pose and had been standing, looking on at the pilgrims to St. Peter's for many a century, with one biblical figure with its bare feet having had its toes almost kissed away by the devout pilgrims of the past and present. The scale of the dome was vast with its magnificent and ornate decorations running around its perimeter. But how did they do it with the tools of the day available then?

During our visit, we were told by the Swiss Guards, who were everywhere on duty, that there would be an audience with the Pontiff in a side chapel that morning and all soldiers were invited.

We walked to the chapel, which was filling up with a good number of Americans from 5th Army. We found some seats vacant and sat down. Before very long, a hush descended on the men and we all came to our feet in respect, as the Swiss Guards carried the Pope, Pius the XII, passed us down the hallway in what you would call an ornate sedan chair that looked very solid and required several men to carry.

After the Pope reached the front of the hall, he stepped out and addressed us in perfect English. "You may think it strange, but till a short time ago I was speaking to an audience of German soldiers in this very chapel. They came here like yourselves, to find peace in a hostile land at war, with brother fighting brother which can never be right in the eyes of God. We can only hope and pray that the war may very soon be over, and that you will all return safely to your homes and live in peace with one another." The Pope then said a prayer for us all and finished with his papal blessing, and returning to his chair, the Swiss Guards carried him away while we came to our feet again.

Rome will have had many millions of pilgrims pass through St. Peter's since August 1944. However, none of the pilgrims could have been affected more by the poignancy of the times and his message to us, along with the feelings we held in the dark days of the war, of our meeting with the Pope.

Afterwards, we went on a tour of the city and paid a visit to the Coliseum, but after coming away from St. Peter's, with its still small voice of calm, and then coming to this place of violence, I was rather disappointed with it all. Rome was indeed a very fine looking city and we visited a building where Mussolini used to speak to a crowd below, from its balcony, with much ranting and raving to stir up his Fascist friends. He was a very vain man and when he was speaking to the faithful below him, he would stand on a wooden platform to make him out to be taller than he really was. We also went to have a look at the Tiber River with its great historical past, but to us it was just one more river.

At the end of the day, it was time to leave the Eternal City and rendezvous at the King Victor Emanuel monument. Sitting on the magnificent steps there, waiting for the transports, we talked about our day before moving back to Tivoli. It had been a wonderful experience for us with its memory lingering on in that most unusual day out in Rome.

Our peaceful stay in Tivoli soon ended. Once more, we moved up the peninsula, always moving nearer to the war. The next stop was many miles north at a place called Narni and, fortunately, we had good billets here in this small village. All our good fortune went a step further when we found out that a Fusilier officer, who had been wounded in action but kept on in Italy to run a bakery, ran the Army bakery in the village. He soon made sure that his old battalion was well supplied with fresh, crusty loaves, the likes of which none of us had eaten in many a long day.

While here, all the men in the battalion who could drive a carrier were detailed to be taken south to an Army transport depot to pick up the battalion carrier quota. The plan was for us to be driven down to the depot in the daytime, fill up the carriers with petrol, oil and water, and then make sure they were in working order. Then we would start our journey back in the evening and drive through the night, arriving back about midmorning the next day.

It was going to be a journey of about 80 miles, and the new carriers must be driven with due care, with a maximum speed of not more than 15 miles per hour till the engines had been run in.

About twenty of us made the trip, taken in a 3-ton lorry, and found the carriers in a vast park. There must have been a hundred or so of these brand new Canadian-built carriers parked there. We were allowed to pick the one we wished to drive back with. We did our own maintenance and checked most things that could go wrong, like the shedding of tracks if one of the track-pins came loose. With petrol, oil and water in the radiator onboard, I then checked the starter, which fired first time telling me that the battery was well charged. Then I was ready for the trip.

Before starting off, all of us had a briefing about what to expect and be expected of us. "The lorry will travel in front and will go very slowly, so the convoy of carriers can keep in touch with one another. When it becomes dark, we can switch on our shaded lights, and hope no enemy aircraft are around. In case of carrier trouble, the battalion's REME (Royal Electrical and Mechanical Engineers) will be in the rear to assist, so we should manage. So now go back to your carriers and start up."

The lorry started off and we crawled out behind with a tail that must have been two or three hundred yards long, and with the noise of the tracks on the road you were unable to hear the engine of the carrier in front. With darkness falling, the carriers switched their lights on and it looked most weird in a country at war, but later in the night the moon came out, showing us the way in most beautiful surroundings as we moved through village after village. When we came to the town of Narni, by the light of the moon, it looked like the most wonderful place to be. In fact, it made a lasting impression on me.

During the drive, I saw one or two of the carriers breakdown and were passed by and left to the mechanics in the REME to take care of them. After being awake for so many hours, it was a wonder that I could keep my eyes from closing with the fatigue I felt. Then the veil of night lifted with streaks of brightness appearing in the sky heralding the dawn of a new day.

With the daylight, it made for less difficult driving conditions and to know we were well on the way. After reaching this stage, I hoped that I wouldn't be breaking down.

We arrived back at Battalion HQ and, after having a late breakfast, were instructed to get a few hours sleep. Some of the carriers limped in at intervals during the day while others were more than a day late in returning. With the carriers now with us, it was time to be issued with our mortars and ammunition before moving on again (and wishing we could take the bakery with us).

Moving on again was just the case of the battalion moving ever closer to the frontline, till it was our turn to become involved in the grand plan the high command had for the division. This next move found us not many miles from Perugia, or for that matter Assisi – a place of great historical renown. Our training increased in preparation for the return back to the struggles that lay ahead.

One day, out on a route march with the company and all the officers present, we were walking along a straight road that led up to Assisi, which could have been barely two miles away. At the time, the road was empty, hot and dusty. Then, in the far distance, we discerned a figure coming towards us and as it loomed ever closer, we were able to see it was a British soldier. Then we saw he was a full corporal and to cap it all, I recognised the face of a man I had known way back in my school days.

On coming abreast of the head of the column, he gave the officers a salute that would have done credit to a guardsman. Then coming alongside us, I called out to him, "Hello Ken!" and he looked among us with startled amazement at hearing his name called out. Then we were gone, marching off into the heat haze, and left the man wondering who had spoken from the ranks to him.

A day or so later, we had a chance to try out our new mortars with live ammunition, but it was in a suspect condition and unsuitable for use in the frontline when firing over the heads of your own men in close support. The platoon commander, Captain Waller, positioned his mortars at the edge of a ploughed field with our own baseplate nesting in a furrow, when it should have been on solid or firm ground.

Each detachment then mounted their mortars and having set their sights on the aiming posts were ready to fire. The captain gave the order, and having taken the 10lb bomb from Number Three, I placed it in the barrel and released it where it rattled down the steel tube till it reached the firing pin at the bottom. Thump—, the bomb sped away with the baseplate being forced back out of the furrow and onto the welt of my boot, giving me a great deal of pain in the process. I jumped back from my position, doing what would resemble an Indian war dance while my colleagues looked at me in mystification at my antics. Pulling myself together, and with a show of bravado that I didn't feel, I said, "Nothing wrong." I turned back to the mortar and carried on, ignoring the pain and nausea I was feeling with the throbbing in my foot.

After the shoot, with the ammunition expended, we packed the mortars back onto the carriers and returned to camp, but now I had a dilemma. My next step should have been a visit to the medical officer after what had happened at the mortar site. However, I could be in some trouble for doing this.

The flaw in paying a visit to the MO was in as much that I would be placed on the battalion sick list at a time when the battalion was expected to return into the line. He would report me to the commanding officer who may hold a court of inquiry into the accident and find against me that I had deliberately caused a self-inflicted injury, prior to our imminent return to the battlefield. In my own mind, I could never accept that tag or branded for cowardice in the face of the enemy.

For my pains, I would have to suffer it, almost like an act of penance. I tended it the best I could with cold water, but that night I had very little rest with the foot throbbing most painfully. In the morning at reveille, I found the foot had turned black and the big toe nail pressed down into the nail bed with dried blood that had oozed from around the nail.

I managed to get my sock and boot on and just hoped that no one would suspect my injury. Walking was hard work, placing my foot very gingerly to the ground every time I took a step and trying not to draw attention to it, but I did manage in spite of it.

Once again, we had to move ever nearer to our ultimate position with the battalion bivouacked in a series of hillocks, in two-man tents. It was while here we had a pep talk from the brigadier, James Scott-Elliot, who was commanding general of 167 Brigade. We sat around him while he unfolded the 8th Army plan for the new campaign, and our own roll in the big new offensive that would be taking place. He went on to tell us that we would be living a Spartan existence. Our carriers would be loaded down with petrol and ammunition, with no time for other aspects of living other than to advance through the enemy lines by what he reckoned would be between twenty and twenty-five miles a day. This was the big push to clear the enemy from the Po Plain and close up to the river.

He made it sound so feasible but we, knowing the enemy of old, were rather sceptical of the whole thing, as we would be attacking prepared positions that the Germans had named 'The Gothic Line'.

It was now the end of August and we were on the move again, taking us this time diagonally across country to the Adriatic side of the frontline and close up to the high ground above the Foglia River. We had arrived and were now ready to deploy when the order was given.

From this vantage point, you could look down into the valley where our 25-pounder guns were sited, firing at intervals over the high hills beyond at targets obscured from our view. It would very soon be our turn to take a hand and not just be onlookers. During the day, we saw a long file of men coming out of the line down the hillside, hardly discernible at that distance, and their progress looked painstakingly slow. It was men of the Queens Regiment who had been in action and were coming out for a well-earned rest, bivouacked in and around the 25-pounder guns.

In the early morning of the 3rd of September, we could hear the roar of tanks, in the main Shermans that were using vast amounts of fuel in low gear, and there were hundreds of them moving along a minor road from where we camped. Even before we saw the tanks, their presence was heralded by a strange phenomenon of a very hot wind that was frightening in the extreme. The tanks were consuming many gallons of petrol per mile, and with over 400 of them, it had caused the wind to blow like a sirocco only much warmer. They came by us in numbers I thought would never end, all moving forward to be in the right position when the infantry made a gap for them in the hope of a breakthrough.

As dusk descended that day, the Luftwaffe paid a visit to the guns in the valley below. The enemy knew they were there and had come to try and silence them after the hammering their frontline infantry had taken from them. What they couldn't have known was that British infantry had been deployed along the gun-lines, so in effect it was a double target for the Luftwaffe. There were several planes that made the attack, coming in very low and releasing their deadly cargo of butterfly-bombs onto the unsuspecting troops. The noise of the bombs detonating was one continuous roar of sound from the valley. The aircraft then having made their pass over the target disappeared into the gloom, leaving behind a rising pall of smoke – and the dead and wounded.

There was no time to dwell on the tragedy just witnessed, for we moved out early next morning with the task of taking a hill feature beyond the hill we had looked on for the past few days. We found we were most fortunate, in that the enemy had pulled back from their old positions and into others, however with better fortifications constructed by engineers of the Todt organisation who had been working on them for a long time. The defences ran across Italy, from coast to coast, and in places rather formidable.

The battalion's next order was to take the next hill feature. Once again, the enemy had retired into new positions, leaving us with one prisoner who had been overlooked by his comrades when they moved out.

Having just climbed the hill, I was detailed by the captain to escort the prisoner to the bottom of the hill and hand him over to the rear troops. We started down and he placed his hands on his head – the sign of surrender – and I could see that he was only a boy of between sixteen and seventeen years of age. I told him with my own hands and a shake of the head to put them down which he was pleased to do. On reaching the bottom of the hill, I turned him over with orders to send him out of harms way. I started back to rejoin my own comrades.

My foot was still giving me trouble with a slight limp, but I was coping with the situation, be it that I wasn't a fit soldier at the time. The battalion was ordered forward to make contact with the enemy, and a passage was found for the carriers to move up the next hill feature. The mountainous terrain looked very difficult for the carriers, being so loaded down. Climbing in bottom gear was hard going. Then we experienced a sharp crack from our carrier that stopped dead in its tracks.

The platoon of mortar carriers came to a halt while the damage to ours was accessed. Some of the drivers confirmed that the half-shaft had snapped, making the carrier and crew immobile till it could be repaired. Captain Waller said, "The platoon must move on!" However, he told our detachment commander, "You are responsible for the safety of the vehicle and its contents, and when it's repaired report back to Battalion immediately. You must make the best of it with what you have."

The carriers moved on, leaving us to our own devices miles from anywhere. We did have some luck, in that we were a few yards away from an old farm building, inhabited by a very old farmer and his wife. We asked his permission to bed down in one of his empty rooms till rescued by the REME. In truth, we did ask but he had no choice in the matter.

The guard we mounted on the carrier was done with conviction, knowing that our colleagues were somewhere in the line. How they were faring we had no knowledge. Insects around here gave us a bad time during the hours of darkness in spite of using the insect repellent and having a fine mesh over our steel helmets.

Next day two of our crew, Norman Sadler and Lofty Bowring, found a chicken wandering about and immediately liberated it. They decided to roast the unfortunate creature in a tin that came with our hard biscuits in the compo rations we received. It was cooked outside over a wood fire, suspended over the flames, and the smell was very enticing as it was cooking. So, we awaited the feast with great anticipation, but waited in vain for our portions were too tough to eat. Did the old farmer have a decoy chicken, very old for an emergency like us, while keeping the young hens safely locked up in a pen?

On the following day, we saw a comic event take place that made me suppose the farmer had been ultra careful in concealing his valuables from the eyes of the soldiery of both sides till the war had passed his land by. However, the farmer had been more fortunate than hundreds of others with their farms totally ruined by the ferocity of the fighting that had taken place.

Out the back of the farm was a field of about 10 acres with a tree standing in the middle, and walking round the tree was the farmer and a man from a neighbouring holding. We were watching them in seclusion and they were obviously having strong words with one another by the gestures they were making with their hands. Then one of them started to pace distance from the tree and our interest aroused considerably by their antics. There was some disagreement between them, when one of them went back to the tree and paced out in a different direction of the compass to his colleague.

After much rumination on their part, they finally decided and, containing our mirth, it was X marks the spot. Having pushed a stick in as a marker, they picked up tools from behind the tree and started to dig in the most careful manner. The outcome of this was that the farmer was retrieving his valuable property from the cache they had concealed from the armies of both sides.

We had visitors in a jeep from the REME who at last had come to work on the carrier and soon replaced the broken part. On leaving, they suggested to us that we try a new route back to the battalion.

We packed our kit back onto the vehicle, took our leave of the old farmer, and with the carrier in reverse, it backed down the slope with us crew walking to make the weight less onboard. At the bottom, we found another track that we hoped would take us back to Battalion HQ.

After travelling someway down the track, we came to a dried-up stream with rather high sides. After looking at the problem, the detachment commander told the driver to give it a try, which he did without success. We removed the digging tools from off the carrier and started work on digging a ramp with a gentle slope for the carrier to climb. In all, we must have removed several tons of soil in making the ramp, even with all of us lending a hand it was to take some time in its construction, but it had to be right.

Raymond, our carrier driver, had been with us in the 10th Battalion. He was first rate at his job, and when he told us that should do it, we moved out of the way. Starting the engine, he eased it onto the incline, where at the top it dropped with a crash onto firm ground. We congratulated him and climbed back onboard, moving on again.

Before long, we were running between low stone walls about 3 feet high, built on both sides of this narrow track and must have been cattle barriers. After about a mile, the carrier stopped dead, for lying in our path was a dead mule, no doubt killed by gunfire. We were now in real trouble with no easy way of escape, so we had a conference on the options left open to us and they were very few.

It was impossible to take the wall down and drive round the poor animal, that would have taken too long, or we could reverse all the way back down the track and dig a ramp on the other side of the stream, but that was really out of the question for the same reason. So, we tried moving the mule, but found to our utter disgust it was crawling with maggots, having been dead a long time. There was only one way out – run over the unfortunate animal.

We all moved to the other side of the track while Raymond very carefully drove his carrier over the carcase. We were standing about fifteen yards away, but the moment he touched it our throats were assailed by the most obnoxious smell that made all of our throats sore with a job to speak. As for Raymond, he said he felt sick. And as for the carrier, one of the tracks and sprocket were covered with the dead flesh. The stench was most nauseating. After climbing back onto the carrier, we had to suffer the smell and hoped that we could find a fordable river, so it could be washed off. Before we came to the end of the track, we could hear gunfire in the distance.

Later, the sight of a river that the carrier could cross granted our wish. But first, Raymond had to screw the starter handle cap in position; otherwise the water would rush in. After being in the river, the smell was bearable but remained on the carrier for many a long day. We later came out onto a secondary road that led at right angles from where we had come, but we had to move towards the sound of the guns. After rolling on for over a mile, we saw a most unusual sight before us of our 25-pounder guns pounding away at a hillside over open sights at about 3 miles distance, and you could see the individual shell bursts on its slope.

At last, we arrived at Battalion HQ who in turn directed us to our Platoon HQ. Once there, we were told a very dismal tale of what had happened since we went missing.

15. Croce and the battle of the ridges.

The battalion had attacked the village of Croce, that was on the crown of the hillside we saw being shelled, but had been forced off by a strong German counterattack who, with tanks, had inflicted heavy losses and on subsequent battalions who had tried in vain to take the village. Croce was taken only when the village was bypassed.

Croce had been a total loss for the brigade. All the battalions involved in the battle had grievous losses with the battalions sorely depleted and with no hope of replacements. Our detachment had thankfully missed all this, with our friends in the platoon telling us that the enemy shelling there had been on the scale of Anzio. The half-shaft breaking on the carrier had worked in our favour for once, and I felt most grateful for it, being spared this episode.

The 8th Army became bogged down in a number of hill features or ridges that ran inland from the coast and were heavily defended by the enemy, curtailing the advance that had been hoped for.

We moved several times with the battalion engaging the enemy, at times losing men who could never be replaced. At one stage, the Army was losing almost a battalion every day in killed, wounded and missing, and this was when you had no reserves. The battalion made a night attack and advanced over 3 miles against light opposition. In most cases, you could only move on when the villages on the hills that had the fortifications were bypassed without a frontal attack.

While here, I was again detailed by the captain to go as escort, with a jeep and its driver, to carry ammunition up to one of the companies we still had left to go into the line. There were no roads or tracks to move on, just rolling landscape covered with thorn bushes.

The driver had obviously been this way before, but was in too much of a hurry for my liking. We managed to reach the company without trouble, dug into the side of a bank facing towards the enemy. Company HQ was established in a large cave, dug out by the Italians who lived around here, and would need some form of refuge to hide and be safe in from the warring factions. That time had come, but now it was partly taken over by the Company HQ staff. It was still full of Italians of all ages who were rather fearful of what was taking place.

We started unloading the jeep, when we stopped at the unmistakeable sound of an incoming shell, which was a large one and could have been a 210mm. They must have known of our presence here, hearing the noise of the jeep engine roaring away. It exploded not far away, making loose soil from the roof shower down on our heads. The next one landed, throwing a large chunk of shrapnel smacking into the wall at the entrance of the cave where I was standing. My better judgment compelled me to move back a step or two inside.

The shelling had now ceased, but the jeep driver had worked himself up into a state of some agitation and wanted to be on his way. He asked me if I was ready, so I jumped in and he was away as if the devil was after him.

I was unaware at the time, but the day before, the carrier platoon officer in his jeep with his driver had been killed by the blast of a near miss. When the bodies were removed from the jeep, those removing them were unable to find a mark on them to establish cause of death. Also, when they lifted the bodies from the vehicle, the men involved said it was akin to trying to lift a jelly out. If the jeep driver now had been aware of this tragedy the day before, I suppose he could be excused, but here he was driving irresponsibly like someone possessed.

The driver now had his foot down on the acceleration pedal in his attempt to escape from the shelling. The vehicle was racing away over the undulating ground, jumping about like a bucking bronco with me hanging on like grim death, when in his hurry he came too close to a thorn bush which whipped over the engine cover and laid-flat windscreen and caught the left side of my face, thankfully not my eye. But even then, he wouldn't stop till he was back at Battalion HQ.

I went in search of a mirror to see the extent of the damage done, where I found lacerations running across my face with plenty of blood. It was very sore, especially where I washed it off, and when I put in an appearance in front of the platoon, some wigs amongst them asked, "What her name was?" I found it most hurtful, and to contend with my foot at the same time. My face became swollen from the effect of the thorns, which must have had some noxious property in them, but I still carried on working in the platoon. I now felt I could be receiving medical attention, but still had a mania against reporting sick.

The war moved on with small gains made, but with terrible loss of life in taking the hill villages that stood in the way of the Army advance, each one needing a major attack to overcome the very stubborn defenders. We were not getting the advance the brigadier had advocated in his pep talk to us the month before. He had let his own imagination get the better of him.

Meanwhile, the American 5th Army had started off on their own offensive towards the city of Bologna. But here again the enemy were fighting for every yard of ground, and the gains made were not decisive enough to call it a breakthrough.

The truth was that large numbers of divisions had been plundered from American 5th Army for the landing in the south of France called 'Dragoon', and the same for the British 8th Army losing divisions sent to the Far East. It became a time of acute shortages in infantry replacements for both of the armies when attacking, when they should be at full strength.

The battalion was on the move again, this time closing up to the Marano River for a night attack, and by the time we moved our carriers, they were across. We moved the carriers under the cover of darkness down a lane leading to the river.

Before going far, Raymond, our driver, complained to the rest of us that the steering on the vehicle was pulling to one side. We all climbed out, trying our best in the dark to discover what was amiss, and looking at the rear of the carrier we found we had an extra passenger, in the shape of a dead cow being dragged along by a rear leg with its hoof caught in the sprocket. We had to move forward and Raymond did the only thing left to us – by hacking the leg off with a machete. Rather ruthless, but there was no respect for the dead or living here.

Moving on again, down the dark slope to the river, we came to the bank where there was plenty of cover for the carriers till we crossed over in daylight. And with its approach, we could see it wasn't a river but a dried-up riverbed we had to cross, rather wide with what looked like vines on the other side.

The day was well advanced when the order came to cross over. Unknown to us at the time, the neutral republic of San Marino overlooked the river with a good view of our crossing place, even if it was a mile or so away. Unfortunately, the enemy had the occupancy of San Marino. We crossed over and deployed among the vines, only to find a few minutes later that the gunnery officer, stationed in the principality, must have spotted us.

A group of shells fell in our vicinity and we looked round for cover, which was close at hand in the shape of enemy trenches. My friend, Norman Sadler, and I jumped into one in double-quick time with a sense of relief that they, the enemy, had given us a refuge. I had to lie on top of Norman, but we were reasonably safe there for the moment. More of the shells came over and we were showered with debris, so we pulled an old door that was lying there over the opening.

However, some of the men in the platoon had a touch of panic creep into them, and they started to run back across the riverbed that was mostly covered in flints. With more shells falling, they were caught out in the open with dire consequences for them in killed and wounded, but in the relative safety of our trench, Norman and I were unaware of this at the time.

During a lull in the shelling, we were able to reach up, out of the trench, and pick grapes from the vines. It was a most unbelievable situation, but then that's war.

After we had suffered a few more salvos, the shelling ceased and later we pushed the door aside and got onto our feet, but didn't leave the trench, instead called out to our friends who should be around us if they were all right. Receiving no reply, we called out again. This gave the two of us the impression we were on our own. We again shouted out loudly, and to our relief had the call returned and located them on the side of a high bank that towered over the dried-up riverbed.

We rejoined the rest of the platoon who were digging into the steep bank for some protection from the shelling. You were unable to dig the traditional slit trench, straight down into the soil, but you could carve a hole out to take your body, leaving your legs hanging over the side. It was the best you could do under the circumstances, and we were out of direct vision of any observer in the 'neutral' state of San Marino. The carriers were now swiftly driven into a natural cutout in the bank where they would be reasonably safe from the eyes and shelling of the enemy.

Later in the day, a Sherman tank came along underneath us, the driver looking for a place to park his 30-ton charge away from the guns of the enemy. He stayed but for a few minutes, then backed off in reverse from where he had come, keeping in tight to the cover of the bank.

We could look down and see where the tank had stopped by its track marks there. Then we were made aware of a shell coming our way that detonated, leaving a crater in-between the telltale track marks where the tank had been standing. If the tank had been there, it would have received a direct hit in the rear, most likely igniting the petrol in the tank, creating a fireball and exploding the ammunition carried onboard. It could have been a very hotspot for us.

Nightfall came and the mortars had still to be deployed to help the battalion if needed. So, we spent the night in our positions on the bank. I was feeling most uncomfortable with my legs hanging in space, which didn't help my bad foot, and with my face still burning and puffy from the lacerations, I was not up to being a very competent soldier. However, the night passed without the platoon called into action, so I was grateful for that.

We stayed in our position for two days just waiting to be called on, but the call never came. It's one thing risking your life to get into a position to support the battalion, but when you get there, you just do nothing. It becomes a wasted endeavour and more so for the killed and wounded who had helped to get us there.

We had to take a different route in crossing the river after the battalion had advanced. This we did at a fordable place, and when on the other side, we were witness to a great deal of devastation in terms of enemy transports, bumper to bumper in the leafy lanes of the other side. As to how they had perished was a mystery. It could have been gunfire or the Germans may have done it, being unable to move the transports out in time to get away?

The battalion, at this stage, was withdrawn from the fighting, and we bivouacked in a wood where we had a spell of very heavy rain and this made things very bad under canvas. While staying here, we received an announcement given by the platoon commander, Captain Waller. He told us that the battalion was going to be amalgamated into the 9th Royal Fusiliers, with the personnel of the 8th Battalion, employed in specialist occupations, found posts in the same positions. The rest were found similar posts in the brigade.

Later, we were detailed off to our new posts. A posse of us went into the 9th Battalion mortar platoon, with my best friend, Norman Sadler, having to leave us. He was going to the 1st Battalion London Scottish, and I felt it a sad loss.

This unexpected move was with immediate effect, and on our arrival at the 9th, the new platoon commander welcomed us, by the name of Captain Sherlock. It wasn't long before we learnt that the captain controlled his six mortars from his headquarters, in radio contact with two observers in their observation posts, forward with the infantry companies. We received the orders from HQ over the field telephones.

The Captain, on his own initiative, had introduced a new concept into the role of the mortars in the battalion. Firstly, he had the map references of the entire gun positions and they, in turn, transferred onto large, squared paper times 10/1 to the original Army ordinance survey maps. This made for greater accuracy in plotting the enemy positions when they came in via the radio from the OP, forward with the troops. A sergeant from the platoon manned the OP, and a man from the signals operated the radio, sending and receiving messages.

It was a new innovation and it worked very well when used later under battle conditions. The large, squared paper was drawn up by the headquarters staff and had to be mathematically correct and square.

We moved back into the line after a short rest, but now it was October and the rain descended in torrents from leaden clouds. It didn't look too good for the offensive, making movement off the roads most difficult with everywhere becoming waterlogged. Mud was now king.

Moving through the town of Savignano, we had now moved out of the endless hills into the Romagna country that was flooded.

The autumn rains had come and it could only help the enemy in their defensive positions. We moved up into the line through this very wet countryside, and would be our first action in the new battalion.

The rain started to slant down, as our two detachments of mortars dismounted from the carriers near an old farm building, ready to support the forward battalion when they made their attack, which was imminent.

A sergeant, by the name of Bill Gooch, took out his compass to take our target bearing and to position the aiming posts for the two guns to lie on. He found that wearing his steel helmet was effecting and playing havoc with the compass owing to its magnetic influence. The rain was still cascading down, but Bill gallantly removed his wide brimmed helmet, placed it on the ground and tried again.

After the aiming posts had been sited and pushed into the ground, already with his head absolutely soaked, Bill stooped down to retrieve his helmet and, unthinkingly, placed it back on only to find a deluge of water descend over his already soaked body. The now dejected sergeant felt a lot worse, minutes later, when news came through that the attack had been called off owing to the inclement weather at the time.

Later, we moved our position forward after the rain had temporarily ceased. We were close to an old farmhouse where we could eventually try and dry our clothing, but first had to dig the mortar pit and our slit trenches in the wet soil.

The 1st Canadian Division were on our right flank and we could hear them taking a terrible pounding from the enemy who were using Nebelwerfers, possibly a battery of them with the number that we could hear falling onto the hapless Canadians. The Nebelwerfer was a six-barrelled mortar which fired rocket projectiles with a range of around five miles, each one weighing seventy pounds. This was a most formidable weapon and greatly feared by the infantry who called them 'moaning minnies' that could saturate an area with HE (high explosive). Indeed, it was psychologically a form of terror weapon with the noise it made on its journey and the devastating blast at the end of it. It always jangled my own nerve ends on hearing them coming our way.

We were called on many times in the next few days to give mortar fire support to the battalion whose companies were now having the brunt of the Nebelwerfers. Our own artillery poured hundreds of shells onto suspected enemy positions, but were unable to silence them since they were mobile weapons. They had a go at us, obviously picking up our own mortar fire on them, but they were wide of the mark. Nevertheless, it gave us an uncomfortable time with you thinking that each round is destined to follow you into your own trench.

The bad weather continued with no letup, so in the end we were issued with oilskins in the vain hope it would keep out the rain in the effort to keep us dry. The oilskins did help, but the rain soon found a chink in our armour. The water was able to permeate down between our necks and the oilskin collar, running down into our body clothing that made life most uncomfortable and cold without us being able to do much about it except suffer.

The area was systematically sprayed with machine gun fire, and at times it was too close for comfort. What with the autumn rains and the cold, and the enemy now standing firm on his new defence line, the campaign that had started with so much promise was now grinding slowly to a halt with everyone totally exhausted and in need of rest.

The American 5th Army, fighting in the mountains, were having the same troubles as us with daily mounting casualty lists and a shortage of infantry replacements. Their drive towards Bologna also came to an end with great loss of life on their side.

After a most miserable and wet stint in the line, we were relieved and moved back to good accommodation in a village but, unfortunately, the 25-pounder gun-lines were in and around our temporary home. They were blasting away at targets intermittently day and night, but to us it was out of the line for a rest. That night we slept the sleep of the just, guns or no guns, with a bed made up of one blanket on a cold floor. To us, it was in effect luxury to be away from the mortal danger you feel yourself in at the sharp end.

Next morning, we started first on our mortar that had to be cleaned and oiled after the atrocious weather it had been standing out in. Also, our rifles too had to be cleaned (the weapons having priority over all other considerations). Next, we turned our attention to our own kit, some of it like our boots was wet and muddy, and our webbing needed re-blancoing. In fact in all we looked in a very sorry state.

The platoon sergeant informed us that the commanding officer was coming to inspect, no doubt, his new intake into the battalion, and we had to parade with pullovers on and wear our unclean webbing. We formed up for his inspection, coming to attention when he arrived in his jeep. Lieutenant Colonel Cleghorn walked down the three ranks of men who were standing in mute silence unless spoken to. He asked questions to some. When he positioned himself in front of me, he looked me up and down, then asked, "Do you mend your socks?" to which I replied, "Yes, sir." Then in a raised voice full of sarcasm, he said, "Then why haven't you mended that hole in your pullover?" My answer to him, the only one I could give was, "It will be done, sir!" He moved to the man standing next to me, and looking him up and down asked, "When did you last have a bath?" and Raymond, our carrier driver, after a pause said, "Six weeks ago, sir!" The starch was taken out of the colonel, by what Raymond had said, and he quickly retired from the parade.

His criticism levelled at his soldiers had been ill-founded and the hole in my pullover was just a snag. What did he expect of us after coming out of the line and what did he expect of us at a moment's notice (groomed like guardsmen on parade outside the Palace)? No, we had just come from the battlefield where you can be killed with or without a hole in your pullover, not for us the nice clean conditions of Battalion HQ.

The very next day, all of us were sent to a mobile bath unit and came out looking like a bunch of red-faced cherubs after having lived in the mud without proper washing facilities at our disposal. Later, we were told to collect all our kit together and load up the carriers and prepare for a journey that would be taken in the hours of darkness, avoiding traffic on the roads in the daytime engaged in convoy work to and from the front.

No one had any idea of our destination, but word got around that we would be going out for a rest, but where? Just before starting out on our night drive, we learnt of our destination, which was south to a town by the sea with the name of Porto San Giorgio.

16. Porto San Giorgio.

It was a wearisome journey, and it was daylight before we arrived in the town of Porto San Giorgio. It looked a pleasant place to us after our 120-mile drive in the carriers, with us in the back with our feet and legs as warm as toast and the top half exposed to the elements. After some time your body feels frozen, a condition you had to endure.

Our billet was very good and the whole of Specialist Company were in quarters there. At some time, it could have been a school with an assembly hall and a balcony that was out of bounds to us. Later, this would be the venue for an officers' dance with the Italian women of the town invited to be escorted by them. The colonel, who was fortunate to have his good lady with him, transformed the battalion military band into a listen-able dance band.

Our training went on as usual, never missing a chance to keep us on our toes or bring us up-to-date on the platoon commander's new method of employing his mortars on the battlefield. We also had a reappraisal of the other weapons used by the infantry battalions other than a rifle, including the Bren gun, Thomson submachine gun and the Piat antitank gun that was a rocket launched projectile.

There was no live firing of the mortars owing to a global shutdown in the production of expensive munitions of war. So, all the guns in France and Italy had to curtail their offensives. The acute shortage of ammunition had come at a critical time in the war, having a decisive effect on the campaigns in both theatres of conflict.

One morning, we had a surprise visit from Norman Sadler, as the London Scottish were stationed nearby, as were the London Irish; the three of our battalions making up the 167 Brigade, all being out of the line for a long overdue rest. I thought my friend looked rather solemn from being the usually cheerful Norman that he was. He looked at us in a rather depressed manner and said, "I have some news about Stan Nicholls. They told me at the Queens Regiment camp that he was killed in his first action with them, when a shell landed at his feet." In the telling of this grim news, Norman almost broke down with emotion, and on hearing it, we were stunned that our close friend was dead at the age of twenty.

A few short weeks before, Stanley, who was on the same troopship, had asked if I would sew his stripes onto his battledress tunic because, he said, I would make a better job of it than him. Now he was long dead, unknown to us during our time in the line. This news made us think of our own insecurity, and with our eventual return into the line, it could just as well be our own fate.

It came our turn to stand guard outside the building we occupied, which was only a short distance from the sea. Our main task on the guard was to patrol in front of the PRI (The President of the Regimental Institute), the equivalent of the NAAFI in the battalion and exclusive for our use. Outside this establishment were several large barrels. These contained wine, procured by the sergeant in charge of the PRI, and he carried a lot of clout in procuring good rations for the officers' mess.

The wine was Marsala, in barrels that must have contained a hundred or so gallons each. It was sold every evening to the soldiery who frequently drank at the bar there, and on closing that night the place was locked up, but the barrels were not. It didn't take long for a member of the guard to discover what the barrels contained, and all the guard, with the exception of the two on duty, were soon sampling it. I was one of the two. Even the guard commander, who was a full corporal and always the most sober of men, joined in the pilfering of this copious supply of free wine.

Before long the entire off duty guard were inebriated, lying all over the guardroom floor in a drunken stupor, not even knowing that they were still on guard. We would all be in serious trouble if the officer of the day came round and found the guard drunk and disorderly, and not acting in a fit and proper manner. We would ALL face a charge of neglect of duty whether the two of us had been drinking or not. All of the guard were a part of collective security and, by rights, the two of us should inform the officer of the guards' unavailability to act in the event of an emergency. The two of us decided to sweat it out and hope and pray that the orderly officer would be too comfortable in his own bed to bother us. It was apparent to us, later in the night, that his bed had proved more secure than his sense of duty. We, the guard, had been saved from a nasty situation.

Sergeant Pepperell, who was short in stature and brains, was the platoon sergeant. He summoned me to Platoon HQ and informed me that I had been detailed to escort Sergeant Noaks of the Vickers gun platoon on a visit to Rome, taking with us a battalion deserter into the military prison there. We were issued with rations for two days, spending a night in Rome.

A driver with a 15 cwt truck was placed at our disposal and, after what seemed a very long journey, we arrived in the Eternal City after dark and placed our prisoner into the custody of the military police at the forbidding prison there. I did feel rather sorry for the man who had lost his nerve in the heat of battle. Seeing his comrades fall, he drifted away from the scene only to be caught later and tried before a general court-martial by officers with no legal training in law or psychiatric conditions that some of the soldiers were forced to endure with.

The driver had to take his truck into the Army motor pool compound for safekeeping and stay with it owing to the thieving going on in the city. This was not only by the Italian populous but also by some criminal elements in, or on the run from, the Army – American and English personnel. Indeed, it was a very sad country with its economy and most of the land in ruins and, above all, an acute shortage of food.

Sergeant Noaks and I found ourselves a billet for the night in a fine Italian building. It had seen better times, but we had a room each which we paid 200 lire for (under four shillings) and had a good night's sleep in a real bed with clean white sheets that were sheer luxury.

We started back on our journey as soon as possible and, after a long day, arrived back at Porto San Giorgio. I reported back to Sergeant Pepperell who having looked me over then told me, "You have been posted, in your absence, to a rifle company. You best get your kit together." I walked away from him feeling rather stunned at the news of leaving my friends behind, and why me? Before I reached our billet, the sergeant's voice called out, "It's not you leaving the platoon, it's someone else!"

After some time had elapsed, I found that no one had left the platoon, or was likely too. He had tried to make me jump after not putting a foot wrong since I joined the platoon. I realised later that he was a bad lot.

It was now the beginning of December, and all our thoughts were about returning back into the melting pot, it just had to be very soon. As far as we could ascertain from news made available to us, via the *Stars and Stripes* and 8th Army newspapers, was that the Italian front was now static. The American 5th Army were stalled before Bologna, after very harsh fighting, and would have to wait till spring when the snows cleared from the high mountains before continuing their offensive. With the 8th Army, they had moved out of the hills into the Po Plain, but had come to a halt on the Senio River flood banks. What kind of role would they find for us?

Our time at Porto San Giorgio ended and we collected our things together with the same kind of trepidation that one always felt at returning back into the unknown. The convoy of battalion vehicles pulled out of the town, and we were sorry to be leaving after our reasonable stay there in peace and security in this war-ravaged land.

It was a cold journey for us in the carriers, but within two hours, we arrived at our destination and told this was just a short staging post before our ultimate return to the sharp end. This was just one of the innumerable hilltop villages which is a sure feature of the Italian landscape and went by the name of Tolentino. We had come northwest from the coast, only about 30 miles, and were not far from the town of Macerata, which the Italians called 'the land of opera'.

Here, in the village, we had a marvellous view of the countryside with no sign of warfare having taken place in the near vicinity that was most unusual in this kind of terrain. This small village could boast of a fine auditorium with balcony seats in a half circle looking down on the stage. The Army film unit treated us to a picture show here.

I remember the theatre most for an inflammatory speech made to the 9th Royal Fusiliers by the brigadier, James Scott-Elliot. He talked about our past engagements with the enemy and the way the battalion had acquitted itself very well in the face of great opposition. Then, lowering his voice, he made a statement to us that was an infringement against the rules of international law while we sat in silent disbelief to his words, which were, "We are taking too many prisoners. I fought in the last war and believe they should be left here and not return to their homeland to cause us trouble in later years." I felt sure that the men, on hearing this, were sickened by the suggestion from such a senior officer who must have been well aware of the rules of the Geneva Convention. The rank and file were.

A few days later, a story circulated round the battalion that the brigadier was going home on Christmas leave while his brigade would have the comforts of Christmas in the line – in their frozen holes in the ground. This story I can't confirm, but I can vouch for what was said in the theatre at Tolentino. (Maybe not the exact wording of the brigadier's speech, but having the same unpleasant message and, most unfortunately, was true.)

We soon said goodbye to the village of Tolentino, and moved north once again. Later in the day, we moved through the town of Forli and into the open countryside beyond, into the Po valley at last, where we should have reached last September if 'The Gothic Line' campaign had come up to its expectations of advancing through the hills and dashing across the plains to the Po River itself. This, the planners had envisaged at the start but was never fulfilled in their time span. It was only after many months had elapsed before the Army had reached this point alone and having sustained fearful casualties along the way.

We were now moving through the flat countryside of the Ramagna, which was a maze of waterways and rivers, and after the heavy rains of autumn, they were in flood and the ground was indeed very wet. The land was ideal for farming and vines were grown in profusion here for the Italian wines.

It was the task of the battalion to clear out the enemy who were still here and drive them back up to the Senio River line, which our forces occupied in places but not along its entire length. We went into our first action and supported the rifle companies with our mortars when called for. The enemy resistance was sporadic, but fatal in consequence when they retaliated against our advance. The battalion made advances of between one to two thousand yards each day with thankfully few casualties. With hard frosts at night the ground became frozen, making it hard work in digging our mortar pits and personal slit trenches. It was a very physical task in the cold winter air, and with very poor rations, in the most part eaten cold, it was never sufficient for our needs.

Now it was Christmas Eve, and after our daily advance with light opposition, we once more started digging our holes in the frosty soil. The mortars were dispersed over a large area, one not being able to see the other. On the completion of our task, we mounted the mortar in the pit along with the cases of ammunition and used them to sit on.

Here, we talked about the reality of our own Christmas and what the folk back home would be doing. With the sun having long set and the stars appearing in the clear night sky, it was going to be a severe frost, and we hoped to be called back later to the headquarters farm. The sound of gunfire had long ceased and peace reigned along the line with the silence of the guns at the front, stilled for the first time in my memory since coming to this land.

We sat in the pit with our field telephone linked back to Captain Sherlock, at Platoon HQ, waiting for a call to lay the mortar onto a target and fire, but the call was never given that evening. Instead, the captain sent a message out to us, a broadcast from the Home Service programme of the BBC, picked up by the Army sending and receiving set in his HQ and relayed out to all the mortar positions. The phone sprang into life with the rendering of a traditional German Christmas carol of *'Silent Night'*, with the words of the first verse going, *'Silent Night! Holy Night! All is calm, All is bright!'* What kind of impression did those words have on the soldiers there who were cold, hungry, dirty and unshaven, but to have unashamed tears form in their eyes at the very privation of life in general? And, of course, the time and occasion indeed – *'All is calm, All is bright!'*

Later that night, we returned to HQ to get some rest before returning to the mortar pit by first light and stand-to (a likely time for enemy counterattack). With Christmas Eve having passed in peaceful tranquillity, I supposed it was too much in expecting the same kind of formula to be applicable over Christmas Day?

We soon found that the spirit of Christmas didn't prevail in the higher echelons of the Army. In their infinite wisdom, they had the battalion move forward into the attack on the morning of Christmas Day 1944. The very thought of peace and goodwill was out of the scope of the planners' mentality who only wished to move their little indicator flags forward on the maps, never mind the day. Our 25-pounder guns started firing from their positions, a few miles in our rear, with the salvos of shells screaming overhead to fall on the hapless enemy who like ourselves would have thought it a day of truce. What did one day matter when the war could soon claim six years to its credit list of death and destruction?

We moved the mortar and ammunition out of the pit and loaded up the carrier, and then moved up behind the advancing infantry till we found a suitable mortar position. Here, we found we were close to a large farm building, which looked the right place for us to shelter from the inclement weather that now prevailed over the continent of Europe. A few men in the detachment, me included, went up to the door, knocked and, after a pause with no one coming to answer it, opened the door and walked inside. We found a large room that occupied the first floor of the house and it was almost full of Italian men, women and children, about thirty in all, and was a gathering together from local farms in the vicinity.

They had come here for self-preservation while the warring factions passed through their land. Now they were safe, since the rifle companies of our own battalion had shortly gone through here in pursuit of the enemy. The people here were standing in silence, only giving us a cursory glance as we trooped in behind them. The Italians were standing with their faces showing a solemn demeanour. The reason for this was in the front of the room, where a priestly looking figure was making religious pronouncements in Italian for the celebration of Christmas with the obvious joy that the family groups here felt, spared from death or injury and their property saved from wilful damage.

All of us removed our steel helmets in respect of the sacred gathering, and stood in silence with the rest of them till their devotions for their deliverance came to an end. Some of the gathering in the room could now return to their respective homes now the foreign invaders, German and English, had more or less passed through their property. The worry they must have felt for a very long time, with the war ever coming closer, had been resolved in their favour. From now on, they should be free from the tyranny of war and, indeed, they were counting their blessings.

After we had sited our mortar and the guards posted, we moved our bedding rolls into the house. The Italian owner of the farm went out of his way in showing his hospitality to the apparent victor. He invited us to sit at his oversized dining table, so we could properly eat our own Christmas dinner that consisted of a tin of bully beef between our six-man crew. The Italian family had a Macaroni based meal, which was flavoured by what could have been goat meat. I hoped that they were doing better than us, back home.

The sounds of warfare were now stilled, and when not on duty outside, we sort the sanctuary of the warm house that held a good fire in its vast hearth. On Christmas night, those not on duty spent an agreeable evening with the Italian families who hadn't returned home. Some members of the families were very good-looking young ladies who sat round the table with members of the platoon and exchanged good humorous banter between one another.

Then photographs were produced of the platoon's loved ones back home, and in this cheerful atmosphere, we parted with our chocolate rations for the ladies and cigarettes for the men. It was a very pleasant Christmas night, being so far from our own families, but spent in the very spirit of Christmas, in peace and goodwill.

After doing our guard duty that night, we put our heads down in the warmth of the old farmhouse. In the morning (Boxing Day), we packed up our equipment and, to our surprise, moved back out of the line for a short rest to a place called Reda, a small village or hamlet in the back of beyond.

17. The Senio River line.

Within the last two weeks, we had been hearing news of a German counteroffensive taking place in the Ardennes, in Belgium, and later would be called the Battle of the Bulge. This was where the American 1st Army under its commander, General Hodges, was having a very bad time with a high casualty list and prisoners taken by the surprise and ferocity of the German counterattack. This was on top of the inclement weather, the worst for many years of deep snow and freezing conditions.

Orders were now coming from our own 8th Army HQ for caution and awareness to a similar attack on our own front. This could be just as disastrous with an order going out to the effect that all tracked vehicles must stand on a bed of straw, in the hope it would prevent the tracks from being frozen to the ground. This was so we could make a quick move in case of an emergency, like the successful German breakthrough in the Ardennes. The high command was very fidgety over this new development and didn't wish it to happen on the Italian front.

The mortar platoon had a good billet at Reda, having an upstairs room for our sleeping quarters, but with rather a cold aspect in our sleeping arrangements. An Italian husband and wife slept in the room next to ours, but had to pass through our room to go downstairs. The floor of our room had a base of cold stone blocks resting between the wooden joists, which unfortunately had gaps between them. This allowed the cold winter air to penetrate our two blankets and chill our bodies, which was most unpleasant. We overcame this the next night by placing on the floor a layer of sandbags, which were always carried on the carriers for any emergency (but not this one), and it did suffice and kept us warm.

After we had been here a day or so and settling in, we were told that we would be returning to the line on New Year's Eve, and take over from the London Scottish who would be coming out for their New Year's celebrations. Looking back over the past year, we had done this for them when we relieved them at the Garigliano River during the time we were in the 10th Battalion Royal Berkshire Regiment. We did, after all, spend a few pleasant days here at Reda. It was better than being outside in a mortar pit in the freezing weather.

One of the members of our gun crew, Lance Corporal Morgan, was reading a novel by Zane Grey, the author of Western stories. This one had the title *Wanderer of the Wasteland*, where the hero of the story finds himself dying of thirst in the desert and in his delirium calls out repeatedly for water. The corporal had been telling us about the plot of the story that evening, before retiring to his draughty bed on the floor.

Now the corporal, when he had fallen asleep, decided in a dream that he was the hero of the story lost in the desert. He started acting the part, calling out in his sleep and waking us all up in the process. "Water ... water ... water!" and then again, "Water ... water ..." until the man nearest to him gave him a good sharp prod, silencing his cry of mercy for a drink of water. The next morning, the corporal was teased over his imaginary incursion into the hostile desert wasteland of his dream.

New Year's Eve came all too quickly for us, and having stowed our equipment back onto the carriers, we waited for the order to move out from our latest sanctuary and return back to the mortal strife. At this stage of the war, we all thought that the New Year of 1945 would herald in, or have in sight, the end of the conflict. But now that the Germans had launched their counteroffensive in the Ardennes, it didn't look very likely anymore. What had they now in reserve when they could make such an advance into Belgium?

We moved out of Reda, into the cold dark night. After a short journey, we passed down a long, straight road and pulled off into a farmyard with its attendant buildings, which the London Scottish mortar platoon had till now occupied.

They were making a lot of noise for a takeover procedure when noise should be kept to a minimum at this crucial time. If the enemy became aware of this, they would very soon be sending their calling card with a vengeance in the shape of a barrage of shells. The trouble with the Scots was they had been celebrating already with vino, possibly liberated, so to speak, from the Italians here.

We had barely moved off the carriers when 'Crack'—, a German tank or antitank gun had fired down the axis of the road, making a hideous noise in its passing. They must have been aware of our presence, with the noise of our seven carriers moving, and retaliated against it with venom. After firing several rounds and not seeing any flaming vehicles to their credit, they stopped firing. It was a miracle that we hadn't continued any further along the road; otherwise some of us in the platoon would never have seen the New Year in. Such are the rigours of war.

We moved into the positions, vacated by the Scots, and soon settled down to our two-hour vigil, while those not on duty outside moved their belongings inside one of the numerous buildings around the yard. I unfortunately found myself with three others on guard duty. The cold was intense, but we had received our nightly rum ration, which you were entitled when in the line during the winter months. I was never a drinking man, but I must confess that the rum issue was always looked forward to in the cold weather. Some say it was given to boost our fighting spirit and called it Dutch courage. But the amount given each time was minimal and just enough to wet the bottom of our enamel mugs, but it was most welcome in the circumstances.

With the end of our two hours of guard duty coming to its close at midnight, we would be entering a New Year. What would it bring for us after the disaster of 1944 and the loss of so many good friends, and the near run battle of Anzio where we had almost been pushed back into the sea? Our minds remained smothered by the very memory of Anzio and its consequences on all who served there, in isolation from the main battlefront, and it would not go away.

Our guard relief came out to take over from us, so it must be New Year and, at that very moment, the darkness was lit up, turning it into day with the light of many flares from Verylight pistols arcing into the black night sky. Machine guns firing tracer bullets, racing up into the dark void of the sky until the phosphorous burnt out. It was an amazing display and it ended as abruptly as it started. The front returned to the stillness of the night. Was it just a celebration on the enemy's part, being an act of defiance for their undoubted success in the Ardennes, or on knowing that the war was as good as lost for them? Whatever it was, it had been well orchestrated to give maximum impact on all who did see it.

The front was very quiet over the New Year, but we were called upon to fire the mortars at times, like SOS calls coming in from Battalion HQ to break up attacks on the company positions. Our own artillery was not as aggressive as it had been in the past, and was not likely to be due to the acute shortage of ammunition for the guns.

One day, while in this position, some men in the platoon were snooping around in one of the barns when they found some very large wine barrels standing on end. In size, they were in the region of around 8 feet high by 4 feet diameter and would each hold many hundreds of gallons of wine. Climbing to the top of one with the help of a ladder, they found to their misfortune that all it contained was wood ash. When the man had climbed down again, his suspicions were aroused to the extent of why would they place the ash in the barrel? After talking it over between themselves, the snoopers decided to investigate it further.

Climbing back to the top again, he placed his hand into the ash and rummaged around, finding that the ash was only an inch or so deep and held in a metal tray fixed onto the barrel. They soon cleared the ash away from the tray and gingerly lifted it out to find, to their utter amazement, that the barrel was full of Demerara sugar! Now sugar was a commodity we were always short of, for cooking and the everlasting mugs of tea. In essence, it kept us going with its high energy content, which sugar gave and our rations were never sufficient for the mortar crews, where the work was very physical and demanding in the extreme and more so in the cold weather. The platoon commander was made aware of the find and each carrier was then allocated one sandbag full of sugar. He also had one on his command carrier.

There was an Army order with a policy stating that you could live off the land if the need arose. After filling the seven clean bags with sugar, it wasn't noticeable that the barrel had been touched, and with the metal tray replaced then filled back up with ash, none of the platoon felt like desperados for taking the sugar. At the very worst here, the farmer could have been killed along with his family, or the farm destroyed by the passage of war in the vicinity. But he was more fortunate than some of his fellow countrymen who had seen their land and property devastated by the intense shellfire.

In the first few days of the New Year, the American forces regained their equilibrium in the forests of the Ardennes and forced the Germans back on to the defensive. It had become a bitter struggle, in weather, the local people couldn't remember in living memory, and the battle had been costly on both sides in men and material. With the Russians now pushing in from the east and the alliance of America and Britain from the west, the end of the war looked close at hand, so now was the time not to be killed. But in this, you had no choice but to carry on and hope for your own deliverance from the battlefield.

We moved from our New Year position, along with our confiscated bags of sugar, as the battalion moved forward once again and would continue to do so till the ground was cleared up to the Senio River.

The enemy, after his rout in the Ardennes, wasn't willing to concede a yard of ground on the Italian front without a fight. The snow continued to fall and with the ground already frozen it looked set for a long, cold winter. Once again, we moved into the inevitable farm with house and outbuildings much the same as the last one. But here, the Italian family had fled and who could blame them with so much suffering in their land.

The mortars were mounted in the confines of the farm, but none at this time were dug in with the tempo of the fighting having slowed down. It was only temporary with each side just holding its breath till the fury started up again.

By now the enemy had been cleared up to the flood bank with one side being occupied by us and, on the reverse side, by the Germans, with just a few feet of soil to separate the combatants from each other. This must have been the only time in warfare when opposing forces could almost shake hands with one another, but this was more serious. If the enemy were attacked and driven from their positions, they would still have to cross the river and climb over the other flood bank, and this could be a great liability for them. However, the closeness of the two forces must have been carefully thought out by the Germans, and they had come to the conclusion it would be safer in being closer to their enemy on the flood bank than across the Senio River. Otherwise, air power in the shape of British fighter-bombers would be able to pound their positions without fear of killing our own troops, but being so close together on the one flood bank made it an impossible target for them.

In our new position at the farm, we were called on at intervals, day and night, to fire in support of the battalion when a request was made from our Platoon HQ and relayed to us over the telephone. By this time, we had about 6 inches of snow on the frozen ground, making life more difficult if that were possible. The roads were getting bad and in need of repair from the amount of vehicles using them, along with the worsening weather conditions.

One morning, a party of Sikhs, who were engineers from the Indian Division, had been working on the road. After they had finished their task, they sheltered from the bleak cold wind by standing round the walls of the farm while waiting for their transport to pick them up. At this point, our detachment was called on to fire on a SOS target.

We ran out to the mortar and Lance Corporal Morgan, our Number One of the crew, picked up the field telephone and we prepared the mortar to fire when we had the range and deflection to place on the mortar gun sight. Then, having centralised the cross-levelling and longitudinal bubbles, we were ready. Number Three then passed me the round of ammunition, which I released down the barrel then, with a thump, the bomb was away. By this time, the Sikhs were moving back onto the road where the transport now awaited them.

Then an order of a change in the range and deflection came over the phone and, after making the necessary correction to the sight, we were ready to fire again. One of the Sikhs was still standing out in the yard, watching us, when he should have been on his transport, moving off back to base, and not standing within a hundred feet of the mortar position.

The order came to fire, and taking the bomb from Number Three, I released it down the barrel. Thump—, the round left the barrel but then exploded no more than 30 feet above our heads and gave us a bad shock. The shrapnel had left us in the crew unscathed, as we looked at one another in sheer bewilderment at our escape from death. After regaining some composure, I reluctantly but gingerly placed another bomb in the barrel, released it and hoped. Thump—, it sped away, and later, after firing more rounds, the order came through to stand-down. If that bomb had exploded in or on clearing the barrel, the platoon would have been minus a mortar crew.

After covering the mortar and ammunition from the inclement weather, we departed back to the warmth of the farm. Then we noticed with amazement that someone was lying down in the snow, but why? We found it to be the Sikh who had been standing on his own, watching us work the mortar. We bent down to him, but his eyes were closed as if asleep, and having a closer look, we found his greatcoat and battledress tunic had been pierced by something very small. We removed some of his clothing and found to our consternation that he had been hit by a fragment of shrapnel in the heart and was dead.

It had come from our exploding bomb and immediately I felt that, indirectly, I had killed this man who had come from India voluntarily to fight on our side. We stayed with him while an ambulance was called, and at its departure, I had a sense of remorse about me. Later, we reported the incident to Platoon HQ who just blamed it on faulty ammunition. It had been a close call for us and I would think about it long into the future, every time I fired a round.

The weather became worse with each new day, with no letup in the snowfall. In a room at the farm one morning, some of the men had just been roused from their sleep on the floor and were preparing themselves for another day, when their calm was shattered by a solid-shot armour-piercing shell that smashed the wall down where they had been lying. They had a most incredulous escape from serious injury or death. It comes no closer.

Word came through from Platoon HQ that we would be staying in our present position for some time yet. So, the order came through to dig a shelter for 3 mortar positions away from the farm building. The 6 mortar detachments then merged into 3 sections. Then one detachment would stay at each mortar position, with four hours on duty in the shelter, at the mortar, and four hours back at the farm.

We moved our mortar back a good one hundred yards or more with the help of the other detachment. First, we dug a pit for the gun about 2 feet deep into the frozen ground. Then having mounted it and left an ample supply of ammunition, we then started on our shelter, close at hand in case of an SOS call over the field telephone for supporting fire. We made the pit for the shelter almost 3 feet deep then, with the loose soil, filled some sandbags and placed them round the pit about 3 or 4 high, leaving an entrance for us on the 'home' side for coming and going. To finish it off, we found some sound pieces of wood in one of the barns and covered the top of the shelter with them, several deep for strength, then piled on the sandbags till we thought the place secure except for a direct hit. Finally, we found a piece of material to cover the entrance.

Before many hours had elapsed, the shelter became frozen in the arctic conditions that still prevailed and by then nicknamed the 'igloo' by all and sundry. For night firing of the mortar, you had an electric lamp fixed onto the aiming post in the shape of a diamond, which had to match up with the gun sight of the mortar if you changed the deflection. It operated by a pull switch on the end of a length of twine to the switch on the lamp that ran back a few yards to the mortar pit.

Our detachment started off with the first guard duty of four hours on at the 'igloo', then four off in the comfort of the cold, deserted farm, but it was a refuge after your spell in the hole-in-the-ground. The night was black and the stars were shining bright in the cold atmosphere, but inside the shelter with the oil lamp going it was far better than being outside. There were four of us in the detachment, the driver was not required and was back at the farm. Sergeant Chambers, who in an emergency would relay the instructions verbally from the field telephone to us in the pit, led the detachment.

Sitting in our fortress, watching our cold breath by the feeble light of the lamp, it seemed more reminiscent of a bygone age like a scene from the Crimea. We sat in our fortress with our legs stretched out in front of us and our backs leaning against the sides of the pit.

After being in this most miserable position for around two hours, one of the crew made a move to go outside and found to his absolute disgust that his oilskin coat was frozen to the 'igloo's' side. We should laugh at the man's misfortune because we were also in the same predicament. After freeing ourselves, we made sure that we moved around more.

Later, we heard machine gun fire going on. Then the phone sprang into life with a call to fire on the enemy. They had infiltrated through our lines on the flood bank and were roving about in the hope of taking prisoners for interrogation into our intentions of a possible attack over the Senio River and beyond. I was first out of the 'igloo', so groped for the pull switch on the aiming base and gave it a pull, hoping to see the light appear on the post a few yards from the mortar pit. It didn't. So, I pulled again only to find it would not work. Getting out of the pit, I went to the post and pulled the twine running up to the lamp and the light came on. Jumping back into the pit, and by the light of a torch, we laid the mortar on and were ready to fire. This had taken a space of less than two minutes to correct the fault, and after having fired several rounds, the order to stand-down came through. Taking the torch, I found that the twine leading up to the post had frozen onto the ground.

After we had settled back down in the 'igloo', Sergeant Chambers looked at me through the feeble light of the oil lamp and said, "I don't think I should be telling you this, Dave, but Sergeant Pepperell was giving the instructions over the field telephone, and he wanted to know the reason for the delay in firing. And, in consequence, he wanted to have the name of the man who had transgressed in his duty. And as a parting shot, with his voice full of sarcasm, suggested that we might have a 'bloody Italian' in the crew!"

In the intense cold of the 'igloo', I felt a kind of fury creep over me, at Pepperell's disregard for what the conditions were like at the mortar and he was in the comparative comfort of warmth and safety at Platoon HQ. I made up my mind that when our four hours of duty came to an end and we returned back to the farm, Sergeant Pepperell would receive a visit from the irate, supposedly Italian mortar-man!

After being relieved by the other half of the section, we made our way back in the snow to the 'farm rest home', or so it seemed after our spell in purgatory at the 'igloo'. Once back inside the farm, I was tired and cold like the others, but I still intended walking to Platoon HQ and have it out with my antagonist there.

I went to Sergeant Chambers and asked for permission to leave, and when I told him what I wished to do, he said, "Don't be a fool! Pepperell would try and get you on a charge for insubordination, even going over the head of Captain Sherlock. Pepperell's not worth it." The others had gathered round on hearing our heated conversation and they all agreed with the sergeant that the man was not worth it, all of them coming down on my side. I was inwardly fuming at the injustice of it, and I would have to wait till the war ended to see this small-minded, arrogant character get his comeuppance.

After spending most of January in this position, with a thaw taking place and everywhere around us becoming a sea of mud, it made life more difficult than when the snow was around. Firing the mortars became a problem with the baseplate sinking into the soft ground, which could lead to inaccuracy in the flight of the bomb and endanger our own troops.

At last we were pulled out of the line for a rest away from the fighting, but were not moved very far with the battalion dispersed over a wide area; in a landscape cultivated with large vines everywhere you looked, in amongst the trees and bushes.

Our two detachments, or section, were billeted in one of the innumerable farm buildings with an Italian family in residence, run by a matriarchal type of old lady who you were bound to listen to with the utmost of respect, but she was a kindly soul. There were ten of us in the section and we occupied one room on the ground floor with enough space to have our bedding rolls. But there was one snag spoiling the luxury of our nest. Owing to the scattering of the company, the cook sergeant was unable to do the catering for us, so our section was responsible for cooking our own food.

I was detailed, along with my friend, Stan Abbey, to carry out this task with the cooking being done on an open fire in the room. With an ample supply of timber around in lengths of vine supports, it was an ideal fuel for our needs. While we did the cooking, the rest of the section had to be out training and stand guard duty, so we two could apply our culinary skills (if any) to the job in hand.

Unbeknown to me, Stan had worked in a bakery for a time back home. He said on our first day he would make some pastry for a pie with the filling of some tins of 'maconicies' – a mixture of diced meat and vegetables. While preparing the meal, we had a visit from the old lady who on seeing what we were trying to achieve went away and later came back with a range of cooking utensils, which we received with gratitude. The Italian adults and children deferentially called her mama, so we did likewise which pleased her.

We also made a chocolate pudding, made from hard Army biscuits soaked in hot water with our chocolate ration added. It looked good and better still after placing some of our looted sugar in, but what would the section say?

We had the section's mess tins lined up ready to fill when they came in from their training session. Again, when mama saw the mess tins, off she went and returned later with a set of dinner plates for our use. These were of good quality and she made understandable gestures with her hands not to break them. When the section came in for their meal, they looked and thought they were dining at the Ritz with the china plates and a nice log fire burning in the hearth. And as for the meal, it was voted a great success, and we were then rewarded for our efforts by the section making us permanent in the job while we stayed here.

The weather was dry but still cold, though nice and warm in the billet, and in the evenings we would sit in with the Italian family under the scrutiny of mama who now called me Davido. We, now in kindness to them, gave what food we could spare, along with cigarettes and chocolate for which they were very grateful and in part added a little colour into their mundane lives. After all, they had suffered terribly in the name of war.

One evening we sat round a large table while they showed us how they make their pasta. They had a hand-built machine, into which they placed a wad of pasta dough and placed a screwed plug behind it, which they then turned with a bar to force the pasta through a metal die. It was extruded out of the die in the shape of fluted pasta with the hole running through the middle, which was then cut with a sharp knife into about inch lengths across the face of the die. I could see that it was hard work to force the pasta through the die, but it typified the harshness of their lives out here, miles away from the hurly-burly of towns and cities, and where electricity was still a dream for them here.

It was around this time that Captain Sherlock had returned home on compassionate leave, but we hoped would soon be coming back. The platoon was now run by an officer from the battalion, a lieutenant with a limited knowledge of the mortar, so was actually run by the platoon sergeant, Sergeant Pepperell.

One afternoon, when cleaning up the utensils after our daily chore of cooking, I was told to report to Platoon HQ immediately. What had I done this time, was my first reaction to the summons to HQ? I found time to smarten myself up, put on my cap and woollen gloves with the weather still being so cold, and started off on my five minute walk there. On arriving, I knocked on the door and a voice called out for me to go in.

The doorknob was made of brass. I gripped it, twisted and pushed the door open, revealing a scene of the HQ staff standing round a hand generator used for the bell on the field telephones. One of the men was working the crank handle like mad to generate maximum voltage into wires running across the floor and fixed to the inside doorknob. They had expected me to place my bare hand on the knob and receive a shock of some magnitude from the electric generator, and they would have seen me dancing around like a contortionist, but their scheme had gone awry thanks to the gloves.

It was a stupid prank played by Sergeant Pepperell. He was doing his best to laugh, but all he could muster was a sickly grin while I looked him over with abject contempt and walked away. How the man had ever bluffed his way to being platoon sergeant, I would never know.

Time finally came to leave the Italian family with our departure upsetting mama and causing tears at the loss of her second family. All good things have to come to an end, but we had all benefited from our stay in the family environment and it stopped us from behaving like things from the jungle.

We didn't move very far, to a village with the name of Ronco, with a river of the same name and high flood banks like the Senio River. With our mortar pit dug, we found some billets in a mostly ruined part of the village next to the flood bank. The men detailed for guard duty were warned about German patrol activity in the area along the flood bank, and to be extra vigilant at all times. One other thing was that the enemy shelled along the bank at times in the hours of darkness. It was strange to stand guard again after being excused for so long with our cooking abilities.

On my first guard duty with a colleague in the detachment on our patrol along the bank, we found a building with its door ajar and decided on the spot that if we could hear trouble coming that's where we would take shelter. It did come and we ran for cover, and on our reaching the door, I put my shoulder to it only to find it wouldn't budge. Crash! The first shell landed, showering its lethal shrapnel in all directions, making the body cringe at the thought of being hit by the hot jagged metal, and then a strong smell of cordite filled the cold night air.

That shell landing had given us strength, or powers we hadn't previously possessed, and pushing with all our might, we forced the door open to find refuge inside. And a good thing we did judging by the number of shells that landed. After the shelling had ceased, we found a large barrel had obstructed our entry. It could have been full of wine, placed there to stop the door being opened when the Italians fled from their homes.

Leaving Ronco, we made several other moves in the area of Ravenna, a city that had fallen to 8th Army back in December, but we never made an entry there. We moved around many towns and villages, supporting the battalion with our mortar fire, operated with a degree of skill by Captain Sherlock who had returned back to the fold and made us all feel better with his brand of leadership. We moved into and through places called Faenza, Forli, Russe, Bagnacavolla, San Pietro, Lugo and San Giorgio. These would always remain in the memory; places of no great significance but still had to be taken from the enemy.

January turned into February, and then moved into March without us knowing what day of the week it was. We moved to a position out in the countryside, miles from any town or village, to a most idyllic spot with a nice pond surrounded by trees that gave us cover from prying eyes to our front. The battalion had dug in a few hundred yards to our front, which was quiet with just patrol activity and the occasional exchange of shots. Neither side was doing much, or so it seemed at the time with the Americans and British closing up on the Rhine from the west and the Russians on Germany's eastern border. So, we also would be making a big push before long, but when?

One night, at around two o'clock in the morning when the men were trying to get some sleep in their slit trenches, the enemy fired a salvo of missiles from their rocket launching Nebelwerfers onto the battalion lines. After the firing of several salvos, they moved back before our own artillery could respond or retaliate in kind, it being too little too late. This happened again, a second night with little response from our own guns.

The next morning, Captain Sherlock called us together and said if the Nebelwerfers returned again that night, the artillery had a fire plan to saturate the area from where the enemy fired their rockets. The Artillery Corps knew the approximate range and target area, from observing the Nebelwerfer flashes when they fired on the previous nights, and had hundreds of guns of all calibres trained and ready to fire the second the flashes were seen.

That night the front became quiet as was normal except with patrol activity, the occasional burst of machine gun fire and the single pop of a rifle. The night wore on and we were beginning to believe that the enemy had somehow discovered about the counter strike, and wouldn't bombard our forward troops that night with their infernal rocket bombs, with that morale sapping, frightening banshee sound that would strike terror into the hearts and minds of brave men. Everyone had all but given in when we saw the telltale lights of the rocket bombs in flight. Then, from our rear, we saw the guns of the Artillery Corps erupt along the whole skyline with flashes of light, and within a very short period hundreds of shells were screaming overhead to fall on the Nebelwerfer battery. The losses on the enemy side would have been catastrophic with the devastation the concentrated shelling must have caused. The German Nebelwerfers didn't return to harass the battalion on the next night – or ever again.

After moving to another position, once again, with the front static and the winter weather almost over, it now being March, we would be getting ready soon for an advance into the Po Plain; and move towards the river with its formidable defences that would have to be overcome before we could cross.

Word got round that we were going to pull out of the line for a rest before the new offensive started and it could be the last of the war, or so we hoped it would be.

Before the move was carried out, the battle patrol, who were also in Specialist Company and led by a Sergeant Marsh, were ordered to take a patrol out. They were to bring back German prisoners for interrogation into their dispositions there, of forces that would oppose us in any attack in the forthcoming offensive.

They moved off under cover of darkness, though not dressed in the standard manner of what a British soldier should look like, but rather more flamboyant with some of them wearing white silk scarves. One of them was wearing a dilapidated top hat. No steel helmets were worn on patrol, only cap comforters, as Army authority was waived aside at their apparent lack of discipline, but that was deceptive. They were highly trained for their role when they were putting their heads on the block, which in fact they were. Their webbing was festooned with hand grenades for easy access if they bumped into the enemy. The mortars were on stand-by, giving the patrol support if needed, and were linked by radio, carried and worked by a man from the signal platoon who went out with the patrol and was a prime target for the enemy (carrying the set with the aerial sticking out of the top of it).

Later in the night, the patrol managed to capture two prisoners and, by first light, were on their way back to our lines. However, they ran into a larger enemy force and had to take refuge in a house, which was empty of its Italian inhabitants who had rightly fled the war zone. The battle patrol were well and truly trapped, but they, the enemy, had not banked on the ingenuity of the sergeant who told the radio operator to "Call down fire!" on and around the house where they had taken shelter. The map reference was sent back to Mortar HQ who then relayed the range and deflection to the guns. Within minutes of receiving the message, the bombs were on the way.

Meanwhile at the house, the sergeant gathered his men into the enemy line side of the building and told them to "Hug the floor!" They were safe from the bombs penetrating through the roof and bedroom ceiling and bursting below, but they were taking an awful risk with their exposure to shrapnel and blast. The bombs rained down on the confident enemy who were thinking they had our men in the bag. After a number of bombs had fallen, the enemy melted away into his own lines leaving the battle patrol in command of the situation.

Eventually, they came back out with four prisoners – two Germans and two geese with string round their necks, being led by the prisoners – who led the detachment, swinging their arms like the rest of the men. What a sight it made. Top hat, silk scarves, prisoners and geese; it was sheer bravado on the part of the patrol, but by now they could have been prisoners of war, or at the worst dead if they hadn't called down the mortar strike.

18. Florence. The final battle.

Within a day or so, we were pulled out of the line, but this time away from the battle area. Moving through the town of Forli, and five miles further on, we arrived at the hilltop village of Bertinoro. It was a wonderful haven after our stay in the line for most of the time since New Year, of around twelve weeks. Here, we were billeted in a monastery, where the good nuns were still in residence and they were most kind to the soldiers who had been imposed on their strict way of life.

From this vantage point on the hilltop, you could see right over into the Po Plain. At night, you could see the gun flashes in the distance pounding away at the enemy positions, and one was bound to feel thankful for being away from it if only for a brief spell.

Then looking to the northwest, you could see a mountain range where the luckless men of the American 5th Army had been fighting just a few miles away from Bologna. This had been their objective in the autumn campaign. In their failure to take this strategic city, 5th Army had paid dearly, with the casualty list being very high, and were missing out on the wonderful accommodation the city would have afforded them in the terrible winter weather that followed. With deep snow and having to be supplied over trackless ground, that was the lot of the American infantryman – exposed in his foxhole, freezing and facing the enemy.

The campaign wasn't lost by the men of the 5th and 8th Armies, but by the complete lack of troops on the ground and the global shortage of ammunition at a vital period in the conflict. The men could never be blamed for a lack of endeavour, it had been beyond our capabilities from the word go. They, the planners, had underestimated the will and the fighting spirit of the enemy in holding their line, and the stark fact that it was held by some of the very best divisions in the German Army.

Bertinoro was indeed a wonderful place to unwind and see once again the culture of civilisation after living in holes in the ground, unwashed, untidy and weary from lack of sleep. Yes, it was time to try and get some real rest and peace that we all needed till eventually called back again.

It was while in Bertinoro that I gained my majority by arriving at the age of twenty-one, and for the first time would be eligible to vote in an election. That was after fighting for the past eighteen months and I think you could call it a real paradox – old enough to fight for your state, but not to vote.

The steep hillsides of Bertinoro were terraced for the most part for the growing of grapes and peaches. It must have looked a fine sight at harvest time, around September. Our training was never neglected, filling most of our daylight hours.

While staying here, all of us had the opportunity of having six days leave in Florence (Firenze), a journey of about sixty miles. Our sleeping accommodation, while there, was a large transit camp where they had concerts most nights and the sleeping quarters were very good. One evening, we decided to stay in camp and see the show there and, to my great surprise, it turned out to be the original cast of Ralph Reader's 'Gang Show'; all dressed up as a troop of boy scouts!

I had appeared in this when I was about thirteen years of age with a cast from our Sunday school on the stage there, and what's more I could remember most of the songs in the show. The main one being '*We are riding along on the crest of a wave and the sun is in the sky; All our eyes on the distant horizon look out for passers by!*' That night it was well received by a very appreciative audience who in the main had been starved of entertainment for a long spell, and for me it was a return back down the years to a time when I was wearing short trousers.

Florence was as magnificent as the word sounded with architectural beauty around every corner you cared to go. In the main square, and looking at the statue of David, was an experience when you think of the countless millions who have gazed with wonder on this lifelike masterpiece, also the magnificent church or domo with its tower alongside. My friends and I decided that we would climb the steps leading to the top of the tower.

After surmounting the difficult climb of what seemed like hundreds of steps, we were rewarded for our endeavour with the city laid out before us, as it must have looked in the Middle Ages. Looking down on the domo and seeing the vastness of it, you could only marvel at how they could build such a structure with the rudimentary tools of the day. It's very easy to look, but not to see and ask yourself questions about how they did the work, and then decide, as well as being their task or livelihood, it was also an act of faith in this grand design of such spectacular splendour.

One day out walking in the city, we came to a row of empty shop windows where nothing was on sale. But passing by one, I noticed a group of middle-aged Italians in a dilapidated property with a darkish interior, and one of them was winding up an old gramophone. I was most intrigued by this scene and waited to hear the result the gramophone would produce when set in motion. He placed the arm over the record on the revolving turntable until the needle made contact, and for the first time in my life I was hearing the overture of Verdi's *'La Forza del Destino'* (The Force of Destiny), this I could hear quite well outside the shop. My friends had moved on while I stayed and listened to this most inspiring piece. Afterwards, I liked to think it was here, outside this rundown shop, that I first found an appreciation of symphonic music.

In the city one evening, we decided to visit a picture house that was run for the forces only. Inside the fine building, we found that half of the audience were Americans from 5th Army, also on leave. After seeing a very good film, the lights came on and we started to leave our seats. However, the Americans there invited us to stay in our seats if we would care to see a United States concert party show, which was accepted with some gratitude.

It turned out to be a great show and very well done with top class professionals. One of them being the up and coming film star, Burt Lancaster, who turned in an acrobatic act, the likes of which I have never seen bettered. A man also gave us a great impersonation of the crooner of the day, Frank Sinatra. He looked so thin and made-up in the image of Sinatra and sang in his manner that you almost believed it could be he. But none of us in the audience carried on in the same way that Sinatra had supposedly affected his lady followers, in the States, when he preformed on stage, working his audience into a paroxysm of passion or frenzy with the swooning way he could sing the numbers. We were of course unaffected, but clapped for the effort of the man's performance, and Sinatra himself wouldn't have had a better accolade. It was a very wonderful evening for us, and no doubt, the Americans didn't know that the British soldiers they had entertained that evening had served in their 5th Army.

Our six days leave in Florence came to an end and we returned back to Bertinoro. From my own point of view, the memories of that most beautiful city took away the harshness of the grim reality of what lay ahead for us.

It was a sad day when we left our picture postcard village of Bertinoro for our return back into the line. Now it was early April, it was about time the Italian offensive started up again. The territory now to be fought over had somewhat dried out after the autumn rains and winter snow. It was now able to support the vehicles where roads were nonexistent in the mainly waterlogged Romagna country, with a maze of rivers, canals and streams to cross over if we were to advance on our divisional front. But first, we had to cross the Senio River and through its flood banks before 8th Army could advance.

On our return back to the line, we held a reserve position till the battalion was called into action. The fighting on the Western and Eastern Fronts was going well, so a big push here by 5th and 8th Armies was now imminent. At this stage of what you could call the final conflict on Italian soil, to be killed now in the last dwindling days of the war was uppermost in people's minds on both sides of the line. All of us only wished in the end to cross the threshold into a world at peace.

The long wait came to an end on the 9th of April, with the breaching of the Senio River flood banks. Explosive charges blasted large holes into the banks, enabling our tanks and infantry to deploy on the enemy side. However, the Germans still put up strong opposition at the incursion into the territory they had safely held for so long.

We moved forward till the battalion engaged with the enemy, in a landscape of rivers, canals and streams. Water was everywhere. We would have been unable to operate in the carriers without the use of the minor roads to keep us out of the water. There were no towns or villages that one could identify where you were, just the occasional hamlet or house in this vast expanse of water, known locally as the Valli di Comacchio (Lake Comacchio).

An order came down from Army HQ for units to come from Brigade to make up an assault force to attack a place called Longastrino, across the lake, in amphibious vehicles called 'buffalos'. Section two mortars were commandeered from the platoon, and I found myself in one of them.

We were whisked off to a training ground where we moved on and off our 'buffalo' to get the hang of it. Some smart officer in charge of the training suggested that we should fire our mortars from the 'buffalos' onto the enemy before reaching the shore. It was pointed out to the officer that firing the mortar from the craft, without making some reinforcement in the 'buffalo', would punch a hole in the bottom. We stayed at the training camp for two days when, for us, it was mysteriously called off and we returned to our respective battalions.

Days later we saw an amphibious force of 'buffalos', at a good distance from us, move off across the lagoon towards enemy held Longastrino. At the same time, we observed several squadrons of Royal Air Force bombers flying in the direction the amphibious force were making for. On arrival at their destination, the bombers released their deadly payloads onto the target of Longastrino that disappeared from our view, obliterated by columns of dust and smoke, and I hoped there wouldn't be any civilians in the town.

After the bombing had stopped and the noise of the aircraft had died away, a new threat came from the devastated town, that of gunfire shelling the 'buffalos'. They looked like sitting ducks to us as they crawled towards the shore. We saw very near misses with columns of water thrown into the air by the bursting shells, then they moved out of vision and none of us ever found out what happened to the men in the 'buffalos'. Some of my friends and I could have been part of that and could have perished out there, on the lagoon, like some men must have done that day.

Our 56 London Division was at the end of the battle line of 8th Army. Our antagonists facing us were the men of the 42nd Jaeger Division of the German 10th Army, and like their comrades of 14th Army, who were now facing the American 5th Army. The Germans had received a message from Führer HQ not to yield any more ground in Northern Italy.

The battalion moved forward, though made slow progress with the engineers having to build bridges over the main rivers and waterways. After the Senio came the Santerno with many more rivers to cross in the days ahead if we wished to advance any further over this part of the Lombardy Plain. The battalion casualty list was, at this stage, mercifully light in number, but when the opposition stiffened at times, the infantry called on the service of the artillery to break up the pockets of opposition before they could establish strong defensive positions.

One such time was when the battalion was pinned down by small arms fire coming from a high bank of a stream. The enemy had dug in well and soon caused a casualty or two when they called in their own artillery to check our advance. One of the victims was a corporal; a stretcher-bearer who would always wear a white blouse adorned with two red crosses front and back. But in the fury of warfare, man's base instincts rule not in kindness and compassion for others but by personal survival. The loss of the corporal, who was carrying out his good work on the battlefield, was a shock to the battalion and in some ways inhibited the men at the sharp end to stick their necks out in future now they sensed the end to the war.

With caution in mind then, the battalion asked the artillery observation officer, who was attached to our headquarters staff, to lay down a barrage along the length of the bank. After the ranging rounds had been fired and corrections made, the divisional artillery 25-pounder guns laid down a most ferocious barrage on top of the enemy held positions.

The shells being so numerous you couldn't identify any single shell burst. Large chunks of grass and earth were thrown up as the shells ploughed into the soft ground of the bank, and from our viewpoint, in a farm building no more than 200 yards away, it looked rather horrific as regards to loss of life. But fortunately, we were wrong. When the barrage lifted, we saw the enemy emerge in great numbers from their deep and safe underground shelters with their hands over their heads, and wisely leaving their weapons behind.

They walked towards us and we passed among them, relieving them of any knives, the equivalent of our own jack-knives, which we collected in our steel helmets and nothing more. They looked very pleased and relieved at their treatment by us, and for them it was now all over.

After the prisoners were taken off our hands, we moved forward not having to fight any major battles. It had all of a sudden turned into a fluid front where the enemy before had to be prised out of his defensive positions, and would eventually culminate into a pitched battle with great losses on both sides. After the way the enemy had reacted to us in the past with their formidable weaponry, this now didn't seen realistic, moving through country they had recently occupied without them pounding the life out of us. I didn't think it would ever be possible to catch the Germans flat-footed, but at this stage it now seemed they could be in some kind of disarray.

At this time, we started to find a great deal of German propaganda leaflets along the way. These depicted, in the most vivid manner to the American and British soldiers, a cruel reminder of what would befall us if we dared to venture across the mighty Po River.

The German propagandists had gone to great lengths with one folded leaflet in colour showing a voluptuous looking Italian woman with a beautiful face, red lips and raven black hair. She was carrying a wicker pannier basket, brimful of bunches of black and white grapes hanging over the sides of the basket in abundance. And there was a background of a wide sweeping Po River and caricatures of the lovely towns of Rovigo and Padova beyond, flowing with milk and honey, extolling all the virtues of life. At the top of the leaflet, in bold disarming words and in very stylish print, was a caption:

'The Po Is Waiting For YOU!'

Then the unsuspecting soldier opens the leaflet. It stares back at him, now in black and white, of a skeletal figure larger-than-life rising out of the river, robed in black with a death's head skull, black hollow eyes and emaciated arms, holding aloft the punctured steel helmets of an American and British soldier. Around the ghostly figure was a most horrendous scene of death and destruction. The German act of retaliation against the venturous soldiers in trying to cross that heavily fortified river. Shells were falling in and around the assault craft, the timbers of which were being scattered far and wide by the explosions. The men inside being thrown into the water and having to struggle with their weighty equipment on, before drowning in the swiftly flowing current.

One other leaflet with a similar picture of death and destruction on the back had a chilling message on its front, stating in bold type:

One more River. But it isn't "One more River" - this time it's THE RIVER!
It is the MIGHTY PO!
Do you remember the hell of the rivers Sangno, Rapido, Liri, Volturno and Garigliano?
Do you remember the lives that were sacrificed in crossing these rivers?
Put these rivers all together and the result will be smaller than the Po!
Also, when you crossed these rivers, the Germans were in retreat and had no time to prepare defences.
But covering the Po, you will find a blanket of death ... Artillery, Nebelwerfers, Mortars and Spandaus.
The whole Po area is a network of canals and is impassable for Tanks.

Rush
In!
Various
Exciting
Revelations
Prepared
Oh Boy!

And here are a few facts about the Po:
At its shallowest part (between Adda and Mincio), it is 7 feet deep.
At the deepest part (near Pavia), it is 20 ft deep.
The width varies from 208 to 1040 yards.
The banks are mostly sheer and between 18 and 30 ft high.
The speed of the Po exceeds 20 mph.

"Po" means death and suffering.

```
P.O.W. means security and comfort!

Think it over,
Only Fools rush in --- !
```

The column of crudely thought out words has the capital letters that spell out 'RIVER PO'. I wonder what psychological effect it had on the frontline soldiers who picked them up around the battlefield with the thought in mind, what for us, could be the closing stages of the war. The frontline regiments were suffering from desertions to such an extent that the Army command was getting rather alarmed. So, did the propaganda leaflets have any influence on some of our troops in the final stages of the war? It seems more than likely.

Each day we moved a few miles nearer to that fatal sounding river, and what would happen there no one dared think. After the town of Argenta had fallen on the 18th of April, we were halted for a short rest while the brigade, for its three battalions, worked out new axes of advance. It was going well on the 5th Army front with the fall of Bologna on the 21st.

In Argenta, where we were resting, the company were billeted in and around what you would call a hamlet with just a few homes and a farm. Our platoon managed to find a good dry barn, which was better than sleeping out in the open.

The evening there started off with a call out on parade, and in its very murky light, we formed up into three sides of a square. The company was called to attention when the company commander joined the parade, then stand at ease was given. Major Woolham addressed his men with the darkness closing down on us, making it feel rather weird. The major, who was a practicing KC in civilian life, said, "I want to tell you all that I am giving up command of this company." By now, the major was just a shadowy shape but he went on. "It's difficult to leave at this time when the enemy would seem to be in retreat, but I know you will carry on the fight under my successor and hope that final victory will soon be won." He continued. "I also want to tell you how proud I have been in command of you all and all your achievements, and I shall feel sad in leaving." Then he concluded with this personal message to us. "If for any reason when you return to civilian life and you find yourself in any form of trouble, come to me and I will help any man standing here on this parade tonight. It would be a way of saying thank you for being a great company. Good luck to you all!"

The battalion was soon on the move again with, thankfully, only light opposition from the enemy. Portomaggiore was taken, and by this time, we had moved through the mainly flooded ground; the landscape now being more of trees, hedgerows and lanes leading nowhere in particular. If the enemy went the way of the advance then they were followed for there were no main roads to travel on, just second class roads in disrepair and not helped by the retreating enemy.

It was at this time that we were confronted with a German minefield of some size, very well advertised by the warning signs with skull & crossbones and words to the presence of mines in German. We found a lot of warnings like this on painted wooden boards and nailed to posts in the ground. The result of the minefield in our path prompted us to leave the carriers and go forward on foot. So, our two detachments unloaded the mortars from off the carriers and, with a case of bombs each, proceeded on our way into the uncharted territory of the minefield.

You could see some of the mines, which were strewn all over the place in a random fashion, protruding through the soil after the heavy rains of autumn and winter. We picked our way very gingerly, with each man placing his feet into the footsteps of the man in front, and just hoping you had taken the right one. It was no easy matter, in trying to keep your balance while carrying a load of nearly ninety pounds of equipment, and to fall with it would cause some grief, not only to yourself but your friends also. Most of the mines planted there were antipersonnel mines, whereas the larger Teller mines could disable a vehicle like a tank. The rest could easily maim or kill a soldier.

After at last clearing the minefield and moving away from our walk in the realms of purgatory, we came into a farmyard where we rested. We were in contact with our Mortar HQ by radio, but at the time were not called on to fire in support of the battalion.

Later in the day, we were pleased at the arrival of the carriers after the sappers had cleared a way through the minefield. But we had, by effort, managed to negotiate our way through and help the battalion forward if required.

One of our carriers standing in the yard was hit by an armour-piercing round, which punched its way through the side of the carrier, smashing the top of the steering wheel and punching a hole out of the other side. The missile, before hitting the carrier, had first come through the roof of the barn, passing through a wooden beam, punching a neat hole in the massive timber, before striking the ¼" inch steel plate of the vehicle. Thank goodness the carrier was empty of the crew at the time. Also, the missile could have hit the bombs in their racks and that could have been the end for us all.

While our section had been struggling through the minefield, the other two sections of the platoon were trying to move forward by a more circuitous route in the carriers, not liking the idea of going near the mines. After traversing numerous tracks and lanes, they came back within range of supporting the battalion with their mortar fire if required.

Eventually, they had pulled into a spacious yard of an abandoned house and a dog called 'Mush', a mongrel, jumped out of his master's arms, over the side of the carrier, and ran towards the house. The dog suddenly gave a sharp yelp and sprawled out onto the ground, then a large explosion followed and the house collapsed into a heap of rubble before the startled eyes of the mortar crews. 'Mush' had triggered off a booby trap by tripping over a fine wire and detonating the explosive charge carefully laid by the retreating Germans, who would have expected far better results from their clandestine labour. The dog had undoubtedly saved the lives of many of the men, in killed and wounded, and the dog itself being dazed but unscathed by the event. We had a new hero in the platoon – 'Mush' our four-legged friend!

Each day we remorselessly moved ever closer to that river, the Germans had so graphically described to us in their gruesome propaganda leaflets. You didn't need much of an imagination to realise that, for many, to cross the river would be a one-way ticket to the end of the line.

We were now advancing in the vicinity of the Reno River, and at this crucial time our signal platoon refused to supply any of their men to be radio operators with our forward observation post. They had always been forward with the leading company of the battalion, and comprised of a sergeant and radio operator. When they ran into trouble, which was always present, a map reference was relayed back to Mortar Platoon HQ, where Captain Sherlock would work out on a large-scale map the position of the enemy in relation to his known position to the mortars on the ground. Having worked out the range and deflection and sent out the message over the field telephone, the mortars would be ready to fire within a minute of receiving the order.

It was known to us, in the platoon, that there had been a casualty or two in the signals in their service for the mortars. They had complained that they had automatically become a target for enemy snipers who could see the aerial protruding from the radio set, carried on the back of the operator. It was if to advertise the fact that he was the man to down if they wished to stop any kind of retaliation, in this case from mortar fire.

Captain Sherlock decided that the mortar platoon would have to fill the role left by the signal platoon and do the necessary job ourselves. We were all trained in radio procedure so it would be left to us. The platoon sergeant looked over his list, and seeing my name decided to look no further and duly detailed me to go as the radio operator to accompany the forward OP.

A sergeant and I joined the lead rifle company of the battalion that moved forward to the vicinity of the Reno River. The pair of us attached ourselves to the Company HQ with a major in command. We advanced with them over fields of lush grassland till we came to the flood bank of the Reno River. Climbing up the side, we advanced along the top, walking in grass that came up to our waists. The river was quite wide at this point and we moved forward with great caution knowing the enemy was on the other side of the river (or so we hoped). I did feel at a disadvantage, walking on top of the bank with the aerial standing up many feet above my head.

At last, the enemy showed his hand by firing on us from the other flood bank, on the opposite side of the river. We all hit the deck when we heard the unmistakeable burst of Spandau fire and the single rifle shots. It was a job for me to get down with the radio strapped on my back and the aerial still showing above the long grass. I slipped the set off and managed to lay the radio and offending aerial in the grass, and then checked that it didn't impede our signal coming in or going out.

After lying in the concealing grass without being fired on again, the major, a South African officer, asked one of the headquarters staff for his rifle, and taking it he crawled away into the long grass till he disappeared from view. Some time had elapsed when we heard a rifle shot, then another, and after a while the major reappeared and in a laconic manner said, "They won't bother us again!"

We moved on with the opposition at this stage being very light. Had they moved the bulk of their forces already over the other side of that most daunting river that we would eventually have to cross? The two of us now moved into another company, and once again attached ourselves to headquarters now they had become the lead company of the battalion.

We joined them in a village with a few farms scattered around, and were taking shelter in some cattle stalls while the company prepared itself to cross some open fields that bordered onto what looked like a canal. I was sitting down in the straw and had removed my steel helmet, placing it on the floor, so I could remove my headphones for a rest. Suddenly there came a loud explosion of a shell hitting the roof of the barn and showering us with pieces of broken tiles. I put out my hand to retrieve my helmet on the floor but found I was too late. It was resting on the head of the company sergeant major who, when it came to self-preservation, had discarded his own and grabbed mine.

More shells came our way causing some panic, but thankfully no casualties, and were fired on from our flank by a single tank which then withdrew and didn't take any more part in the battle. It could have been far worse if the tank had been more aggressive. But even then, the tank crew may have been thinking along the same lines as all of the combatants that the war had run its course so why get killed at its end? I retrieved my helmet from the sergeant major who said he was sorry and thought it was his. So was I, my hair being full of tile dust.

It was suggested by the company commander that we should fire the mortars in support of the company attack on, and along, the canal bank which was their objective, a distance of not much less than half a mile with no cover. The sergeant gave me the map reference, which I sent back in clear to Platoon HQ, and within a very short time ranging rounds were on their way passing overhead. After the bombs had landed and observed by us, we sent back the necessary corrections and were then ready to fire when the infantry advanced.

The infantry, in extended line, started walking across the open ground with grim faces and not a word spoken between them. Some were smoking and, but for the weapons they carried, they could have been on a Sunday afternoon ramble back home. The headquarters staff, we included, started off after a short interval.

When the line of infantry was halfway to the objective, the company commander gave us the order to fire and neutralise any of the enemy on the line of the canal. This order was relayed back and soon the bombs were falling onto the target, but then the enemy showed his hand by shelling the line of infantry, throwing up black plumes of acrid smoke when they landed. I saw one man carrying a Piat (antitank weapon) have it dashed from his hand and made useless by a shell fragment. Several other men were injured in the attack, but when we lifted our mortar fire, when the infantry were about 250 yards from their objective, they soon moved forward and secured the line of the canal. Afterwards, we moved on north.

The next day, advancing through countryside planted with vines, we inadvertently found ourselves in front of the retreating German forces, and only became aware of their presence when they began infiltrating back through our own lines. A most bizarre situation, seeing them stealthily work their way through the undergrowth of vines like ghosts in their field-grey uniforms, but carrying weapons which they started using when they saw us barring their escape route. After a sharp exchange, it finished just as abruptly as it had started with the enemy in flight and disappearing into the endless vines.

The infantryman's dread of standing on a mine came to one man in grim reality when he was advancing with his company. His friends called him 'Jap' for his likeness to the men of that nation and he had the misfortune, with the end of the war in sight, of treading on an undetectable German wooden shu mine that severed the man's foot at the ankle. He must have been one of the last casualties inflicted on the battalion in the war.

The sergeant and I at this stage were relieved from our duties of the observation post and taken up by two other members of the platoon. Both of us returned to our own detachments.

The battalion moved on with the amount of opposition from the enemy being almost nonexistent and was now looking as if their front could be in a state of collapse. But what did they still have in reserve? After fighting against such an efficient Army for so long, none of us could believe that they wouldn't turn and fight like they had on numerous occasions in the past. When things at times had looked bad for them, their troops had always been rallied together by superior generalship, with the tactical skill of men like Kesselring and Von Senger who had some of the best divisions anywhere in the German Army under their command in Italy.

It was at this point, the enemy started the abandonment of his transport and major stores of all kinds. The transports could have been left through lack of fuel. Our platoon decided to commandeer a German open-sided lorry that we used to carry our reserve of 3" mortar ammunition, also a German motorcycle that was in very good condition and had a very quiet engine sound. This was added to our dispatch riders in the platoon and was ably ridden by Len Midgley from one of the mortar detachments.

With the inability, or so it seemed, for the Germans to mount any kind of attack against us, the prospects looked very good now for the end of hostilities, whereas the writing must be 'on the wall' for them.

The Army were concerned with clearing out the enemy this side of the river before crossing, but now it seemed a formality. We had now left our carriers and were moving forward on foot making a sweep towards the river, making sure there were no pockets of resistance left.

Later, we came upon a group of Italians, mostly women, making gestures with their hands (a common trait with the Italians). They attracted our attention to a large mound of earth, which must have been 30' to 40' feet square and obviously made as a shelter by the Italians as insurance for their safety when the war reached them. That was not all; some of the women were muttering "Tedesco, Tedesco" with something like fear in their eyes. The word for German, in Italian, was the word they were muttering so we were on our guard for any trouble. If there were any Germans in the shelter, why didn't they show themselves?

I made my way to the steps leading down into the shelter and started down them in a gingerly way, hoping to prove the Italians wrong. I didn't volunteer for this but found myself doing it against the reason of logic, and if there were Germans in the dark interior, they should have quickly emerged with their hands above their heads. Descending the steps, I would have made a good target with the background of daylight behind me. When I reached ground level I could make out a dim light from an oil lamp inside, which cast its feeble rays of light over the shelter's occupants, and I realised that I had been rather reckless in descending the steps in the first place.

At a glance, I could see a goodly number of the enemy taking refuge here, and holding my rifle in a non-menacing manner, they looked me over and slowly raised their hands in submission after they could see the other members of the detachment coming down the steps. Then I saw something standing on the straw-covered floor that sent an involuntary shudder down my spine – the sight of a Spandau machine gun – a most fearsome weapon that had been used against our infantry during the war, and would hopefully never fire another round. It could have been used to dispose of all of us in the detachment within seconds if they had had the will to use it.

Fortunately, for us, they were more forgiving in adversity than the brigadier would have shown mercy to them, remembering his vile statement on prisoners in the theatre at Tolentino. Having removed the prisoners from the shelter, they were marched off into captivity while we moved on.

19. Bells of peace. Tito. The Holocaust.

At last, the battalion not only reached the Po River but also crossed over it. It was the 25th of April, and after our fill of German propaganda on the horror that would befall us, if we had attempted a crossing, it came to us all with great relief of our apparent deliverance from what could have been a bloodbath. We in the mortars had to wait our turn in crossing the river in our tracked vehicles.

By this time, the battalion was well and truly established on the far bank, as were the rest of the brigade. They had pockets of resistance to overcome on the other side and asked for our assistance with mortar fire. We fired many rounds in support of the battalion before the enemy were dislodged, who then laid down their weapons.

By now, the engineers had finished their construction work on the Bailey bridge and the vehicles could cross over. The bridge itself was a miracle of construction, many hundreds of yards in length with pontoons in the river supporting the many arches that spanned the whole river and its approaches. The pontoons had strainer wires on them to stop them from drifting in the strong current of the Po. It was the most extraordinary feat of engineering skill that I had ever seen in the war, and built in record time. One can't think of the consequence of it constructed under withering enemy fire, the loss of life would have been catastrophic with injured men falling into the water with no hope of rescue.

When the tracks of our carrier touched the approach of the bridge, they made a booming, hollow sound, but it reassured us knowing that we were safe looking down on the river when it could have been so different before the enemy were broken. None of us at the time could have known that we had fired our last mortar bombs in anger.

We moved on, into the countryside north of the river, through villages where we put up for the night and moved on in the day. After several days of moving on and finding no sign of our old adversary, we came to a large town where we found a Fascist HQ, not a very imposing place but interesting for what it contained.

The original occupants had fled, not wishing us to catch them in a place full of regalia of a deposed regime and had conveniently left it behind. Of course no one had ever been a Fascist was what they wished us to believe. I found a black silk neckerchief with a white border and motifs, also in white, of the emblem of Fascism – a bundle of faggots and an axe. Also, there were some oval badges with the same emblem and a background of the Italian colours of red, white and green. Then I gave myself a shock by finding a large photograph of the Fascist Dictator, sat at the head of a large ornate table, surrounded by stern looking members of his cabinet or Fascist ministers. But the thing that held the most fascination for me was the bold flourish of the signature on the photograph, that of Benito Mussolini.

I decided that the photograph was a wonderful souvenir to keep along with the scarf and badge. Then I realised, with a touch of sadness, I would have to leave it behind, for I was reluctant to roll or fold it up as we were still on active service and not in a department of antiquity. Forced by circumstances, I replaced the picture back where it came from, but it made me feel very dejected and always wish I had liberated the picture from the Fascist HQ. It would have been quite a prize.

This day I would always remember, not for the loss of the picture but for something that happened – something that changed all our lives. We were waiting for orders to move on and at the time I was with my friend, Stanley Abbey, doing some local sightseeing but within clear view of our parked carriers. It was very wondrous at the time that we were standing close to a church tower, when the bells started ringing out with peal after peal that kept on and on. Stanley looked at me in astonishment, and I at him as to what was going on. The bells had been a symbol of imminent invasion, so what was this? It soon dawned on us that the bells ringing out were proclaiming to the populace that peace had been declared, meaning the end of the War in Italy on the 2nd of May 1945.

The battalion moved on, filling up the vacuum left by the retreating German forces. Fighting was still going on in Germany with very heavy attacks by the Russians in the suburbs of Berlin, but for us it was most thankfully over. The German resistance was crumbling with the ferocity the would-be conquerors were now applying in taking the prize of Berlin. Our Army moved north, as was the American 5th Army, with our own battalion moving forward in 3-ton transports while we brought up the rear in our slow tracked vehicles.

We were coming to the outskirts of a village where we would be spending the night before moving on next day. Most of us were sitting up in the carriers for once, admiring the beauty of the Italian countryside without having to cower down below the steel sides in some safety from the enemy. We were distracted from our grand Italian tour by a sharp crack above the roar of the carrier engines in the convoy. And once again—Crack—then another; the unmistakable sound, to the infantryman, of a near miss from a bullet. By this time, we had rearranged our bodies below the protective sides of the carrier. Many shots were fired at us and we thinking the war was over, it came as a shock.

On our arrival in the village, the battle patrol were sent out in skirmish line to flush out the culprit, but later came back without discovering the would-be assassin. It was most fortunate that we had been a moving target; otherwise, it could have been a very different story. We moved on our way north every day, stopping in villages at every opportunity.

We started seeing sights we never thought possible, of columns of German troops looking very dejected and being marched into captivity by their guards. They looked very bedraggled and unkempt in what were once smart uniforms, made more so by the removal of all insignia of rank and regiment. None of them were wearing their identifiable steel helmets, just their forage caps, making them look less menacing now. I could see no sign of hope in their dejected faces, only the despair of the vanquished, and I thanked God I wasn't one of them.

The platoon, to their credit, made no ribald remarks from the safety of our armoured vehicles, but looked on in passive silence at the passing human flotsam and jetsam – the end result of all major wars.

I could feel no kind of elation or triumph for being the victor, but felt a kind of disenchantment about the whole sorry mess, with the magnitude and consequences that the end of the conflict would bring to millions of displaced persons in Europe.

After a day or so of witnessing groups of marching men, always in good order and well disciplined, we moved into a village for our usual night's stay, and while here we received news that the War in Europe had come to its close. With this unbelievable news still sinking in, most of the men in the platoon started to look around for something to celebrate with. Battalion said that two bottles of beer would be issued free to each man by the President of the Regimental Institute; extra would have to be paid for. I didn't drink so I handed mine over to two willing recipients.

Just being a bystander, I looked on with great interest as the drink started to take its toll on the revellers. Then things started to get out of hand when they removed a complete mortar off one of the carriers in the yard and, after a struggle, managed to mount it. Having got so far, someone then placed a full bottle down the barrel as if a bomb, and on reaching the bottom it struck the firing pin and smashed. Someone called out, "Misfire!" So, they played out the procedure of a real misfire by unlocking the barrel from the baseplate and lifted it up so the offending bomb would slip down and be caught at the muzzle, but this time it was glass and beer.

It proceeded to get more dangerous as the game went on and after a number of bottles had reached the bottom, the yard was strewn with glass and many pints of beer. So, when some idiotic person suggested firing some live ammunition he soon had some willing helpers who were going through with it. Then it dawned on the less inebriated members in the platoon that if they fired the mortar they could kill some unsuspecting persons, or have a mishap there and kill or maim everyone standing in the yard. In the end common sense prevailed with the mortar placed back on the carrier plus a beer-stained barrel.

As for myself, I had been most grateful to the men in the platoon that somehow we had survived against the odds. But just now, I couldn't bring myself to join in and celebrate. My mind was full of other thoughts and I needed to leave the party and be on my own.

I slipped away without anyone noticing; out into the rough, untracked countryside, and being a warm spring evening I found it most pleasant and a distraction from a hazardous past. It was a good time for quiet contemplation, and yes, the war was well and truly over, but would there be peace in the lands that had seen so much strife? Only time would tell.

As I walked away from the noise and bustle of the constant living with others, my thoughts inevitably turned towards the friends I had known and had left the shores of England with, but would not be celebrating today or any other day. Their time had run out and they were destined to remain in the peninsula forever, whereas we would hopefully have the joy of returning home to our loved ones.

Thinking back over the campaign, the impression it had created in each and every individual's mind, of anxiety, doubt and fear that was always present when near the enemy. That part was now thankfully past, but there was nothing that would ever compensate for the loss of your close friends and would stay with you forever. There was a sense of guilt that you had been spared and you would never be able to comprehend why. I had tears running from my eyes at my own thoughts, but I was unashamed at showing the emotion I was feeling at the time.

After our end of the war news, the battalion moved on north, arriving in an area of desolate landscape where we would bivouac for a while, out in the back of beyond but in the vicinity of Trieste and Monfalcone. The ground was covered with large boulders as if cast there at random by a giant. The ground was so hard it was difficult to push the tent pegs in, and this at one time could have been a volcanic area.

It was Sunday and all denominations were called on to attend a service of thanksgiving for the war's end beneath the canopy of God's sky. We assembled for the parade and formed into three sides of a square with the officers standing on one side at the front. The battalion padre, who looked resplendent in his regalia, made the rest of us look drab in our khaki uniforms. We were standing at ease, waiting to be called to attention by the adjutant on the arrival of the commanding officer, Lieutenant Colonel Cleghorn, who had given me a roasting for having a snag in my pullover on the day after coming out of the line, and without having a bath for six weeks. It was now after the time the service should have started with no sign of the CO, so we waited in silence with no one moving or talking.

After five minutes had elapsed and still no sign of him, the officers began to look rather agitated at the absence of the man who up until now was five minutes late for his own parade. If it were any of the seven hundred men on parade who had been late, they would have automatically found themselves on a charge for insubordination and, unfortunately, standing before the man who was now late. What kind of person would be late for a thanksgiving service when the men under his command had fought and died to reach this far, and had won him the ultimate prize of a victory of arms after a very long and hard campaign? Now being late showed he had little or no empathy with his men who were now waiting for him.

Time dragged on for the assembled battalion who were getting warm in the morning sun, and when the time reached half an hour, we could hear hoof beats in the distance. Then the CO loomed into view on a horse surrendered by the Germans to us as spoils of war, and he was making the most of it. He jumped from the horse with great style and agility, and sauntering onto the parade, he returned the adjutant's salute and told him to "Stand the battalion at ease." He then told the padre to "Carry on."

The service of thanksgiving was lost on the men who were inwardly fuming with resentment at their treatment by a senior officer. He had calmly ridden off into the countryside for a jaunt while we had to wait for his pleasure. He alone would have sanctioned the service of thanksgiving and the time and the place for it.

We started to get a large influx of soldiers from Yugoslavia (now the former Yugoslavia) into the area. Our intelligence told us that their government had their sights set on the port of Trieste, and were willing to fight for it if necessary. Tito, the Yugoslavian leader who had fought against the Germans there, wanted some kind of payment and now also laid claim to the port of Pola, down at the tip of the Italian peninsula. Pola was ceded to the Italians after the First World War, but now he wanted it back.

The war had been over just a week and all of a sudden we could hear the drums of war again, or was it a continuation of that war or the third one looming over the horizon? To say the very least, we were perplexed by such thoughts and only wished to return to our homes.

We in fact were very vulnerable here from an attack and there was some cause for alarm. Tito's troops were all over the place. Moreover, they were well armed. Most of them had captured German weapons and carried bandoliers full of ammunition draped around their shoulders, and many of them had machine guns. They all looked tough and formidable, a quality they had displayed against their enemy over the years and must in numbers run into many thousands of men, whereas we were only brigade strength at about two thousand. If the balloon went up, we could find ourselves in very deep trouble.

The brigade was put on a state of alert and nobody felt very happy about the situation. However, even in this kind of potential danger, we could still smile in adversity, and this happened after a column of Tito's Army walked passed us over the rough terrain. Bringing up the rear was a cannon on two spoked wheels about the size you would find on a pram (baby carriage), and could have been! The barrel was bolted onto a shaft that held the wheels, and one man was pulling it along with a rope while a second man held the barrel steady and pushed. The calibre of the cannon was under an inch in diameter, but we all had to smile when we saw a cork pushed into the muzzle attached to a loop of string, making it look like a child's pop gun. That made us all feel better with a good laugh, but only when they were out of earshot.

We started to get the most distressing and disturbing news imaginable from the *Stars and Stripes* and 8th Army newspapers – that of death camps found in Germany. This was devastating news, even for war-hardened soldiers who had seen the pose of death in many forms along the way. The sole purpose of the camps was for the complete extermination of the Jewish race in Europe. It was news to us of a most barbaric nature and was a hard job for us to stomach after the Germans, having opposed us in conflict, had always fought fairly on the battlefield, or to us had seen to be so.

We looked at a full-page picture that had appeared in one of the papers, which depicted a Jewish boy of about four years of age dressed in the garb afforded them by their tyrannical masters, complete with mobcap to match. The poor child was sitting in squalid conditions on the floor with his back resting against an oven, which would have later consumed him but now mercifully closed down. In death, he was clutching a handful of straw, symbolic to us all that we would do the same to retain our hold on life.

He had died most likely asking and crying for his mother, which is what any of us would have done in the same circumstances. He never enjoyed the comfort his mother could have given him at the end. And her life would have ended just the same, only the pangs of despair and suffering would have been more vivid for her to bear at the last. What kind of people could perpetrate such a heinous crime against humanity and expect to get away with it? For several days, the newspapers were full of the most gruesome details and the most horrible pictures imaginable, the result of which could only have been carried out by people who had a most sadistic kind of nature, like the Gestapo or some SS units. The whole thing was most unforgivable with the sheer magnitude and scale of the crime against the Jewish nation.

We moved on once again, not very far but to a better strategic position. We were still on a state of full alert with double guards and orders to remain most vigilant.

Early one morning, the men who had just completed their night of guard duty were mustered on parade with the rest of the platoon for some rifle drill before breakfast. After falling in, we were brought to attention by the sergeant. Then he gave the command to "Port arms." This entailed moving the rifle diagonally across the chest, left hand on the stock and, with your right hand, pull back the bolt and then place your hand on the butt.

The sergeant shouted out, "That was downright shoddy! Close your bolts and squeeze the trigger." Bang—, a shot rang out, the noise vibrating around inside my steel helmet making me dazed and shaky. Some of the platoon broke ranks and gathered round, but to their relief found me unscathed. The round fired had missed my head by inches and my friend was just as shocked as I, and but for one fact that he was holding his rifle at the correct angle across his chest when he pulled the trigger, otherwise, my name would have appeared on the proverbial village war memorial. My friend, who coming off his guard duty, had forgotten to remove the rounds from his rifle magazine, such was the stress we were under at the time with the constant uncertainty of what Tito had in mind.

We had become a blocking force in stopping the Yugoslavian Army from infiltration through our lines into Northern Italy. But the problem was they outnumbered us by 10/1.

After a week or two's stay, without any kind of leave to Trieste or Udine, the battalion would be on the move once again. Orders had come through that the brigade with its three infantry battalions, of the Fusiliers, the London Scottish and London Irish, were being sent down into Yugoslav territory to the town called Pola, which was 70 miles into Tito's heartland.

Within days, we had packed and started on our journey down the Adriatic seaboard, but the countryside looked rather inhospitable and baron with large boulders and stunted undergrowth everywhere. It was a long, hot journey with the convoy only moving at around 20 miles per hour with the platoon riding in our open carriers, and we were soon covered in a fine grey dust. This soon penetrated into our clothes, and what with the heat of the day made life unpleasant with the dust churned up by the carrier tracks as if it were boiling. We had put up with this many times before, it was nothing new but it was uncomfortable.

At long last we came onto a bend in the road and there, in front of us, we saw a most magnificent panoramic view of Pola set in the sweep of the bay. As far as I could see, the stately buildings were of a similar character and hadn't been damaged like the rest of the country by the rigours of war.

Moving down the hill into the town, we passed by a large amphitheatre in its entirety; a wonderful sight. It was very pleasing for us dust-ridden soldiers to find such a place, which we would have to garrison for more than 8 months, but that was in the future. Eventually, the convoy up ahead moved off in various directions with dispatch riders showing them to their new quarters in the town. Our own dispatch riders came up alongside the carriers and turned us off the main road, a distance of a few hundred yards, moving passed wonderfully cultivated gardens with the flowers in full bloom. It could well have been a park.

Moving on, we came to a very fine building with two floors. This was the main school of the town, but was in fact a polytechnic, and to us war weary soldiers it looked palatial. We, of course, were now in Italian territory; Pola having changed hands after the First World War and Tito wanted it returned forthwith to Yugoslavia.

Having parked the carriers in the school grounds, the platoon climbed down, over the sides of the vehicles, but then we were forced to cling onto the steel sides till we regained our land legs. The mortar crews sitting by the sides of the Ford V8 engines had had their legs and lower body immersed in a heat of around 120°F for over 5 hours. This was jolly fine in winter but not in summer. The condition became known as 'petrol feet' and was most unpleasant till the limbs regained the circulation.

After a while, we gathered up our kit and went inside the school. The grand edifice of the outside was just as wonderfully built inside with a wide, curved oak staircase leading up to the higher level, which the platoon was going to inhabit, and found a spacious room with a high ceiling that must have been 20 feet high. We began to wonder if we were in the right place. Indeed, it was a most wonderful place, which even contained an upright piano, in good order, allocated for the sole use of the mortar platoon. The dormitory would hold the whole platoon less the half-dozen sergeants who would have their own quarters. Divisional engineers were going to make everyone a folding camp bed before the winter set in, so for the time being we were to sleep on the wood block floor. No problem after being without a bed for so many years.

We started training straight away with the situation of the enemy being at the gates, waiting for some provocation to launch an attack against the intruders of their old territory. It was a very grave issue and could blow up like a powder keg with our brigade in the middle. Pola was a most beautiful town, however in the early days of our occupation we had little time to enjoy where we were stationed, as it was nominally a danger zone and we were never, at anytime, allowed to forget it.

The company had to stand guard duty at times and we were always marched to our respective posts by the battalion band. The guard positions were Brigade HQ, the Bank of Italia and all other important places in the town. The most paramount consideration was to our training with the mortars. We worked long and hard with them in the hot sun and were all proficient with the weapon.

One day, we were called to a platoon meeting by the captain who told us, most unexpectedly, that the platoon was being disbanded with the men being posted into the rifle companies of W, X, Y & Z. It came as very bad news for us, with all the mortars placed into store and the rest of us leaving for our new companies. We decided from the start that we would try and make a go of it. All of the men in my age group were sent into W Company, which seemed to be full of new recruits fresh out from England. They looked and acted just like boys. To all of us who had served in Specialist Company during the war, we felt that we had been forced into taking a retrograde step.

In our new company, we seemed to be in everlasting discussion with talks by our platoon officer, also new out from England and showing it. We spent very little time at drill and never did any kind of fieldcraft, not the workings you would expect in a top rifle company that had always carried out such sterling work in the defeat of the enemy in the peninsula.

Everything seemed out of kilter with what we should be doing as a rifle company, here facing possible danger and surrounded by a large force of a potential enemy. It was only recently that we had seen tanks in the hills beyond the town – and they were not ours.

One afternoon, the officer held a question and answer lesson from the education section of the Army, ABCA (Army Bureau of Current Affairs), in which he had a list of questions set by the bureau for testing the intelligence of the soldiers present. He found that the majority of the questions asked could only be answered by the new intake into the company, from the mortar platoon, and not by the new recruits.

Then coming to one question on his list, he hesitated while he read it through to himself. He eventually said to us, "I don't know why they should include such a question like this because it's obvious no one here will know the answer." He went on. "I suppose I should read it out, the question being: Dorothy L. Sayers, the author, has written a religious play. Can anyone here tell me the name of the play?" He faced us with a sardonic smile, thinking he would have to wait forever for the answer. I caught his eye and he said, "Well?" I replied to him in a confident manner, "*Man born to be King*, sir!" He looked at me in a most incredulous way and asked, "How did you know that?" The platoon at this stage was dismissed for the day.

The platoon carried on without any firm training programme. I suppose it could have been the result of the old veterans of the company, who had survived the war, were now leaving to return to their homes. Then one day, out of the blue, came a stunning piece of news for us, be it the late members of the mortar platoon. The news was that we should remove our kit from W Company and report back into Specialist Company immediately. W Company, for us, was now in the past.

We collected our kit together and made it back to the school that we returned to with some gratification after our banishment. We were called to a meeting where Captain Sherlock addressed us with some well-chosen words. "I am very pleased to see you have all been returned back into the mortars, which is your true employment, and will now carry on from where we were told to call a halt." The captain carried on. "You may well wonder why you have been reinstated." And here a note of triumph came into his voice, which he couldn't suppress. "Brigade here made a grave mistake by disbanding the mortar platoon to strengthen the rifle companies. Army HQ in Trieste got wind of this and told Brigade, here in Pola, to revert back at once to the correct battalion formation, which includes the mortars." The captain looked very pleased with himself and proud to have his platoon reinstated.

20. Escort duty. The Atomic Bomb. Home leave.

At this time, some of the men in the battalion with high age groups, who had seen some active service, were being returned back to England for leave before being sent out to the Far East and the war with Japan. Eventually, most of us would end up there in accordance with a promise made by Churchill to the American President that all British troops would be sent out to the conflict there at the end of hostilities in Europe.

It was indeed wonderful to return back to the school again. Even the old Italian caretaker was delighted, seeing that in the time we had been there none of us had caused him any concern. Training still carried on to a very high degree with the threat of Tito's Army ever-present in the hills around the town.

Sergeant Pepperell, up to his old tricks again, sent for me. He informed the wary private standing in front of him that I had been placed on escort duty with a full corporal in charge and a driver. We were to take a battalion prisoner to the military prison in Klagenfurt, Austria, where he was to serve a three-year sentence. The journey would take several days. We would be leaving Pola, then go via Trieste, Udine, Villach to Klagenfurt, and our transport – a 15cwt truck. It was patently obvious by now that the platoon sergeant had his claws in me, for what reason I had no idea. No one else had been detailed off for this work since he had sent me to Rome, so I must be a target for this most obnoxious character.

We left the next day with enough rations to last us three. With the corporal sitting in the cab alongside the driver, I had to sit in the back with the prisoner and the responsibility that goes with it. I started a conversation with him and asked him the reason why he was going into the military prison. He told me in a very guarded manner that just before the war ended, he had lost his nerve when the battalion was in the frontline and deserted from his company. After living off the land for a while, he was picked up by the redcaps and sentenced. I felt very sorry for the man, now that the war had finished, but if I failed and he escaped I would be taking his place in the prison.

The road from Pola to Trieste was completely devoid of traffic or inhabitants along the way, making it seem very eerie. Nearing Trieste, we passed by the Italian liner *Rex*, the once proud holder of the Atlantic Blue Ribbon for the fastest crossing, now lying on its side rusting away in the shallows. How the mighty had fallen. We went through Trieste, then Monfalcone, and a halt was called for the day, not many miles from Udine, at a small village there.

The driver and the corporal must have talked about our overnight stopover between themselves because stopping at one habitation in the village, they were welcomed with open arms by the many occupants inside. Obviously, one of the two must have had a clandestine liaison with a member of the household when the battalion was stationed in the area. Life is full of surprises.

Of course, I was lumbered with the prisoner and left to me to keep him company during the night, so was compelled to use the handcuffs. After a restless night, we packed our kit and moved on, through Udine and later crossed the border into Austria, and into the most wonderful countryside I have ever seen. But for the prisoner on hand it would have been a grand tour. We passed through the outskirts of Villach, and later came to Klagenfurt where the military prison was situated.

The corporal now showed his authority by handcuffing the prisoner and marched with him up to the huge wooden doors and knocked on same. They were then admitted into what could have been called the punishment yard. Everything inside the prison is always carried out at the double, such is the punishment, and is appropriately called 'Three

Years Hard Labour' for desertion. I would call it a most sadistic regime and one in which our platoon sergeant would be in his true element. The door slammed shut behind them and I could hear them running off at the double to the reception office.

Ten minutes later, to my astonishment, the door swung open and the corporal came out, still handcuffed to his charge, telling us they wouldn't accept the prisoner on the grounds that the papers of his conviction were not in order. So, with the same complement we came with, we started on our journey back to Pola, but not without stopping for the night with the same Italian family and my job once again of being the jailer.

That evening, when alone with him, we talked about his position now and the refusal to accept him into the prison at Klagenfurt. He may have had a psychiatric problem and they could have thought he needed medical treatment and not prison. I impressed on him that he had a good chance to get off the charge when we returned to Battalion HQ. Later, he gave me his word that he wouldn't scappare (Italian for run away) while in my custody. That night, the prisoner and I again slept on the floor in our blankets, whereas the corporal and driver were sleeping in pastures new.

On waking the next morning, I felt justifiably relieved to find he was still with us. We were soon on our way, and after leaving Trieste behind, we moved down the coast road, passing once again the hulk of that once great luxury liner, beached after being damaged in the war with its name still discernible on the rusting vessel. What a way to end its days after being so admired a few short years ago when it had sailed into New York harbour to the acclaim of all the ships there, and now? Once again, there was a complete absence of traffic on the road, mechanical or human. It was very strange and you realised just how cut off you were down in Pola.

After an uneventful and bumpy ride in the back of the truck, we were glad to reach our destination. After wishing the prisoner good luck, he was handed back over to the regimental police at Battalion HQ. I was never to see or hear of him again. I then reported back to Sergeant Pepperell.

One morning, shortly after my return, I looked on the school (now company) noticeboard in the hall and started to read a bulletin pinned on there. At first, I couldn't fully comprehend what the message was all about which said 'Atomic Bomb dropped over Japan', and went on to say it had the power of a hundred suns and had caused great destruction to the city of Hiroshima. This was dated 6th of August 1945. There were no other details, but it created a great deal of controversy among the men. A further bulletin appeared which said a second bomb had been dropped on Nagasaki, and once again caused great devastation. This was dated 9th of August. A day later, on the 10th, the bulletin just said 'War with Japan at an End: Japan accepts Surrender Terms.'

We all felt a keen sense of relief at the news. However, a few days later, relief turned to anger after hearing how the Japanese had treated our Allied prisoners of war. Nevertheless, we had been spared from crossing the ocean to fight the Japanese, and felt well and truly thankful for what you could call our deliverance from a savage and brutal enemy.

We were, however, very alarmed at the high casualty figures the two bombs had wantonly incurred on the civilian population. None of us had the intellectual capacity to try and unravel the new science of mass destruction, or its moral implications, but we all felt a sense of unease about the new weapon that had fallen into our hands.

I have found in life that justice comes very rarely, but it does happen. One morning, Sergeant Major Cartwright summoned me to Company HQ. On arriving there, I went inside and found several members of the company in a state of undress and I was ordered to do the same as the others. Removing my tunic and shirt I was now dressed like the others in vest and trousers. Looking round the group, I could see two sergeants, a full corporal and lance corporal, and the rest of us other ranks present.

I was most intrigued to find myself in the company of Sergeant Pepperell who looked rather subdued in his white vest. Then the sergeant major called the motley looking crew together. "Stand in a straight line, in any position you like facing me and stand at ease." He went on. "This is an identity parade which you have been asked to attend, with all positions of rank removed and with a variety of people standing in the line-up. Keep your eyes to the front and don't smile."

He left the room and then returned with two redcaps escorting a tall, well-dressed Italian man who looked very uneasy at the assembly of frozen-faced men. He started walking down the line having a good look at each individual person and looking at me, he gave a cursory glance and moved on. When he had completed his scrutiny of the possible criminals, he went into a huddle with the law enforcers. After a lot of speaking in whispers, the Italian pointed to the sergeant major's list on the clipboard, he then made a swift exit along with the police escort while we were left to dress.

Later on, we were told the reason for the parade. A soldier had illegally sold a motorcycle to the Italian gentleman. Soon after, the military police arrested the man and questioned him about where the motorcycle had come from, hence the identity parade.

Days later, it was revealed that the motorcycle referred to by the police was the German machine that belonged to the mortar platoon, and not belonging to any individual. However, it had been sold and the money pocketed by none other than the man who had harassed me since the day I joined the platoon. Now it was his turn to be degraded. In the confinement of Battalion HQ, the commanding officer reduced him to the ranks for his part in the matter and now he was plain Private Pepperell. At long last, he had received his comeuppance and was swiftly moved out of the battalion.

We had a visitor come into the port – HMS *Ajax*. The government, no doubt, wished to show the flag as a means of reminding Tito that we were willing to defend the outpost. With its eight six-inch guns, *Ajax* was indeed a formidable show of strength and at a very crucial time.

The battalion was invited onboard ship, a company at a time, for a tour round the prominent parts of the vessel. I decided to take advantage of this and look over the now-famous ship, after its encounter with the *Graf Spee* at the battle of the River Plate in December 1939. Before I left the ship, I asked a sailor if any member of the current crew had fought in the battle. He smiled and shook his head.

Off one of the landing stages at Pola, you were able to discern an object lurking under the surface in about 15 fathoms of murky water. It was only when the sea was calm and the sun in a favourable position that the secret of the depth was revealed to be an Italian submarine. But how had it sunk and by whom? The ship was upright with the conning tower and hull apparently undamaged. What kind of fate had befallen this vessel, and were any poor souls still entombed there? We were never to find the answers to these sad, but intriguing questions.

The mortar platoon training still carried on with a visit from a man from Brigade to teach us the rudiments of the infantry range finder. We had a full gathering for this with the exception of those on leave back in England. After the demonstration, which had taken place in one of the classrooms at the school, we were asked questions about the lesson and its roll for the platoon.

At the end of the lesson, the captain thanked the demonstrator for his explanation to a very complex instrument, which then received a good round of applause from the platoon. Captain Sherlock then dismissed the platoon with one exception – I was to stay behind. I considered this a rather strange order. I thought to myself, what have I done this time? The men filed out through the door till the last one had gone, leaving me alone with the officer who then closed the door shut.

He looked me over, not unkindly but with a smile and said, "I have a proposition I would like to put to you, but at the same time I'm well aware of your record concerning promotion. That aside, I can offer you a return back to England for a month's leave, otherwise you will not be eligible until the end of the year for one with your age group '50'." He went on. "If you accept my offer, you won't return back here to the 9th Fusiliers, but instead report to Netheravon, in Wiltshire, which you may know is the 3" Mortar School and Training Depot." He paused before going on. "You should become an officer in no time if you go there. In fact, I guarantee you will be made an officer!" After another pause, he said, "What are your thoughts about it?"

I tried to pull my scattered wits together before replying to the captain. "Sir, you held a meeting here this morning with the full platoon being present. Half of them are NCO, many of them being full sergeants of long-standing, and most of them with good war records. With respect, sir, why me and not one of them?" The officer looked at me before replying. "If I had wanted one of them, I would have asked that person, but no I have asked you because I know you have the right record for success in the position." The captain then ended with, "Well, I would like you to take up the offer because I know with your background you can do it and I have faith in you, so sleep on it tonight and tell me in the morning."

The interview was over and I returned back to our dormitory where I was asked why Captain Sherlock had wanted me. I never told anyone or ever did to what we discussed that day in the schoolroom at Pola. I spent a sleepless night going over in my mind what the captain had asked of me.

Next morning, I reported back to the platoon office for a word with the captain who on seeing me arrive there asked his staff if they would leave for a while. He closed the door behind them and asked me, "What have you decided?" Standing in front of him, I was keenly aware that he had done this for my own advancement in the Army, but I had made up my mind. "Thank you, sir," I said, "for your kindness shown towards me in the offering of this position and your confidence that I could carry it through, and I do indeed feel very honoured." I went on. "But I only have one wish now, sir, and that is to return home to my parents." On hearing this, the captain was most understanding and generous with his praise and finished by saying, "You were the man for the position. And I can assure you now, I shall not be asking anyone else to take your place." After saluting the captain, I left the office, feeling for once very unsure of myself at what I had done.

The golden summer slowly turned into autumn, and with the return of the darker evenings, the platoon spent many happy evenings gathered round the piano with Len Midgley at the keyboard entertaining us by playing requests. These played out to the accompaniment of the platoon's male voice choir! Not quite up to the standard of the Huddersfield Choral Society, but music to men who had been deprived of the simple things in life for so long. Indeed, it was a most enjoyable time in the platoon when we received our camp beds made by the Royal Engineers, keeping their promise to get us off the floor by winter.

We had a visit from the Army commander of the Mediterranean land forces, Field Marshal Alexander, who was going to give us a pep talk in the amphitheatre with its vast arena. Still in the warm sunshine, the brigade gathered around him on the massive tiers of seats, where once the Roman legionnaires had sat with their wives while they watched the acts of mayhem performed below them, between the combatants trying to kill one another, and had taken place here even before the birth of Christ. Humanity, alas, hasn't progressed very far since that time.

The field marshal looked around the brigade before speaking. "Coming here today, I must first congratulate you on the outcome of the war your brigade played as part of the very successful 56 Division.

But we still have a job to do here, and how important it is to hold on to the territory here, in this port at Pola, which is still Italian and will hopefully remain so in the future." He went on. "I know this to be a very isolated outpost and rather cut off from the main land forces, but I think I know my British Tommy very well and would fight if challenged, and–" his next words were made inaudible by the resounding clangour of ringing bells from the church standing alongside the amphitheatre.

The field marshal looked very irate at having his talk drowned out by the would-be saboteurs. Alexander turned to his staff and quickly dispatched his retinue of officers and redcaps to quell the mutinous insurgents who would dare do such a thing. The bells continued to ring out, and then ceased abruptly in mid peal, the chimes becoming discordant when the ringers were stopped in what must have been a show of force. It would have made a good libretto for an Italian comic opera.

The GOC carried on with a few well-chosen words after this escapade, and then turned his attention to decorate a few officers in the brigade. One of them was the company commander who had complained bitterly about the cigarette packet thrown into his slit trench by one of his own men when we were fighting for our very survival that day on the Anzio beachhead, and he hadn't shown much in the way of leadership at the time. Now he had a DSO pinned to his tunic by Alexander, and I could well believe the old saying in the Army that most of the decorations come up with the rations and, indeed, it had been demonstrated to me that it was so.

After the brigadier brought the parade to attention, the field marshal was whisked away to the small airstrip just outside the town to fly to his next engagement, wherever that was.

The men were still going on leave to England when their age groups came up. After having a month's leave in the homeland, they were compelled to return to the battalion as there was no general demobilisation in the Army. The troops were still required for garrison duty. All good tradesmen were exempt from this if they were plumbers or electricians holding a City and Guilds certificate, or a higher qualification could obtain a class B release on application. All of them urgently required back home to help repair the six years of neglect and destruction the legacy of the war had left us with.

We still carried on with our training and guard duties, the main one being at a check-post several miles out of town where we would stand guard day and night for a week before being relieved. The main object of the exercise was to check all that went out and all that came in along the road. Most of this traffic was just horse and cart, and civilians coming through with farm produce to feed the mouths of the inhabitants of Pola. Most of them crossing the demarcation line were of Italian origin and had smallholdings. They farmed on the perimeter of the ceded territory and they looked and obviously lived in abject poverty.

During our tour of duty there, we were to see many sad sights of people just clinging on to life with nothing to spare. What would happen to most of the populous around here if it returned back to Yugoslavia?

The month of November was well advanced when several of us were relieved from duty at the check-post and told to report back to Company HQ at the school. This sounded very interesting and was. My age group '50' (the Armies' 'Age and Service Group' method of releasing soldiers after the end of the 1939-45 conflict) had come up for leave in England – after being abroad for nearly two and a half years. I was going to start the journey back home on Sunday.

Come Sunday, having said goodbye to our friends left behind, the leave party piled into the back of the transport and were soon away with the expectation that we could be home by Wednesday. We had to travel back over the same route designated to us by the Yugoslavian government, as it was the only approach road to and from Pola. On this road, once again, there was no sign of activity till we came to the outskirts of Trieste and the lonely rusting hulk of the *Rex*.

We stopped in Trieste for a cup of tea and our haversack rations (a sandwich) and then carried on to the nearest railhead. We then boarded our train, which had seen better days with no comfort and just a means of getting personnel from A to B. It was pitiful, but the one saving grace was that we were on our way home. The air offensive had almost brought the railway to the brink of destruction over the last three years. There was no direct route back home, so we would have to make it by a more tortuous journey over rails cobbled together just to get the trains moving again.

We slept on the moving train that night, arriving in Milan next morning. Then we were ordered off the train to await transport to take us to a transit camp outside the city. While waiting for our transports, the vastness of Milan Central and its network of tracks and sidings enthralled me. In fact, the largest station I have ever seen.

Later, the transport delivered us to the camp which you could say was also a vast complex specially built for the troops in transit, either going home for good or just on leave. Here, the camp commandant explained to us that there was a hold up in troop movement owing to the severity of the bad weather in the English Channel, and we would stay here until further notice. To add to our misfortune, everyone was confined to the camp as Milan was strictly out of bounds or off limits to all troops in transit, and if anyone should disobey this order he would be immediately returned to his unit.

We had been deprived of visiting one of the most beautiful cities in the world with the cathedral and La Scala theatre – a must-see for any visitor. It was the equivalent of visiting Cairo and to ignore seeing the pyramids. The sense of frustration increased when the Monday eventually turned into Friday. Then, at last, we were told we would be leaving the next morning.

After going back to Milan station, we boarded our train that would now take us all the way to the port of Calais. We left the vast complex of the station and slowly moved towards the mountains in the far distance. Later, passing through the town of Domodossola, we made our entrance into the Simplon tunnel – at that time the world's longest. Moving through this very masterpiece of Italian engineering, we at last came out into the light at a place called Brig, in the Rhone Valley, Switzerland, and later passed into France.

We had meals on the train, arranged for us along the way, and slept on the train during the hours of darkness. This had certainly been no Cook's tour journey, more like a Spartan existence in keeping with the travel of the day.

The evidence of massive destruction was everywhere you cast your eyes and would take many years to rectify. The long dark night changed into the dawn of another day that most of us would wish to remember forever with gratitude for having the chance of returning.

We came into a network of sidings, which could only be the terminus at the port. With the train having stopped, we were ordered off by some officials who then directed us towards a hallway at the end of the platform.

Inside the hallway was a large sign, which stated in a most uncompromising manner that if your kit contained any kind of enemy weapons or equipment, it must be handed in to the military police. Failure to do so would result in you being returned to your unit. As we moved through the hall, several of the men were picked at random and searched by the police. Standing in a queue, we passed into a long room where, sitting at tables, were about ten studious looking gentlemen in civilian clothes. Some of them were smoking their pipes, no doubt to make us feel for once in a very long time that we had returned back to civilization.

This was the documentation centre where you presented yourself when a vacant space appeared at a table. I walked up to a now vacant space and was asked for my pay-books, part one and two, by the man sitting there. He then asked me for my name and regimental number and, checking his list over, he wrote me out a leave pass and stamped it. Then he gave me four weeks leave pay and accrued back pay that gave me a grand total of almost five pounds sterling.

Walking away from the table, I looked at the pass, which told me that I must start back from my leave on the 26th of December, Boxing Day 1945. How insensitive the people in authority can be in spoiling a first Christmas at home since 1941, but I just thought that was in the future.

Walking out of the building, I came onto the quay where a cross channel ship was waiting to return us back home to our kith and kin, but it still seemed to have the reality of a dream. We didn't have long to wait for them to clear the backlog in the centre. With the last man up the gangway, it was pulled away and we moved away from the jetty to the delight of the soldiers onboard.

We stayed on deck, not wishing to miss a minute of the experience of our return. The sea was calm and we made good progress towards the white cliffs. After landing at Folkestone, and a short walk, we came onto the station platform where we were shepherded onto a London bound train that was awaiting us – a special for troops only. After what seemed like a long journey and the light changing to the dark, we arrived at Waterloo station so I had to say goodbye to my friends (until the 26th of December). They would now be making tracks to all points of the compass, whereas no one was going from Marylebone station with me.

Having arrived via the tube at Baker Street station, I walked the short distance to Marylebone and was fortunate to find a train waiting in the station. It was Sunday night with not many people around, so I found a compartment for myself and sat facing the engine on the left-hand side. I had a reason for taking this seat. The train pulled out of the station on the last leg of the journey and for the first time I felt very lonely and, indeed, I was after being in the company of others for so long. The train stopped at every station, their names now discernible after the blackout when the lamps had been removed for the duration of the war. Progress indeed.

The train stopped at Beaconsfield. One more stop to go and I would be well and truly home. The carriage door opened and two young ladies stepped into the compartment and sat in the far corner on my side, followed by two middle-aged men who also sat in the far corner with their backs to the engine. After the train had pulled away from the station, I pressed myself into the corner with my face to the window, wishing to see a sight, at times in the past, I thought I would never have the pleasure of seeing again.

The train entered the Beaconsfield tunnel and I cupped my right hand over my eye, the better to keep out the glare from the light inside the compartment, hoping to see the sight for which I had waited so long. Still in the darkness of the tunnel, I could see in the reflection of the glass window that one of the men in the corner was attracting the attention of the ladies, by making a gesture with his finger pointing to his breast. This indicated to them that I was wearing medal ribbons. He was enacting in pantomime to his audience (and at my expense with sarcasm written all over his face) that the soldier boy sitting by the window was showing off. He was completely unaware that I could see the mischief he was making.

But here, my thoughts turned away from the hurtful incident as the train emerged from the tunnel. And there it was, the lights shining along the length of the valley, a vision I had conjured up in my mind many times but only now to look on again. Instinctively, to me, came that wonderful song, sung by Deanna Durbin, which went, *'I can see the lights of Home; Riding to me on the Foam!'* The man in the corner was temporarily forgotten.

After seeing all I wished to see, I thought it a great pity that the miserable little man couldn't have been with me to share my reason for wearing the ribbons. He would have been mortified at the prospect of such an invitation. He would have also seen the thin red bars on the top of my sleeves to denote that I served in the infantry; all wasted on the small-minded little person who had set out to dent my self-respect.

The train finally pulled into the station at High Wycombe. I was the first onto my feet and started gathering my kit together, purposely barring the way to the door to my would-be tormentors. It was my turn now, and having slipped my arms through the webbing straps of my valise, which held among other things my greatcoat, I shouldered my kit bag and gave the man a cold hard look that must have left him in no doubt that I had been watching his playacting all along.

Turning, I opened the door and stepped onto the platform where I was greeted by my sister who had, at the arrival times of trains from London, waited for me for most of the day. Twenty minutes later, I was home, reunited with my parents, and in the sanctuary of my own thoughts I thanked God for my safe return. It was wonderful to be home, yet I did feel the claustrophobic effect of living in rooms again after being used to so much space. That aside, it was nice to be away from the hurly-burly of living in the company of forty other men and their minor squabbles, which at times became rather tedious.

During the leave, I found time to visit all members of the family and also visited my old company. With all the visits I made, no one ever asked me about my service overseas or what I had been doing in all that time. They were completely in the dark about my service. However, in fairness to them, I was never allowed to include in my mail home any place name or engagement I had taken part in against the enemy. The platoon officer, who had to read through the mail before allowing its despatch back home, would have censored anything of that nature. All you could write about was that you were either all right or injured and hoped everything was well at home. That, of course, made for a very uninteresting letter, but anything else was strictly forbidden like keeping a diary.

So, my family could have thought that I was employed in some nice safe haven where I could sit out the war in peace and tranquillity – but not my father. One day, alone with him, he started up a conversation by asking me what had it been like in the war and if I had been in any kind of danger. I could see that he wished to know. Thinking about it, I decided to relate the tragedy of what befell the battalion after our arrival on the Anzio beachhead on the 4th of February 1944, when a week later the surviving members of the regiment could be counted in tens and not hundreds. The result of this meant the battalion was disbanded and the remaining men going to other battalions in the division.

He listened very intently to what I was telling him, but in so doing felt very shocked being a peace-loving man himself with no kind of aggression in him. After a pause, he said, "Son, I can see that we owe you a big debt which can never be repaid."

The month soon sped by leaving me with the last full day, that of Christmas, which was spent in the old traditional way, even if it was a time of rationing and shortages in the shops. That day, my mother even surpassed her own high standard of fare provided for us and was the climax of my homecoming.

21. The London Scottish. Venice.

On Boxing night, I returned to the station and started back on my journey to the battalion with its strict discipline, after a month bordering on what I would call luxury. Meeting with my friends at Waterloo, things were inclined to look better and more so after we reached the Channel.

Officials of the port authority asked if any of our group had applied for Class B release, if so to check with the office before leaving the country. One of the men did, but he came back empty-handed and must return with us.

We crossed the water and walked to our train, waiting for us in the siding. Six of us, moving into one of the compartments in the dark, found to our consternation that a window was missing. Other people had occupied the others, so we were stuck with what we had. It was cold with that open window, but we managed to fix a groundsheet into it, keeping out most of the cold air. Before the train pulled out, a feeble light came on that only served to increase the gloomy surroundings and exposed our breath in the cold air. The compartment, like the rest of the train, was decrepit and should have been replaced many years ago. It was downright austere like most of Europe and well beyond.

After a while, I groped inside my small pack and produced a gift, given to me by my mother for use on the journey. A half bottle of whisky, which soon found eager hands and gave them a sense of warmth and well-being. Our sleeping arrangements were soon worked out, where by two would make beds in the luggage racks that were only string netting and would use their warm greatcoats. The rest of us would sleep with our backs in the corners and our legs along the seats, which had seen better days, and we snuggled into our greatcoats.

After a bitterly cold night, the train ground to a halt and we awoke from our fitful sleep to find it was daylight. We all had stiffness from the cold and at first found it difficult to move around, no doubt brought about by our civilised living in the past month, of good food, warmth and the affection of good parents. We had been well and truly spoilt in our absence from Army influence.

The train had made the stop for us to be fed and ablutions, then we were on our way again having no idea where we had just stopped. Once again, it was the trappings of a Spartan life after living on the edge of a decent society for the last four weeks. Now it was in the process of gradually being stripped away from us.

We spent a second night on the train with meals provided along the way till we reached the end of the line where battalion transport was waiting for us, taking us back down the coast road of the peninsula to our base at Pola.

We soon got back into the old routine by the end of the year and the beginning of 1946 – another to have to negotiate in the Army. What would it bring for us? It started with Specialist Company having to move out of the school to a recreation ground that had accommodation there for the men and our transport. We had always enjoyed our time at the school, a real home from home and were reluctant to leave, but they needed the school back for the children. For us, it was only about a ten-minute walk into town, so it was no great hardship.

The older men in the platoon with low age groups were now leaving, which I felt was rather sad. Also at this time my friend, Norman Sadler, in the London Scottish and also in our brigade here in Pola, received his Class B release to return back to his father's farm. But with the older men leaving, this created an imbalance in the platoon as well as having to say goodbye, for the last time in the majority of cases, to the kind of men you would trust with your life.

On top of this drift into obscurity, we found out that the brigade, after our eight months stay, was being pulled out and replaced by another. What was left of the brigade with its three under-strength battalions would be based around the Trieste area, still to be a blocking force against Tito's ambitions. Our move came in February, with us saying goodbye to the most beautiful place one could ever imagine. What was left of the battalion moved to a place called Lazzaretto, a few miles down the coast from Trieste.

The company was billeted in an old sanatorium that had seen better days. The rest of the battalion along with headquarters were scattered around, and the rest of the brigade – London Scottish and London Irish – were stationed in an old Italian barracks in Trieste.

We still carried on with our training, and I personally kept fit by accompanying Sergeant Torrington on his road runs, thinking nothing of dragging me along on a ten mile run. I should point out that the sergeant had been Southern Area Army Champion in England before going abroad. He was a wonderful distance runner and also a good friend and kept me fit at the same time.

After being here just a few weeks, we had a visit from the brigadier, and sometime after, we were informed that the battalion was being disbanded and the once proud 9th Royal Fusiliers would be no more. The rest of us would be parcelled out to the two other battalions in the brigade. At this stage, I was beginning to believe I had made an error of judgment in turning down Captain Sherlock's offer, back in Pola.

Once again, we were back on the move with most of the company being drafted into the 1st London Scottish Regiment. Most of our officers, Captain Sherlock included, went to Brigade HQ to await their own demobilisation. I hoped mine would come before too long. Having to say goodbye to some of the men eventually came to be very unpleasant. It may have been a step nearer to my own Army release, but at the time it had a demoralising effect on the rest of us still left to carry on. But now we were about to discover the whys and wherefores of our new battalion.

On our arrival at the barracks, we were rather stunned by the size of the parade ground where, no doubt in time, we would be put through our paces by some over enthusiastic NCO. The London Scottish occupied the buildings on the topside of the square with the London Irish on the bottom. The transport of both battalions was lost in the vastness at the far end of the square, which must have measured at least 200 x 100 yards.

I thought it strange that we were about to occupy the same billets that had once housed Mussolini's troops – the man who had sowed the seeds of the Second World War by the conquest of Abyssinia (Ethiopia) in 1935/36. The state of war was brought about entirely by Mussolini, who concocted the case about the barbaric aggressor who in some cases only had the most primitive of weapons in their armoury including spears. He later goaded Hitler, encouraging him to start on the road of world domination by their collective pact. Now here we were about to take up residence in the halls of the vanquished.

All of us in the new intake of the London Scottish were employed in our old positions held in the Fusiliers, joining up with what was left of the Scottish mortar platoon. They had a shortage of carrier drivers and gun-numbers.

There was just one small problem; communicating with one another as most of the Scots came from the Glasgow region and having a dialect you all but need an interpreter on hand. And on the parade it was almost impossible to obey the word of command. We would all have to work at it.

It didn't take long to settle down with our new colleagues. We found the platoon sergeant along with the company sergeant major to be very fair-minded, which helped a great deal. Then we had Regimental Sergeant Major Fraser who was the Army contender for the hammer-throwing event and was just along the corridor from the mortar platoon dormitory, ensuring us peace and quiet around the clock. Both of the battalions here had their own pipe bands (bagpipes) that you would hear for most of the day practicing on their chant pipes.

From our windows, we had a grand view of the town's stadium, about two hundred yards away. But we had the advantage of slightly looking down on the arena, which was wonderfully floodlit for the late evening's entertainment, being trotting track races and were able to look on and see it in clear detail. The charioteer, or jockey, sat in a flimsy contraption on two wheels which could have come from a bicycle. At the distance we viewed them from, you could well believe the jockey was sat suspended in midair behind the horse. If the horse at anytime during the race should break into a gallop, it would be disqualified.

About six horses would take part in each race and it looked very spectacular and exciting. An event for the many thousands of Italians watching who had nothing much to cheer about in the humiliating existence Mussolini had imposed on them with his grandiose idea of power. With food shortages and the southern half of their country virtually destroyed by war, poverty was rife in the land and it showed in their faces.

Now, with the departure of every group of men leaving here for home, we had an added poignancy to contend with, in the shape of a single piper from the band playing the lament at 6 o'clock in the morning to the tune of *'Will ye no come back again?'* In truth, we who braved the early morning departures were standing there waving our friends goodbye with our eyes misty with tears. One would never forget the severity of the times. The friendships were forged, now the links were being broken and one could deeply feel the loss, which was heartfelt.

It was Easter Sunday morning, and some of us in the platoon decided voluntarily to attend a nonconformist church service held in a hall, in the London Irish section of the barracks. An American 5th Army padre, a large man with an apparent sense of humour, conducted the service. During the service, the padre based his sermon on a Biblical text and illustrated the subject by a quotation in modern terms of: "You can't have your cake and eat it!" explained in a masterly way. In plain Christian language, you should never take out of life what you are not prepared to put back in, and to hold the love and respect of others and not to think too much of yourself. It must have gone down well with the members of the congregation, for at the end they queued to shake his hand and receive the Easter blessing from the portly padre, who he and his words I would long remember.

Brigade informed the battalion that we would be taking part in an anniversary parade to commemorate the surrender of the German armies in Italy 1945, and would take place on the 2nd of May 1946 in Trieste. This was most likely a show of strength against the Yugoslavian threat in the area, which was very real. So, from hereon, training would begin in earnest and become a priority over all other matters.

Men selected off the grand parade included those who were too short in stature or not smart at drill. Also, those of poor appearance were cast aside. These men didn't mind missing the hard work, but the psychological effect on some of them must have hurt after being such good soldiers when it really did matter. About 150 men would be marching in each group plus their bands. We were required to be on the parade ground three or four hours a day, and now it was coming to the end of April with the weather becoming very hot, but drill was the order of the day.

The colonel commanding the battalion lived with us on the parade ground. He watched us at all times and had no intention of seeing his battalion go on this most prestigious occasion just to see it outsmarted by other units on view.

It was the end of April now and it was very hot. Standing and marching in the heat became too much for some of the men on the parade. Two such men, standing to attention with their rifles, succumbed within minutes of each other in the searing heat. From being bolt upright to falling, still clutching their rifles, and hitting the hard gravely parade ground with a most sickening thud, then sliding forward with the momentum of their bodies in a dead faint. Their comrades standing next to them broke ranks to help their stricken friends. But in each case they were lambasted for their attempts at being good Samaritans by the RSM who shouted words of abuse and severely reprimanded the good men with the final words, "Just leave them alone!"

After we had been restored to some resemblance of order and the muttering of descent from us had all but died away, the colonel gave his permission for a detail to remove the two men and take them to the regimental aid post. We could see the unfortunate two were bleeding from abrasions and cuts to their faces and from their noses, also the rifle hand. They were carried away looking absolutely wretched and may have sustained more injury than on many of the battlefields they had fought over.

During our time in Trieste, we had several outbreaks of a riotous nature inspired by the people of the town who had sympathy with the Yugoslavian extremists, and at times it almost got out of hand with some very ugly scenes taking place that were never reported in the papers. At one time, a story was circulating that a Yugoslavian extremist group in Pola had killed a senior officer from the brigade that had taken our place there. It was a very volatile situation for us, which was bad enough to have our home leave cancelled for a time.

On the final rehearsal for the parade, the men, who had sweated away and were very fatigued from it all after two or three hours of drill, were eventually halted by the RSM. He, in turn, saluted the ever-present colonel who then cast his eyes along the ranks of his composite company and said, "I think that will be satisfactory. I don't believe in flogging a dead horse." He went on. "Tomorrow, you must spend your time going over your kit you will be wearing on the day, which I expect to be faultless on the day of the parade. Dismiss them, Sergeant Major."

On the morning of the 2nd of May, there were warnings going around that Tito's Yugoslavian compatriots in the town would try and attempt some kind of disruption on the parade, so everyone was told to be very vigilant. All the men in the battalion, not on duty, were to be spectators to the event and to be on the lookout for any trouble. All of the British infantry taking part in the parade would have their rifles with them, but only for show with no ammunition carried. So, if any incident should happen of a violent nature involving the use of firearms, how would the marching infantry units be able to retaliate in kind with empty rifles?

After giving this some thought, I approached Company Sergeant Major MacLean and voiced my fears to him of being caught out by such an oversight. He just said to leave it with him, and returned soon after telling me that he had passed it on to the company commander. The company commander in turn spoke with the battalion commander, then via the chain of command to the brigadier, the divisional commander who then passed it on to Army HQ. They, thinking the request had come from a very senior officer, sanctioned that a clip of five rounds of ·303" ammunition will be carried in the pocket of all infantry marching in the parade. The top brass would have felt very humbled had they known the germ of the idea had originated from a humble private soldier.

Marching in the parade, I could feel the clip of five rounds pressing onto my leg and I felt a sense of security by its presence. The instructors in weapons training were always telling us that your rifle is your best friend; a most macabre thought, but a rifle without ammunition?

Back in our barrack room later in the day, a Glaswegian lance corporal (whose dialect you could almost cut with a knife) openly boasted to us in all sincerity that he had watched the parade from the saluting base, and having seen all the units pass by had seen none better than the London Scottish contingent, saying it was even better than the Guards Battalion. Praise indeed.

With the Italian summer now well advanced, mosquito nets were now issued out to us from the stores to drape over our beds at night. No one wanted to suffer the dire consequence of a bout of malaria, and having seen it at close hand over the years, it was something to avoid if at all possible. It was very strange but with the introduction of our mosquito nets, we started to find red sores on our bodies when we woke at reveille. This was very disturbing. Everyone was baffled by this new phenomenon with the sores now turning into small bumps.

All this made the majority of us attend the public baths each night by taking the tram down into Trieste, but this meant having to run the gauntlet while on the tram with the Italians having just had their evening meal (well spiced with pungent garlic). It was overpowering in the extreme and we were glad to arrive at our destination.

You could have a bath in a single cubicle with towel and soap provided, but you had to pay for the privilege. It was well worth it, to get immersed in the luxury of a nice warm bath and feel clean once again, in an attempt or hope of ridding yourself of the irritating sores that were gradually covering the body.

Lights out in the Army, when in barracks, really did mean lights out and no one was allowed to switch the lights on till reveille, even if needed. One night, a man in the platoon awoke us from our sleep. Feeling some discomfort, he struck his cigarette lighter and cried out in some panic at seeing numerous small creatures scurrying for cover, off his body, out of the revealing light of the flame. He had the presence of mind to dispatch one or two by crushing them with his fingers against the body, which left red splotches of blood – his own.

Obviously, the parasites were lice and were gorging themselves on the blood of our bodies. Without the constant protective inoculations of Typhus B, we could all be in some kind of jeopardy. I had personally received the injection on the 11th of March 1946, and would thankfully place all of my colleagues in the clear. By the light of day, we stripped our canvass beds, bedding, kit and personal possessions, which were few, but couldn't find the offending bugs or any trace of them.

That evening, after our duty for the day, we caught the tram again for what was now the order of the day – a bath. While in Trieste, we purchased boxes of matches so to lighten our darkness under the mosquito nets when the cause arose.

After lights out, we waited in our beds for the invasion of the parasites, darkness allied to the reason for them moving. The very enticement of sleep had overcome some of the men, but those who had remained vigilant, myself included, were soon to see matches being struck inside the mosquito nets, making strange pools of light in the darkened room. I could now feel something or things crawling over my own skin. Striking a match, I found to my disgust the culprits, swollen with blood and scurrying away out of the light. Having killed all that I found, like the others in the room, I soon fell asleep and on waking next morning found the usual eruptions of red spots from our night visitors.

This situation was reported repeatedly, but found it was endemic in this particular part of the barracks. If my mother had been made aware of her son's predicament with the lice, knowing her attitude towards foreign bodies on the person, I doubt if I would ever have been allowed back into the home.

Out of this chaotic state of affairs from which we could find no answer, some of us in the company were given six days leave, in Venice of all places. This was a heaven-sent opportunity to get away from this kind of plague that had descended on us and wouldn't go away. When we departed in the transport for our leave, we did feel some guilt at leaving our friends behind with the problem as they had still not discovered the source of the outbreak, but were still looking. About twenty of us made the journey, which was around one hundred miles, and was well worth it. Seeing it was called 'the Jewel of the Adriatic', when passing over the causeway into Venice proper, we soon discovered how well it had been named.

The transport stopped and we transferred ourselves to a launch that was to take us through a canal, into the Grand Canal. We passed squares and buildings and under bridges, like the Rialto with its ornate decorations, the Doges Palace and San Marco Square, all of them world renowned for their architectural beauty. We passed views of great splendour, which before the war had only been the prerogative of the rich. In truth, we hadn't paid money for our tickets through a Thomas

Cook agency, but I think we had the moral right to look over places of interest for which so much blood had been shed.

Venice had been an open city and there was no apparent war damage, but they had suffered by the result of the war. Our launch passed through the canals and out into the open sea with a short trip to the lido – a narrow strip of land with all the facilities needed for holidaying on a grand scale. There were tennis courts, open-air swimming, picture house and a host of souvenir shops with models of gondolas complete with gondoliers.

It was a most fabulous place, and the haunts of the privileged of the past now opening their doors to people who would have been barred from this exclusive place. I think the soldiers had as much appreciation and wonderment of this most unique place as anyone could have. The beds in the Hotel Excelsior were lavish to what we were used to, in fact it would spoil us for going back to our own lice-ridden quarters, back in Trieste. Also, our view from the fourth floor window was magnificent, looking out over a placid Adriatic sea with the temperature for being in the water just right.

This was the setting to which British honeymooners came before the war, and one could very well understand why. Seeing the canals by moonlight was most romantic and seen from a gondola moving smoothly over the water, which danced in the reflective light of the moon. What more could one ask for?

Looking round the shops, I was first tempted then bought my mother one of the silver-plated model gondolas, which was very eye-catching in this time of austerity. My friends and I had a very pleasant leave, away from the daily routine of training; that was drill, and lately our nightly visits to the public baths in Trieste to rid ourselves from the ravagers of our bodies during the hours of darkness that we were so powerless to stop.

Most of our time at the lido was spent in the water, which was warm and therapeutic to the sores we still carried. We hired a floating contraption with two floats joined together by seats, which you could row from and, very foolishly, we ventured far out into the open sea to get a panoramic view of the lido with Venice in the background. One of our party of about four of us had been towed out about a mile from the shore, clinging to one of the floats, and when he decided he would like a rest from being in the water, he started to climb onboard.

This was a big mistake and I, who had been rowing at the time, found myself in the water under the boat. Having made it to the surface, hanging onto a float, I could see the pair of oars drifting away. These were soon retrieved. Between us, we held a council of desperation, knowing only too well that we couldn't right the boat or be rescued, as no one would have seen it happen.

I and one other would balance ourselves out by climbing simultaneously onto each float. We did this, each of us straddling a float and using the oars like a paddle, then started off for the shore that looked very distant. Indeed, the view of the city was magnificent but our thoughts at the time were only on survival. What with the drag of towing the two men and the resistance through the water by the seats being underneath us, it was like having an anchor holding you back. It must have taken us a long time and had exhausted us by our efforts of paddling, but after our long haul, we finally reached the beach. After regaining some of our strength, we righted the boat and returned it to the owner. I think we all felt thankful for getting away from what could have turned into a nasty incident.

With our leave sadly at an end, we reluctantly returned back to Trieste and the dreaded lice once again. After our arrival back to our barrack room, we received the good news that the whole block had been fumigated in our absence and finding, out of all places, where the enemy had been lurking – inside the supporting bar pockets of our mosquito nets! On opening them, they found on removing the wooden support bar the pockets teeming with lice of all sizes. Some of them so bloated with human blood they could scarcely move. For us the ordeal was now over. We could sleep in peace at night from the foreign invaders.

It's an Army policy not to let the troops get well established for any length of time in a garrison roll. We had just settled down to our Trieste based way of life, when they warned us that a party of about forty would soon be leaving the battalion to set up a new headquarters for the Central Mediterranean Land Forces in the city of Padova, about twenty-five miles due west of Venice. Trieste had proved a very good place for us, apart from the episode involving the lice. Otherwise, we had very good sports facilities like cricket and football, which we indulged in on the spacious trotting track.

The men in the company nearing their Army release were not on this list for Padova, but I and some of my friends were and kept on standby till required. This didn't stop our training, despite the fact of us moving to Padova and operating in an infantry roll and not of specialists.

One morning, we were told to drive the mortar carriers down to the docks where a Royal Navy tank landing ship was berthed. We were to practice moving on and off the ship, rather futile when we were reverting back into the infantry. Having driven the carriers into Trieste, we then drove them onto the docks where we had instructions on the correct procedure of moving on and off the ship. The drill was that you must first get the carrier square with the ramp, rev the engine to climb over the ramp resting on the jetty, then cut the engine revs and drop into the ship's well. After that, move onto the steel ramp that was at an angle of about 30° from the horizontal, which led up to the top deck of the ship.

It was very steep and going up the ramp you would be unable to see where you were going. Being so laid back in the seat you would only see the sky. The naval officer would only beckon you forward when you had a clear run with the vehicle you would follow, now safely up on the deck.

It came to my turn and the officer at the ramp waved me forward. Giving the engine some power, I climbed over the ramp and dropped into the well before climbing, very gingerly, up the ramp to the deck. All was going well and I must have been within feet of the top, and the flat deck thereafter, when into my vision appeared an officer in white uniform with outstretched arms forcing me to stop or run him over. Removing my foot from the accelerator, I pressed on the brake pedal and pushed in the clutch. Knowing that I was in trouble now, I put a light lock on the steering wheel, which locked the tracks, and for good measure switched off the engine.

I had done all that I could do and was now stranded on the ramp, the officer having decided to vacate the scene. Someone behind me started climbing the ramp, causing it to judder with every footstep and making the carrier slip sideways to the edge of the ramp. I could say, without hesitation whatsoever, that my life was put in jeopardy by the action of the officer who had stopped me. The carrier was slipping with a kind of finality towards the edge, taking me with it. While I hung on like grim death, knowing that I must hang on to survive, trying to climb out would be fatal. After what to me was a most wretched moment in my life, with the thought of dropping thirty feet or more in the carrier into the well of the ship in a situation not of my making, I could only feel resentment at the fool who had caused it.

I was now clutching the steering wheel like you would to life itself when a sailor's head came into view at the top of the ramp and he called out, "I'm going to put a cable on the towing bar. When it takes up the strain release the brakes, and we can let you down backwards."

When I felt the cable pull taut, I released the lock on the steering wheel and removed my foot from the brake pedal, but it still yawed towards the edge till the cable on the winch came into play and pulled the carrier straight on the ramp. At the bottom, the cable was released and, starting the engine, I reversed it back over the ramp and onto the dock.

A sergeant, unbeknown to me, came over and gave me a right dressing down interspersed with some vile language, and even my explanation to him, about the naval officer stopping me on the ramp, made no difference whatsoever. He, like the rest of them, was blind to the happening. No one else would have witnessed it, being unsighted outside the ship, except the officer who had caused it to happen and they never apologise for the mistakes they make.

I could only look back on the event in that I was the victim of an injustice, which would rankle in my thoughts for many a long day. It could very well have taken my life.

22. Padova. Guard Battalion.

The day came when we had to leave Trieste for Padova, and with some regret at leaving our friends behind who would soon be returning to England. Saying goodbye to trusted friends leaves you with a sense of emptiness, a finality of friendship that had been very genuine in the making.

Our party consisted of two officers and around forty other ranks. The officers were fresh out from England and had only recently joined the battalion. I could see there was some animosity between them that later became apparent when we stopped for a break on our journey, in a town with a Red Cross canteen.

We all trooped inside and sat down at the tables after collecting our tea and bun from the canteen. One of the officers, Lieutenant Pammet, who seemed a very jovial kind of man, came over and joined us at our table. He told us, in the course of our conversation with him, that he had been in the Tank Corps before transferring into the infantry.

Then he unexpectedly started to talk about his fellow officer, Lieutenant Wolfe, and told us in no uncertain terms that he was a fool. Lieutenant Wolfe was sitting at a table on his own, thankfully oblivious to what was being said by his colleague in arms. Before we left the table to go, Lieutenant Pammet said to us, "Just you listen to this," and to our complete amazement, he called out, "Lieutenant Wolfe!" On hearing his name called out in this most unexpected and ungentlemanly way, Lieutenant Wolfe sat bolt upright in his chair, looking out for this insolent person who would dare to call him. Failing to locate the mindless offender, he turned very red, whereas the perpetrator of the incident had a smile and an attitude on his face that butter wouldn't melt in his mouth. It was the first and the last time that I saw an officer take the rise out of another.

We arrived in Padova and stopped in a square with the name of Piazza Spalato, flanked on three sides by very elegant buildings. One of the buildings was the former Fascist headquarters of the province, now earmarked for the main CMF headquarters.

There was an Italian caretaker, who spoke very good English, in charge of the project and held all the keys to the buildings. All of our meals were provided at the railway station at the end of the Carso Del Popolo, a magnificent wide thoroughfare that we travelled along many times during our stay in the city. The food there was, in general, a lot better than the food we received at battalion level. Most surprising of all was that we were waited on at the table by a German prisoner of war who was dressed in a British Army uniform, minus the hat with no badges or insignias to identify him by.

Our sleeping quarters, which were only temporary, were in the large building opposite to the HQ across the square. Large boxes and packing cases started to arrive daily and were stored underneath the cavernous archways at the front of the new GHQ. At the main door of the building, on the supporting pillars of the centre arch, stood two eagles, larger than life facing one another with unfolded wings, and were cast in bronze.

It was a most imposing place, but what intrigued me most was some ornate lettering on the front, about eighty feet above the ground with the middle lettering covered with an awning. The words visible read ISTITVTO NAZIONALE --------- DELLA PREVIDENZA SOCIALE.

About a week later, looking round a run down bookshop for some souvenir postcards, I found one with the building in the days of its former glory and the word covered over was FASCISTA (Fascist). I was rather perplexed by the Italians going to all this trouble to hide the word when they all claimed, to a man, they had been against Mussolini from the very beginning and what he stood for. Anyway, I suppose it's only natural to suppress your true feelings when confronted with the issue in conversation with a victor. Well they all did, saying he was a brutal man.

We, at this stage, were told that our main reason for being here was to take care of things arriving from headquarters, in Caserta. The whole unit spent most of its working days getting things into shape for the eventual arrival of the 'armchair' soldiers from the south, and looking after the Army records inside the large crates. We also posted guards, night and day, to stop any kind of pilfering from the numerous containers arriving each day. These now piled six to eight feet high and were accumulating under the ornate archways.

After several visits to our feeding point at the railway station, I struck up a kind of relationship with the German who served us at the table in the mess room. He was many years my senior and an interesting person. He also seemed well educated.

One day, he told me that he had come from Hamburg and very proudly showed me a picture that had seen better days, of his wife and baby who he had not seen since well before the war ended. He also told me that he had been a reporter on a newspaper there, but he never mentioned about the bombing that had all but obliterated the city. What was most upsetting for him was that he had no idea when he would be returning back home to his family. Once again, I felt fortunate that I had never become a prisoner of war and been degraded in that manner. He had no social life and was restricted to the confines of the railway station. In knowing this, I did feel some compassion for the man, even if he were a former adversary.

There was a picture house near to the square, which was exclusively for the use of British soldiers. It was a comfortable place and we used to attend there at least twice a week, but there was a snag in never knowing what film you would be watching.

Before our time came to leave Padova, I suggested to my friends that we could very well shepherd the German, who could speak excellent English, into the night show at the picture house. They were all in agreement, but there was one complication in that he had a British uniform but no cap and badge, and if seen by the redcaps, one of us would have a lot of explaining to do. That could only mean trouble, as they didn't deal in compassion in their line of business. My friends agreed to be cover, but not to be responsible. So, at one of our mealtimes, it was put to him and he jumped at the chance of such a luxury. The risk was great, but I was now committed to giving him an evening out.

Keeping our word, one evening we escorted him from the station surrounded by some very wary soldiers down the Carso Del Popolo, dreading at every step to bump into a redcap patrol. Having reached our destination, we spirited him inside using the same ploy for cover. Once inside and sitting in amongst rows of other soldiers, he became less conspicuous, especially with our own hats removed. Then the cover of darkness, as the lights dimmed and the flickering light flashed onto the screen.

We all felt more relaxed in the darkened auditorium with the titles coming up on the screen, informing us that the film was called *The Captive Heart* starring Michael Redgrave. It was a black and white film made in the same year – 1946 – and sounded like a very romantic film.

I was shortly to be proved wrong, when in the first scene you were taken to a battlefield showing a British officer lying dead in the mud, when along comes Michael Redgrave in the roll of a Czech soldier serving in the British Army. Removing all identification documents and discs from the man's body, Redgrave then takes over the identity of the unfortunate officer. The next scene is of a German prisoner of war camp with Redgrave now in captivity, assuming his new credentials will help him escape the clutches of the Gestapo who are looking for him.

Of all the films you could see, it had to be a propaganda film. So, I leaned over towards the man from Hamburg and, whispering in his ear, I apologised most profusely for our indiscretion, but he just looked back at me and smiled. It was a good film and when it was over, he told us that he had enjoyed every minute.

To finish the evening off, we moved him to a coffee bar nearby. Drinking the wonderful beverage, we all agreed it was the best we had ever tasted. We applied the same cover for him, returning back to the railway station in our midst. Good fortune had favoured the brave, or the foolish, whichever way you care to look at it. When we said goodnight, the gratitude showed in his face and after shaking each of us by the hand, he walked back into his prison yard of the station. Anytime spent on making a friendship is time never wasted, and it's true not every German would have been in the Gestapo.

Padova was no doubt a lovely city, and when the news did come through that we would be leaving and on the move once again, we all felt some regret at the prospect. Our work here was now finished, and I could see that we were now in the way of the deskbound soldiers who required the quarters we had occupied during our stay.

The order came through that the London Scottish and London Irish were disbanding. The remainder of the men would be going into one unit, which would be called No.1 Special Guard Battalion and would be stationed at Riccione, about six miles south of Rimini and eight miles from the neutral state of San Marino. The 167 Brigade that once had a total of around two thousand five hundred men was now reduced to battalion strength of around eight hundred.

We were returning to one of our old battlegrounds of 'The Gothic Line' campaign of 1944. It was a well-remembered place with memories of hardship and suffering in a struggle that never lived up to its expectations of a great success, during our advance to the Po River and beyond.

We left Padova on our journey south, which was about 120 miles distance. On arrival in Riccione, we found the remnants of the two battalions already in place and functioning in their guard duties. Most of our party from Padova were immediately posted out into other units in the battalion. My friend, Stanley Abbey, now a full corporal and I were ordered to report to the adjutant, a major who had been in the London Scottish.

We presented ourselves to Battalion HQ and taken into the adjutant's office where we exchanged the customary salute, after which he told us to sit down. After giving us a good looking over, he said, "I've been waiting for your return to the battalion, and I can tell you that I have been going through your service records and they are both, so far, exemplary." After letting the statement sink in, he went on. "I would very much like you to help me by joining the Regimental Police here. After the amalgamation of the two battalions, discipline is now at rock bottom and we have a problem on our hands." He continued. "Most of the men in this new battalion are fresh out from England, and have no war experience and seem to lack the awareness of good soldiers. Things are beginning to get very sloppy and that's why I need your help."

He looked at me and said, "According to your record, you have refused all kinds of promotion, but you must have rank to work in the Regimental Police. How do you feel about it?" "Well, sir," I said, "I will join the police with my friend if he's in agreement. But the other thing, I can't accept and I do feel very sorry about it, sir." The adjutant was very quiet, and then said to me, "I do need your help, so you will become the first Private soldier to be enlisted in the Regimental Police. And I ask you both to keep your eyes open and your ears to the ground. So, if you now report to the Provost Sergeant, he will fill you in on your new employment. I do know you will set a good example, that's why I personally asked for you, so good luck."

After leaving the adjutant, we looked at each other in disbelief at what we had done, but we felt it a new challenge and out of the ordinary. We found the police station and presented ourselves to the sergeant who was from the London Irish and had been in charge of their police. He was also a regular soldier and had served in the Army all his life. After having explained what our duties would entail every day, he then gave us a red armband with the black lettering of RP on them, and told us to walk round the battalion area to get acquainted with the job by showing our faces in every conceivable place we could find.

Corporal Abbey and I went out on our walk displaying our armbands, exposing our newfound power we had acquired without having to ask for it. Whatever kind of power I now possessed, I would always make sure that it would be fair and I know my friend would do likewise. We fitted rather well into our new positions. No one ever calling into question or made any judgment to the lack of stripes on my arms, they just accepted the RP emblem without comment.

The sole reason for the forming of No.1 Special Guard Battalion was to enforce the captivity of around 16,000 men, of Ukrainian origin, who in some adverse way got caught up in the war and were now unable to return back to their homeland for fear of reprisals against them.

I was rather depressed at the sight of the inmates inside this great compound, covering many acres of ground for its 16,000 prisoners. They were quartered there behind strong steel mesh fencing about twelve feet high with watchtowers at intervals around the perimeter. It looked a forlorn sight with some of the prisoners walking about inside in an aimless and uncaring manner. There was also a deep ditch around the outside of the perimeter fence with un-scalable sides, and a wooden bridge over the ditch at the entrance, which was strongly guarded, as were the towers.

No one would venture in there at night other than special circumstances with a strong guard detail, fully armed and prepared for any emergency. The incarceration of them here, we were told, was for their own good and you were dealing with desperate men.

Camp guards weren't the responsibility of the regimental police, but good behaviour and discipline in the battalion was, and I found just showing yourself was a good way of keeping order. No one questioned my lack of rank, but would always take me at face value (or was it the armband with its most authoritative letters?).

At the regimental police station, a prisoner was brought into our custody and placed into my care in the guardroom. He couldn't have been more than twenty years of age and looked in a very dishevelled state, wearing civilian clothing that didn't look tailor-made for him. It fitted where it touched. His clothing, like him, was very dirty and in need of soap and water. The prisoner and I were alone in the room that served as a cell, which contained the bare rudiments for the prisoner. He was sitting on a long wooden trestle and it was easy to see that he was a very frightened man. Out of curiosity, I asked him what he had done to be in police custody. I certainly wasn't expecting the story he related to me, but felt sure afterwards that he had badly wanted to do so.

He had been in an infantry battalion for some time and after several engagements with the enemy, seeing his friends cut down and with the prospect of death ever-present, he gradually lost his nerve. When on returning back into the line, he could face it no longer and in the chaos that reigns at the sharp end, he just walked away. Where to, he had no idea, only to distance himself from the maelstrom of men trying their best to silence one another; away from a place where no sane person would want to venture.

Walking till he had moved away from the incessant gunfire, he slept rough in the hedgerows. In the end, he came to an outlying farm. While sleeping in a barn there, he was found by the farm owner who gave him sustenance at a price.

The Italian farmer, knowing he had a British soldier who was on the run, turned it to his own advantage and craftily gave him some old clothes in exchange for his uniform. In doing so, the soldier had virtually become a prisoner of the farmer who could now use him (and did) like an unpaid farmhand who would be given food but made to sleep in the barn.

Time dragged by for the deserter, not knowing what was going on in the outside world. And the irony of it was that he had deserted from the line just a few weeks before the end of hostilities, and hadn't been aware of the victory we had won. He worked on the farm under the instructions of his master without respite of any kind.

One day, he was picked up at the farm by the military police, I suspect on a tip-off, and brought here for us to guard before being picked up by them, and later charged for a crime that anyone of us could have committed when you feel your very life could be forfeit. Unbeknown to him at this time, he had been in bondage eighteen months after the war had ended, thanks to the farmer. The military authority frowns on desertion from the line, and the punishment for the said crime is very harsh with 'Three Years Hard Labour' served in a stockade under severe conditions.

While telling me his story, I had rested my foot on the trestle he was sitting on. Throughout, I could feel the vibrations from his trembling body running from the trestle and into my own leg.

When his story was finished, I asked him to show me his hands and I was taken aback by the condition of them. A pair of hands I had never seen the likes of before, even a navvy would have more delicate hands. His were horny and covered with calluses grimed with dirt, broken black fingernails or what was left of them. They looked pathetic and I realised that he had been telling me the truth. Furthermore, in that time of self-imposed exile, he had never been in touch with his family in England and could be looked on as dead or missing. In my humble opinion, he was like a broken man in mind and spirit. After all, the war was now over and he had been punished enough. He needed psychiatric treatment, not three years in the stockade.

Later, two redcaps arrived in a jeep. Both of them looking in ruddy health and well fed and, most likely, had never been near the line or knew what it was all about, like their dirty, broken-down prisoner. He was led away in handcuffs, looking a most pathetic figure between the two immaculately turned out policemen.

What did happen to this man who had lost his nerve at the most crucial time of the war – its end? But I feared the worst in that he would be found guilty of desertion from the frontline. Nevertheless, I believed the sad story he related to me in the guardroom.

The battalion billeted in what had been a hospital complex and now housed most of the men in the Guard Battalion. One day, just walking around showing myself, I was approached by the adjutant who asked me to look into a claim by one of the men that he had injured himself, by falling down one of the ornate staircases in the building. However, the adjutant thought the man to be drunk at the time. On the quiet, I asked around and found the soldier had been drunk at the time of falling, but none of them would come forward and be witness to the fact. Later, I reported back to the adjutant and told him that I had drawn a blank. He was rather disappointed, and so was I.

Having had our leave cancelled way back in the summer to the United Kingdom, due to the intransigence of Tito and the disputed territory, out of the blue, leave was now made available to the CMF. My close friend and I were fortunately placed on the first party going home on what would be nineteen days leave. Though having just settled down into our new roll, being away for the next month had come at the wrong time, but headquarters had given their blessing for us to leave.

So, once again we started off on our journey home with the first leg done by a 3-ton transport, along with about thirty other men, which carried us to the railhead, which this time was in Austria. The scenery from the train was magnificent with views from the higher ground being most beautiful. Then we moved out of the sunshine into a squally shower of rain, and at its end something very wonderful happened. The interior of the compartment was suddenly bathed in a heavenly light as the train moved through the end of a rainbow. Dropping the window, I felt compelled to place my hand in the miracle of the coloured bow. It was most unbelievable. Our journey passed from daylight into darkness, and eventually we fell into a kind of sleep with the motion of the train rocking us into our slumber.

We were awakened from our fitful sleep to find the train halted in a siding, and a voice called out, "Breakfast time!" in the dark outside. But to us it seemed rather early in the morning for breakfast, which was confirmed by an irate voice that cried out, "It's only four o'clock in the morning!" And so it was.

The food would be waiting for us just a short walk away. As to where we had stopped, what we could see of it in the dark, it looked like an old Saxony town. We were directed to a building that must have been a hall of some kind, and moving inside into the light, I could see the tables prepared for our meal. All of us looked full of sleep, unwashed and unshaven. In fact, we looked like a common rabble and anything but soldiers.

After receiving our food and drink, we sat down at the tables and to our amazement a band started playing from a small balcony, up near the ceiling. And it sounded really bizarre when the tune was recognised as being *'Gee it's great to see you looking swell Baby!'* Most inappropriate at four o'clock in the morning, but you do have to have a sense of humour. The band was just trying to earn a crust. The Austrian musicians were trying to make a living in their ruined economy, which would take a long time to return to its former state. If the story of the band had been related to me by anyone else, I don't think I could believe it. Nevertheless, it is true.

After four days of journeying, I reached home once again and most enthusiastically welcomed by my mother and father who then told me I had missed my sister's wedding by a week. Talking with them generally about nothing in particular, they told me it had been a very wet summer, one of the worst on record. Thinking back, I recall it had not been kind in sunny Italy.

I decided to pay a visit to my old friend, Norman Sadler, who had left the Army on a Class B release way back in February to work on his father's farm. In conversation with Norman, he said the year had been a disaster and confirmed what my parents had told me. The crops in the fields had been unable to ripen and cattle feed was now at a premium. Walking over the fields with him, even fields with a slope, they seemed saturated with water and nothing would dry out. I said to him, "Do you know, Norman, what the Italians blame the wet weather on? They say the 'Bomba Atomica'!" He looked at me and just said, "Could be."

My leave was soon over and I started back to what would hopefully be the last time. After four days of travel, I arrived back at Battalion HQ and reported for duty.

Within days of returning, a motorcycle was stolen from the battalion motor pool compound, which was constructed with steel mesh fencing and was about eight feet high on three sides with a gate. The fourth side was the open sea with the mesh running out into the water. The three men on guard duty at the time were held responsible and they were confined to barracks pending their court-martial trial.

They were also made to report to us, in the guardroom, three times a day. After booking them in myself on many occasions, they didn't seem to me to have any kind of criminality in them and I began to feel rather sorry for the three who were all fresh out from England, and clearly frightened about the court-martial, fearing the worst.

One evening, after booking them in with all of them standing to attention in front of me (not my idea), I asked them how they would feel if I were to intercede on their behalf to get the booking in lifted from them. They told me it would make a great difference for them to enjoy the same privileges again, which they had lost after their supposed misdemeanour on guard duty, and they all claimed they had carried out the duty in the proper manner.

After saying I would do my best for them, I next approached the adjutant and told him my thoughts about the three, also saying I didn't think they would abscond and all had been faultless at their attendance in the guardroom. The adjutant did admit about the booking in had, by this time, lost its purpose and agreed with me to look into it.

That evening, I went to the guardroom with the intention of telling the men of my talk with the adjutant, on their behalf, and the time came for them to make an appearance to be booked in. They were late tonight, the first time in several weeks. Why? The clock moved on with still no sign of the three and, for once in a long time, I felt apprehensive at what I had done now they were missing and I could be involved in their disappearance.

After some time had elapsed and doubt was crawling all over me, I somehow had to find the courage to report the men missing. Seeking out the provost sergeant, I found him off duty in his office and expected a good ragging when I told him the three men were missing. He never let me get that far by saying, "The Adjutant told me the men have been taken out of detention, so you won't have to worry about them now." A great burden lifted from my shoulders by his words and then he said,

"Would you make yourself available for tomorrow night. Another motorcycle's been stolen from the compound and I think we know how. What's more, I'm going to set a trap for them." I walked out of his office feeling very gratified at the result. I felt let off the hook.

On my rounds next day, I was confronted by three jubilant soldiers who thanked me most profusely for interceding on their behalf. But they would never know how I had suffered when they failed to report.

That night, the sergeant briefed us in his office about the seriousness of the situation and said, "Battalion wants some answers." He also told us, "All the guards on duty at the time of the two break-ins swore on oath they had been alert at the time and had been most vigilant, claiming that nothing had come through the gate or been lifted over the fence." There was no lighting at night in the compound, so whatever had happened here it must have come from the open sea. The rising tide in the Mediterranean is insignificant and hardly noticeable, and the wire mesh of the compound's sides ran into the sea, but the depth of the water here measured only in inches. So, if the motorcycles had been stolen that's where they were spirited away, but how?

The plan for the evening was that we would split into two parties, each having the two sides of the compound under surveillance. I found myself with two others and the sergeant who I noticed was carrying a holstered revolver.

We waited patiently in the dark, cold night from our hiding place, only talking in whispers when necessary on our night vigil. It was in the early hours of the morning and we had all but given in when we heard a slight noise from the vicinity of the waters edge. The sergeant, not showing much intelligence, decided to switch on his torch. This revealed two Italian men paddling through the shallows into the compound who, on being spotted, came out running like greyhounds out of a trap.

Splashing through the water, they then ran along the sandy beach and darted into an alleyway by some old buildings alongside. I ran after them in hot pursuit, leaving the others way back, but I could just make them out in the dark.

Bang—, a shot rang out from behind me, then another, and I was between the sergeant and the target. This made me abandon the chase, being fearful for my own safety in not wishing to receive a bullet in the back. The sergeant must have been mad firing at random with me in front of him, and he had no right in trying to shoot the Italians. Nevertheless, we had stopped a third motorcycle from being stolen by way of the Italians wheeling them through the shallows, along the beach and then away. The compound was fenced off at the sea end. The three guards were exonerated from all blame, and the sergeant, being a regular soldier, was posted to a London Irish battalion.

With Christmas over, time moved on, and we were at the gates of another year once again. Four of us decided to attend the watch night service at a small church in the town, which would be conducted by our own padre. We arrived at fifteen minutes to midnight, to find just two others there with relief on their faces at our arrival. So, we started the beginning of the New Year 1947 with the adjutant and his wife; a memory I would long cherish.

23. Home posting. Aberdeen. Full circle.

The year started badly with snow on the ground, but back in England it was far worse making it the most unpleasant winter weather in living memory. In Italy, the snow didn't linger for any length of time, but it had a great nuisance value in that we were never warm enough. Cold weather had never been on the agenda for keeping the troops warm in sunny Italy, so we had to make the best of it. There was very little police work, which seemed to curtail with the arrival of the inclement weather. No one wished to venture out into the cold night to visit Riccione (Rimini still being off limits to the troops), but it was a much larger town.

With the first week of February gone, we received a staggeringly good piece of news in that our repatriation back to the United Kingdom would be imminent. Apparently, the higher echelons of the military establishment had overlooked us. After the events of D-Day, the 6th of June 1944, with the landings in Normandy by the Allied armies in the invasion of Europe, we were looked on, in Italy, as a forgotten front.

But the invasion of Europe had started the year before, with the landings in Italy by the American 5th Army and the British 8th Army; landings across the Straits of Messina, at Reggio di Calabria and Salerno, from the 5th of September 1943. The higher echelons were now going to make amends for their lack of charity in the past by sending soldiers home with long overseas service. We had been here, in Italy, a very long time through the years' 1943/44/45/46 and now into '47.

I would personally miss the land, even for its faults, but always remember it for the beauty and wonderment of Rome and the vast scale of splendour in Florence and Venice, the culture and music in the land of Verdi and Puccini. However, leaving Italy, I never intended to return having too many sad memories that could never be erased from my mind.

Within days, we were released from duty and reported to Battalion HQ, only to find out there was a snag for us on the way home. It was this – when we arrived back in London, instead of going straight home on leave, we would have to go to King's Cross and catch a train for Scotland for the sole purpose of obtaining our leave passes – a round trip of one thousand miles. Britain, at the time, was suffering from the most atrocious winter weather on record, and what with an austerity crisis at the same time it looked a very unnecessary journey to have to make. But that, unfortunately, was the Army.

So, with us going home but still in a Scottish regiment, we had to present ourselves to our depot, which was the Gordon Highlanders Barracks at the Bridge of Don, Aberdeen. For us it was going to be a 'home' posting; 'home' being over five hundred miles away from the address they had in my pay-book.

We said goodbye to our friends in the Guard Battalion with mixed feelings, in the knowledge that we would never see them again. In the next few days, we travelled back over some of the routes we had been over before, but this time it was much colder the farther north we went, seeing the snow in the fields again. We crossed the Channel, which to us felt like arctic conditions after the warmer climes we had left behind, in Italy.

We caught our train for London, and arriving there, proceeded to King's Cross where we found to our disgust that the overnight train to the north was completely full. With all the compartments filled to capacity, we still needed to catch this train; otherwise, it would add another day to our returning back home. So, with our kit bags, large valise and small packs, we crowded into the cold corridor of the train – a very fitting homecoming for the heroes of yesteryear. Removing our equipment, we then sat down on our kit bags and tried to settle down for a long, cold journey.

We found it impossible to sleep in the narrow confinements of the corridor, which was used quite frequently by the occupants of the compartments who wished to visit the small room at the end of the corridor. The train travelled on through the cold winter night and by the light shining from its interior, you could see a white landscape out there.

The long night ended with our arrival at Edinburgh's Waverley station. We then transferred onto the Aberdeen bound train for the last leg of our journey, having come almost four hundred miles in the most atrocious conditions in that corridor. We now had a journey before us of about one hundred and twenty-five miles before we came to our journey's end, but this time we were going to ride in style with a compartment at our disposal.

Travelling through the white countryside, we at last reached the Granite City. We trooped out of the station and looked around for someone to give us directions to our final destination. A kind-hearted man told us to board the tram, which would take us to the terminus at the Bridge of Don. It was quite a journey and would have been a long walk with all our kit, and stepping off the tram, we could see across the bridge at the Gordon Highlanders HQ beyond. Would they keep us here or return us back to London?

We reported into headquarters at the barracks where the leave passes were processed to start from the next day, the 21st of February to the 21st of March 1947, and we had to return to the Gordon Highlanders Barracks to finalise our Army service before demob.

After a quick meal, we were away within an hour of our arrival. Going back to the station, we most fortunately found that the train there, waiting in the station, would be going direct from Aberdeen to King's Cross with a seat all the way. It was midday so with any luck we would be home by late evening. We had a good run down to London, and on arriving said goodbye to one another till we met again to return to whatever they had in store for us, north of the border. Once again, I left on my own for Marylebone station, just an hour from home and my parents.

My leave was anything but a holiday where it snowed every day. I worked on the job of snow clearing, having to move many inches of snow away and each time finding it a problem on the steps with it frozen solid underneath. The roads and pavements were in a treacherous state. The main roads were glazed with compressed ice, and with what traffic there was on the roads like buses finding it hard to negotiate on some of the hilly routes in the town.

Even the railways were suffering with this constant snowfall, of frozen points and the tracksides piled high with drifts. At this stage, they even started to experiment with two jet aeroplane engines mounted on a low-sided wagon preceding the train. The engines worked in a reverse position, the jets' thrust directed downward onto the track, melting the ice and disposing of it in the hot blast. The whole operation was carefully monitored for any damage to the existing trackwork whether wood or steel. It did work, but mercifully the bad weather abated at long last putting the whole idea, you could say, on ice.

With the inclement conditions, it did restrict to some extent what you could do. So I spent most of my time indoors, reading and listening to music on the radio, only venturing out into the cold to shop for my mother and my own amusement of attending all of the four picture houses the town could boast of.

Within a few days of my return to Scotland, the snow in the south eased off and the long-awaited thaw set in with the inevitable result of some bad flooding in some parts. Then like all good things, my leave expired but I did know this was my last time I would be under orders to leave my home. In the meantime, while still dressed in khaki, I had to try and attune myself to returning back into civilian life. I had been made aware that some found it very difficult to adjust back to a life where you must think for yourself, after being ordered and directed into the most improbable circumstances. It would in all probability make the undisciplined civilian throw a fit.

In any line regiment, the very nature of the employment of troops necessitates overbearing discipline. Without which, when confronted by the enemy, you would offer no resistance and melt in the face of your very tough adversary. Therefore, discipline must be strict if you have any hope of survival. So, after five years of this way of life, it could be a job to just shrug it off and conform to the steadier tempo of civilian life.

I met my friends at King's Cross where we were fortunate to find a compartment this time, and having settled down exchanged news about how we had faired in the big freeze and all admitted were glad to see the back of it. It turned out later that we had spoken too soon by observing traces of snow alongside the track in the lights from the train. As we progressed on our way north, it seemed to get ominously worse and crossing the border it looked very wintry. Changing trains at Waverley station, we felt the icy blast of, to us, the return of winter. On our journey to Aberdeen, we could see the snow but it had thawed in places. However, it was still bitterly cold. The bad weather had followed us all the way from Italy and looked set to stay with us for some time yet.

Leaving the platform at Aberdeen station and moving up the steps to the main road, the piercingly cold arctic wind cut into us, making it feel more like the Windy City of Chicago rather than the 'Granite' one. When the strong wind caught your kit bag, you felt like being blown off your feet. The cold felt so intense after the mild southern counties of England. We piled into the waiting tram with our kit and duly arrived at the Bridge of Don.

After reporting into the headquarters office, we were shown into a spacious dormitory where we found other men, like us, just awaiting their own demob. There was just one thing wrong with our accommodation – the Gordon Highlanders band was across the corridor to us. The annoying thing was their practicing on the chant pipes and the drummers incessantly tapping away on the windowsills, making a sound that would eventually drive you to the boundary of distraction at the infernal racket.

Now having poured scorn on the band, I must say that when spring arrived at last, we did attend the beating-the-retreat ceremony which was held every Friday evening on the parade ground. My friends would go with me to see the spectacle of the band marching and counter-marching, and just being there was a mark of respect to our friends who would never be coming home. They were watched by a goodly throng of soldiers, some of them being regulars at the barracks who came with their wives and children. The band was resplendent in their full regalia with Glengarry caps and wearing Gordon kilts. But the music said it all with tunes like *'Highland Laddie'*, *'The Flowers of the Forest'* and *'Will ye no come back again?'* It was always a very moving episode, coming at the end of my Army service.

We were called on parade every morning, with the exception of Sundays, to be counted and inspected, to see if we were still keeping in touch with Army standards like being shaved, short haircut and smartly turned out. Even then, we were getting rather bored at the inactivity of the useless and wasteful life we were being forced to live out till the time of our release when '50 Group' came up.

There were no educational projects we could join that would help ease us back to civilian life, however there were such courses available to the Armed Forces but not on offer to us. So, when my friend and I found they wanted volunteers for a farm project, we jumped at it without hesitation. It was far better to work than being bored to death. The project was to make fresh food available to the NAAFI canteen in the camp, making it self-sufficient.

We started right away and found the job to our liking, having plenty of land in the camp that could be used for food production, for we still had strict food rationing in our country that would remain in place for many years. An Aberdeen farmer was in on the project and supplied us with a motor-driven cultivator, or hand-driven plough, which came in very useful for making furrows for the planting of half a ton of King Edward potatoes. We also went out to his farm for loads of manure to enrich the soil we had there.

After several weeks had elapsed, we became very involved in the work but had no extra privileges for doing it. However, we looked on the work as a labour of love. We also dug other plots of land and planted various seeds and plants, but before we could see the fruits of our labours, we were informed that we would be leaving the barracks on the 25th of May for our demob on the 26th at the military dispersal unit, in Aldershot.

All the men down for demob were summoned to the headquarters office where we were seen individually by the commanding officer of the Gordon Highlanders depot, a lieutenant colonel of the regiment. After saluting him, he started to read out what he had personally written for me in my 'Soldier's release book, class "A"'.

It read:

Military Conduct. Exemplary.

Testimonial. Should do extremely well in

any position requiring hard work and trustworthiness.

And a second from the No.1 Special Guard Battalion:

Military Conduct. Exemplary.

Testimonial. This man, who on many occasions refused promotion, is extremely clean and smart and absolutely trustworthy. Conscientious in his work, he has proved an outstanding Soldier.

Signed Lieutenant
K E Hanson

Naturally, I felt very pleased at their assessments of my time in the Army, and read more like citations than a testimonial. The colonel rose to his feet, shook my hand and wished me good luck. After saluting one another, I walked out of the office holding my release book, which had taken five years of my life to obtain, but even then, I was a fortunate one.

It was Whit Sunday, 25th of May, and the day of our departure from the Gordon Highlanders depot. We would leave to catch the evening train and make our arrival at King's Cross to be first thing in the morning, then a short journey through London to catch the train for Aldershot. We were told that the staff at the demob centre would be on duty, even working on the Bank Holiday Monday, so we should get home that day.

Aberdeen, for me, had been a most rewarding posting, even if it was referred to as a 'home' posting, coming at the end of my Army service, but did in no way colour my judgment that it had to be good because we were going home. On the contrary, I found the Granite City most hospitable in the way they looked on the soldiery stationed there with great respect. And with the Gordon Highlanders being one of the British Armies' finest regiments, the Aberdonians were very proud of the connection with the city.

After spending so many years in the training to annihilate part of the human race, I was glad that I found working on the agricultural project a good form of therapy, in tapering back into a civilian role.

We left the camp with mixed feelings, and caught the evening train. On our arrival in London, we made tracks to catch the train to Aldershot where we were picked up by an Army transport, which made the short journey to the military dispersal unit. Here, we were asked to form a single line into the warehouse entrance by one of the civilian staff who was then joined in the entrance by a civilian with a tape measure hanging round his neck, and he was obviously a master tailor.

You would just walk up to him, he would then place the measure round your neck, look you up and down, and then tell you to go to a particular section in the warehouse where you would find all the civilian clothing you would need. It was uncanny in the extreme that he could tell, by placing the tape round the neck, the size of all your clothes, and it worked out right for me. To buy clothes in the shops, you needed clothing coupons and the allowance was not a very generous one, so you had to horde them if you wished to buy anything out of the ordinary. So, we had to choose wisely, they would have to last a very long time.

After having our release books filled in and officially stamped by the clerical staff, we were soon on our way back to the station to catch a London bound train. After arriving back in the capital and stepping off the train onto the platform, we just looked at one another in a kind of disbelief that it was time to say goodbye. We said our sad farewells, and shaking each others' hands parted company with one another, a sad business to end such friendships after being so long together in times of adversity.

Taking leave of the now dwindling number of friends still left on the platform, I proceeded towards Marylebone station. On arrival there, I caught the train for my hometown. On reaching the destination, I walked the remaining distance to my parents' home and opened the gate, the one I had opened to leave on that cold, dark November morning way back in 1942, and in so doing I had come full circle to my Army service commitment.

When I next opened the gate, it would be as a civilian.

Finito!

Conclusion

After sixty years, the citizens of the city of Anzio have seen fit to present a Certificate of Honour to the soldiers who fought on the beachhead. I feel it ironic now to be honoured in this way, when the British government of the day refused the offer of the Anzio medal (given to the American soldiers who served on the beachhead by their government). The certificate now goes part way in redressing the balance.

In this day and age of the rapid advances in science and technology, one is able to unravel secrets of the past which you had no inkling till the present day. Now, with the aid of the computer and the Internet, information becomes available about what befell your former brothers in arms, and comes to life with vivid reality when you feed in the few details you know of your friends and other battalion members.

The hurt that you feel for them surfaces when you read on the computer screen, or see the details in red, black and white on the printout, the stark grimness of the situations in which they were killed.

The following citations relate to a Debt of Honour Register, courtesy of the Commonwealth War Graves Commission; in memory of their name, rank and number, the battalion and the battle in which they fell, and age and date they died. It also gives information about parents and/or wife, town from and cemetery of burial. In all, it's very sombre reading, about the citizens of the nation who gave their lives for what was, considerably, a just cause of the time.

However, how many today wish to remember the sacrifice made on our behalf when you hear the trite saying spoken now of "Just let me get on with my life"? They wishing to absolve themselves from all moral obligations we should have for one another in the troubles of the present day. What would have happened if all the men who were called up into the services of the realm had voiced that same, selfish sentiment way back in 1939? What would have been the outcome in Europe? The cosy conditions of today would never have existed had that been so.

Items found on the Internet with what I would recall with some sadness at the disclosure of the details I had carried in my head and unable to wipe away, that of 'Smith—42' killed near the Garigliano River, with the citation:

In Memory of Cedric George Smith, Private 14410242, 10th Battalion Royal Berkshire Regiment, who died on Wednesday 19th January 1944, Age 19. Son of Fred and Bella Smith, of Weoley Castle, Birmingham. Cemetery of Burial, Minturno, 60 miles North of Naples.

Just two weeks later when the battalion had been rushed to the Anzio beachhead, I along with my friend had answered a call, out of the night, for a stretcher. This was when we had been portering our 3" mortar off the carriers, along with the cases of ammunition, running the gauntlet along a 200 yard stretch of shell-swept scrubland to our mortar pit in a bomb crater on the top of a railway embankment.

The caller had been Captain Zangen, the medical officer from his aid post established in the embankment, tending to a wounded man who we recognised to be Sergeant Scott. After helping him with his efforts to save the man's life, who had a severe head injury, we left the aid post to carry on with our own task. Looking up Sergeant Scott's name, I found he had died after we had left him. His citation said:

In Memory of Arthur James Scott, Lance Sergeant 5344364, 10th Battalion Royal Berkshire Regiment, who died on Friday 4th February 1944 at Anzio. Cemetery of Burial, Anzio War Cemetery, South of Rome.

Sadly, there are no details of next of kin or of his age, which unfortunately portrays a man on his own with no one to mourn his passing, but those who endeavoured to save him.

The next casualty, just two days later, was my best friend, Bob Manley, with the citation:

In Memory of Robert David Francis Manley, Private 14335572, 10th Battalion Royal Berkshire Regiment, who died on Sunday 6th February 1944, Age 20. Son of Robert David and Elizabeth Clara Manley, of Hackney, London. Cemetery of Burial, Anzio War Cemetery, South of Rome.

The final entry, from the Debt of Honour Register, must be that of my good friend, Stanley Nicholls, whose lance corporal stripes I had sewed onto his battledress sleeves for him on the ship returning us to Italy, and after docking at Taranto, we never saw him again. We read his citation:

In Memory of Stanley Victor Nicholls, Private 14511591, 2/7 Battalion The Queens Royal Regiment (West Surrey), who died on Friday 8th September 1944, Age 21. Son of Edward Horace and Dora Nicholls, of New Southgate, Middlesex. Cemetery of Burial, Gradara.

He was a lance corporal, but it had never been officially entered in his pay-book. Gradara is just a few miles south along the coast road from Riccione, my last posting in Italy. I only wish I had known the facts here when I was stationed there.

There are many others who deserve mention here, who died in the service of their country, but I remember them with affection when they parade in my thoughts in moments of solitude. All of them still with young faces that never age, or will I ever forget, and it makes you feel you are never alone.

No atheist ever dug a slit trench.

About the Author

David Ivan Vere was born in 1924. After a secondary modern school education, he started work at the age of 14. He worked in the manufacture of electrical measuring instruments till his call up into the Army in 1942, where he served in four separate Infantry Regiments till his discharge in 1947.

He then returned to his old company, where he was transferred to the Development & Experimental department, which came under his control in 1965. The department worked in close co-operation with the Royal Aircraft Establishment, Farnborough, on solar cell arrays for spacecraft. He also carried out experimental work for Harwell on reactor thermocouples, and many other projects in the medical field, obtaining patents along the way. He retired in 1989.

Print
5874

781425 953812